Early Readers, Scholars and Editors of the New Testament

Texts and Studies

11

Series Editor

H. A. G. Houghton

Text and Studies is a series of monographs devoted to the study of Biblical and Patristic texts. Maintaining the highest scholarly standards, the series includes critical editions, studies of primary sources, and analyses of textual traditions.

Early Readers, Scholars and Editors of the New Testament

Papers from the Eighth Birmingham
Colloquium on the Textual Criticism of the New
Testament

Edited by

H. A. G. Houghton

gorgias press
2014

Gorgias Press LLC, 954 River Road, Piscataway, NJ, 08854, USA

www.gorgiaspress.com

Copyright © 2014 by Gorgias Press LLC

2014   ܐ

ISBN 978-1-4632-0411-2   ISSN 1935-6927

Library of Congress Cataloging-in-Publication Data

Birmingham Colloquium on the Textual Criticism of the New Testament (8th : 2013 : University of Birmingham)
    Early readers, scholars, and editors of the New Testament : papers from the Eighth Birmingham Colloquium on the Textual Criticism of the New Testament / edited by H.A.G. Houghton.
        pages cm. -- (Texts and studies, ISSN 1935-6927 ; 11)
    Proceedings of the Eighth Birmingham Colloquium on the Textual Criticism of the New Testament, held in the Orchard Learning Resource Centre at the University of Birmingham, March 4-6, 2013.
    Includes index.
    ISBN 978-1-4632-0411-2
    1. Bible. New Testament--Criticism, Textual--Congresses. I. Houghton, H. A. G., editor. II. Title.
    BS2325.B57 2013
    225.4'046--dc23

2014030210

Printed in the United States of America

TABLE OF CONTENTS

LIST OF CONTRIBUTORS

Amy Anderson is Professor of Greek and New Testament in the Institute of Biblical and Theological Studies, North Central University, Minnesota. She specializes in mentoring undergraduate students in palaeography and textual criticism. She has published several books, including *The Textual Tradition of the Gospels: Family 1 in Matthew* (Brill, 2004).

Simon Crisp is Coordinator for Scholarly Editions and Translation Standards with the United Bible Societies, and an Honorary Fellow of ITSEE at the University of Birmingham. He has published widely in the areas of Bible translation and text-critical studies, and is one of the editors of *The Gospel According to John in the Byzantine Tradition* (Deutsche Bibelgesellschaft, 2007). He is currently working on a critical edition of the Euthalian Apparatus.

Hans Förster holds a doctorate in church history (University of Vienna 1997), compiled a Dictionary of Greek Words in Coptic Documentary Texts (Berlin, 2002) and has published Greek and Coptic Papyri. He is currently preparing a critical edition of the Sahidic Version of the Gospel of John in co-operation with the *Editio Critica Maior* of the Gospel of John.

Hugh Houghton has co-organised the Birmingham Colloquia on the Textual Criticism of the New Testament since 2007. He is a Senior Research Fellow at the University of Birmingham, currently leading a major research project on the biblical text of early commentaries on the Pauline Epistles.

Rosalind MacLachlan is a Research Fellow on the COMPAUL project, funded by the European Research Council, investigating the earliest commentaries on Paul in Latin and Greek as sources for the biblical text. She previously worked on the *Vetus Latina Iohannes* project producing a new edition of the Old Latin text of the Gospel of John.

Oliver Norris is a doctoral student at King's College London. His PhD is on the biblical and patristic sources used by the fifth century poet Sedulius, with particular focus on Sedulius's connection with the North African homiletic tradition.

Thomas O'Loughlin is Professor of Historical Theology in the University of Nottingham. He has just finished work on a book on the Eucharist looking at how early practice raises questions for contemporary ecumenical understandings. He is also part of a project, involving scholars in Birmingham and Nottingham, to examine the origins and impact of the *Protevangelium Iacobi*.

Rebekka Schirner works as Wissenschaftliche Mitarbeiterin at the Institut für Altertumswissenschaften at Johannes Gutenberg–Universität in Mainz, Germany. She wrote a PhD thesis on Augustine and his way of commenting on and dealing with different Latin versions of the biblical text. In affiliation with the *Vetus Latina* project "The Old Latin Text of the Acts of the Apostles" in Mainz, she is currently also working on a study of Augustine's citations of Acts.

Matthew Steinfeld is a doctoral student at the University of Birmingham. His research and part-time work contribute to the International Greek New Testament Project and the COMPAUL project at the Institute for Textual Scholarship and Electronic Editing.

Ulrike Swoboda finished her master's degree in theology in 2012 and is currently Wissenschaftliche Mitarbeiterin in the project "The Gospel of John and its Original Readers" funded by FWF (Austrian Science Fund/FWF-Project 24649) at the University of Vienna.

Satoshi Toda holds the degree of *doctor litterarum* from Leiden University and is currently Associate Professor at the Graduate School of Letters, Hokkaido University (Japan). He specializes in the history of ancient Christianity as well as the literatures of the Christian Orient. His publications include *Vie de S. Macaire l'Egyptien. Edition et traduction des textes copte et syriaque* (Gorgias, 2012).

INTRODUCTION

The study of the New Testament text is far broader than the reconstruction of its earliest attainable wording. As historical artefacts, manuscripts preserve information about the context in which they were produced and their use in subsequent generations, as well as pointing back towards an earlier stage in the transmission process. References made by Christian authors to the textual culture of the early Church, in addition to their biblical quotations and more general scriptural allusions, transmit information about the treatment of the documents as well as attitudes to (and the form of) the canonical text at the time. The task of the modern textual scholar is as much to map the continuity of the New Testament tradition as to reach behind it for a primitive form which was unknown to most later users.

The papers in the present volume represent the breadth of current investigations in the area of New Testament textual criticism. First, there is the study of the treatment and reception of scriptural books in the early Church. **Thomas O'Loughlin** uses a single phrase from the beginning of the Gospel according to Luke to advance a hypothesis about the production and care of biblical codices in the very earliest Christian communities. **Hans Förster** and **Ulrike Swoboda** attempt to reconstruct how the Gospel of John may have been understood in the generations immediately following its composition by examining concepts which may have posed problems for the earliest translators who produced versions in Latin and Coptic. The codification of the four gospels underlies the paper by **Satoshi Toda** on the system of concordance developed by Eusebius of Caesarea in the late third century. Toda shows how the tables found at the beginning of many gospel books, as well as the section numbers in the margins of each evangelist, can shed light on both the biblical text used by Eusebius and the exegetical presuppositions with which he worked.

Early readers also had to be textual scholars in order to establish the quality of the manuscripts they used. **Rebekka Schirner** makes a persuasive case for Augustine's text-critical abilities, which have long been eclipsed by those of his contemporary Jerome. She shows how the Bishop of Hippo applied a consistent set of criteria when faced with differing readings in biblical manuscripts, modelling the principles of responsible scholarship for his readers and listeners. **Oliver Norris**'s careful study of the two principal works by the fifth-century Latin writer Sedulius suggests that for his poetic retelling of the life of Christ, the *Paschale Carmen*, Sedulius used a gospel harmony with Old Latin readings. When rewriting this in prose, as the *Paschale Opus*, he adjusted the biblical text to match Jerome's Vulgate. **Rosalind MacLachlan** provides a reintroduction to the Budapest Anonymous Commentary on Paul. Although this manuscript was copied in the late eighth century, its Old Latin text of the Epistles goes back some four hundred years earlier. This may also be the case for the exegetical comments assembled in the margins by a scholarly compiler. MacLachlan shows how the current layout of the manuscript derives from a change in format which sometimes disrupts the original conception.

Research on early readers and editions of the New Testament relies on the careful assembly and analysis of the surviving evidence. **Matthew Steinfeld** offers some preliminary reflections on his survey of Origen's citations of Galatians. He confirms that introductory formulae do not guarantee that a verbatim quotation follows, as has already been observed for other Christian authors. He also notes differences between Origen's citations of the same verse and suggests how these may be reconciled. **Amy Anderson** provides data from her transcriptions of the manuscripts of Family 1 in Mark. This early edition of the Gospels is particularly notable for its significant readings in the text and margins.

Finally, we move onto modern scholars and editors. **Hans Förster** considers the interaction between textual and literary criticism in New Testament scholarship. His comparison of the Gospel according to John with other ancient writings indicates the stability of the text, which he attributes to its early canonisation. He also looks at variations in the miracle stories and how these might be connected with an early 'signs source' proposed by literary critics. Extensive archival research by **Simon Crisp** illuminates the history of the British and Foreign Bible Society's edition of the Greek New Testament in the middle of the twentieth century. The questions and issues associated with this publication are, he suggests, common to much editorial work.

The common origin of all these contributions was the Eighth
Birmingham Colloquium on the Textual Criticism of the New Testament,
held in the Orchard Learning Resource Centre at the University of
Birmingham from 4–6 March 2013. Although the Colloquium had a broad
theme, 'The Tradition of the Old Testament: Treasures New and Old', the
offered papers resulted in a coherent whole as shown by this volume.[1] An
even greater range of participants attended than in previous years,
representing institutions in no fewer than eight countries. As usual, guests
were accommodated at Woodbrooke Quaker Study Centre, where the
famous textual scholar and editor J. Rendel Harris was once Director of
Studies. The colloquium excursion was to the city of Leicester, where we
examined the Leicester Codex (GA 69) at the Public Records Office in
Wigston Magna before proceeding to the city centre, visiting its Roman
baths and the car park where the bones of Richard III had recently been
discovered. The speaker following the conference dinner in the University's
Staff House was Mark Pallen, Professor of Microbial Genomics at the
University of Birmingham: he recorded his fascinating presentation on *The
Great Trees of Life: Genes, Gospels and Languages* and made it available later that
evening on YouTube, where it can still be enjoyed at http://youtu.be/
8Ykj5wQs7vU.

The proceedings of the Fifth Colloquium were published in the
present series in 2008 as H.A.G. Houghton and D.C. Parker (eds), *Textual
Variation: Theological and Social Tendencies?* (T&S 3.6. Piscataway NJ: Gorgias,
2008). The inaugural volume in the series with papers from the First
Colloquium, first published in 1999 by the University of Birmingham Press,
has also recently become available in a Gorgias Press edition, preserving the
original pagination: D.G.K. Taylor (ed.), *Studies in the Early Text of the Gospels
and Acts*. (T&S 3.1. Piscataway NJ: Gorgias, 2013). The Sixth Colloquium
was held in London jointly with the British Library as the conference
marking the launch of the Digital Codex Sinaiticus (www.codexsinaiticus.
org) in 2009. The proceedings will be published separately by the British
Library. The Seventh Colloquium took place at the University of
Birmingham in March 2011, on the subject of 'Early Christian Writers and

---

[1] The paper delivered by O'Loughlin on the chapter titles of Revelation in the
Book of Armagh (VL 61) was already scheduled for publication in Pàdraic Moran
and Immo Warntjes (eds), *A Festschrift for Daibhí Ó Cróinín* (Studia Traditionis
Theologiae 14. Turnhout: Brepols, 2014); we are grateful to him for offering an
alternative which matched the present theme.

the Text of the New Testament'. A selection of papers from this gathering
are included in M. Vinzent, L. Mellerin and H.A.G. Houghton (eds), *Biblical
Quotations in Patristic Texts* (SP 54. Leuven: Peeters, 2013); others have been
published elsewhere.[2] The excursion that year to Lichfield Cathedral
included a visit to the Cathedral Library and a chance to see the St Chad
Gospels; the conference dinner included a presentation of the newly-found
Staffordshire Hoard by Dr David Symons, Curator of Antiquities and
Numismatics at Birmingham Museum and Art Gallery.

The editor would like to express his thanks to the contributors to this
volume and all participants at the Eighth Colloquium, a gathering of friends
and colleagues new and old. David Parker continues to preside and inspire
as founder and co-organiser of the colloquia, while Rosalind MacLachlan,
Catherine Smith, Christina Kreinecker and Alba Fedeli provided invaluable
assistance before and during the conference. We are grateful to Clare
Underwood for making our visit to the Public Records Office possible and
to Peter Chinn for organising the accommodation at Woodbrooke. The
publication of this volume in *Texts and Studies* would not have been possible
without Dr Melonie Schmierer-Lee and George Kiraz of Gorgias Press.
Our gratitude also goes to the Hungarian National Library (Endre Lipthay,
Archive of Manuscripts), the Freie Theologische Hochschule, Giessen and
Cambridge University Library for permission to reproduce images of items
in their collections.

H.A.G. Houghton
Birmingham, March 2014

---

[2] e.g. Tommy Wasserman, 'The "Son of God" was in the Beginning (Mark 1:1)'
JTS ns 62.1 (2011) pp. 20–50; Dirk Jongkind, 'Some Observations on the
Relevance of the "Early Byzantine Glossary" of Paul for the Textual Criticism of
the Corpus Paulinum' *NovT* 53.4 (2011) pp. 358–75.

LIST OF ABBREVIATIONS

ANTF	Arbeiten zur neutestamentlichen Textforschung
AGLB	Aus der Geschichte der lateinischen Bibel
BFBS	British and Foreign Bible Society
BETL	Bibliotheca ephemeridum theologicarum lovaniensium
CCSL	Corpus Christianorum series latina
CSEL	Corpus Scriptorum Ecclesiasticorum Latinorum
ExpT	*Expository Times*
GA	Gregory–Aland (cf. Kurt Aland, *Kurzgefasste Liste der griechischen Handschriften des Neuen Testaments.* Zweite neubearbeitete and ergänzte Auflage (ANTF 1. Berlin & New York: de Gruyter, 1994).)
GCS	Die griechischen christlichen Schriftsteller der ersten drei Jahrhunderte
HNT	Handbuch zum Neuen Testament
JBL	*Journal of Biblical Literature*
JECS	*Journal of Early Christian Studies*
JSNTSup	Journal for the Study of the New Testament - Supplement Series
JTS	*Journal of Theological Studies*
LSJ	H.G. Liddell, R. Scott et al., *A Greek-English Lexicon.* 9th edn (Oxford: Clarendon Press, 1996).
NA27	E. Nestle, K. Aland et al., *Novum Testamentum Graece*, twenty-seventh edition. Stuttgart: Deutsche Bibelgesellschaft, 1993.
NA28	E. Nestle, K. Aland et al., *Novum Testamentum Graece*, twenty-eighth edition. Stuttgart: Deutsche Bibelgesellschaft, 2012.
NHC	Nag Hammadi Codices
NHMS	Nag Hammadi and Manichaean Studies
NovT	*Novum Testamentum*

NRSV	New Revised Standard Version
NTS	*New Testament Studies*
NTTSD	New Testament Tools, Studies and Documents
PL	*Patrologia Latina* [= Patrologiae cursus completus: Series latina]. Edited by J.-P. Migne. 217 vols. Paris, 1841–1855.
RP	Maurice A. Robinson and William G. Pierpont, eds, *The New Testament in the Original Greek According to the Byzantine/Majority Textform* (Atlanta GA: Original Word Publishers, 1991).
RSV	Revised Standard Version
SBLDS	Society of Biblical Literature Dissertation Series
SBLNTGF	Society of Biblical Literature New Testament in the Greek Fathers
SD	Studies and Documents
SP	*Studia Patristica*
T&S	Texts and Studies
ThHKNT	Theologischer Handkommentar zum Neuen Testament
ThKNT	Theologischer Kommentar zum Neuen Testament
TR	*Textus Receptus*
TU	Texte und Untersuchungen
UBS	United Bible Societies
UP	University Press
VC	*Vigiliae Christianae*
WUNT	Wissenschaftliche Untersuchungen zum Neuen Testament
ZNW	*Zeitschrift für die neutestamentliche Wissenschaft*

1. Ὑπηρεται ... του λογου: Does Luke 1:2 Throw Light on to the Book Practices of the Late First-Century Churches?

Thomas O'Loughlin

If we reflect on the practicalities implicit in any of the text traditions of the earliest Christian communities, we appreciate at once that there must have been systems for the preservation, copying, and diffusion of those texts. The relationship of the gospels of Matthew, Luke, and John to Mark is a case in point. Both Matthew and Luke had independent access to copies of Mark (and thus we have the Synoptic Tradition), while John also had access to Mark's account and dovetailed his own narrative with it. These patterns of use imply that in the last decades of the first century the text of Mark was being both preserved and disseminated in the churches. These same churches were also preserving and diffusing the letters of Paul after his death – and indeed adding to them – and so building up the Pauline corpus and tradition. And while we have but an indeterminate fraction of what was written by those Christians, the fact that we have as much as we do points to deliberate practices of preserving writings within the churches at a time when our evidence for formal structures within those communities is minimal.

This interaction between Jesus' early followers and written texts has long been a concern of scholarship.[1] Since the work of C.H. Roberts, we

---

[1] One could argue that this is both behind all concerns about canon (so starting with Eusebius) or text (and so with Eusebius if not Origen), but I am thinking of modern concerns about books as cultural objects in a society, and works such as H.Y. Gamble, *Books and Readers in the Early Church: A History of Early Christian Texts* (New Haven and London: Yale UP, 1995).

1

now speak with confidence about the material form, codices, taken by those early texts.[2] Much attention has in recent years been devoted to the networks for their diffusion over 'the holy internet';[3] and this in turn has allowed us to see texts such as the gospels as having an appeal across the churches.[4] Similarly, the patterns of survival of those texts enable us to observe the beginnings of the processes that would eventually lead to their 'canonisation'.[5] That said, the emergence of the four gospels (Matthew, Mark, Luke, John) as a distinct grouping of texts, or the gathering together of Paul's letters, with the implication that they had some special authority is perhaps better described as 'proto-canonisation' in a second-century context.[6] Given the obvious extent of this engagement with written texts, it is somewhat surprising that we have virtually no direct references as to how those early communities obtained, retained, duplicated, or published their books.[7] The only exceptions to this silence is the Deutero-Pauline reference to an exchange of letters between Colossae and Laodicea (Colossians 4:16), presumably from the later first century,[8] and the mention in the Pastorals of

---

[2] C.H. Roberts, *Manuscript, Society, and Belief in Early Christian Egypt* (Oxford: The British Academy and Oxford UP, 1979).

[3] M.B. Thompson, 'The Holy Internet: Communication Between Churches in the First Christian Generation' in R. Bauckham (ed.), *The Gospels for All Christians* (Grand Rapids MI: Baker, 1998), pp. 49–70.

[4] This is the theme underlying the essays in *The Gospels for All Christians.*

[5] See G.N. Stanton, *Jesus and Gospel* (Cambridge: Cambridge UP, 2004), pp. 63–109.

[6] Before we find references to 'the four gospels' as *somehow* forming a unit – which we could link with Tatian's choice of them more than a decade before Irenaeus we have the special status attributed to *both* Matthew *and* Luke in the *Protevangelium Jacobi* (see T. O'Loughlin, 'The *Protevangelium of James*: a case of gospel harmonization in the second century?' in M. Vinzent (ed.), *Studia Patristica: Papers Presented at the Sixteenth International Conference on Patristic Studies held in Oxford 2011.* (*SP* 65). Leuven: Peeters, 2013, pp. 165–73).

[7] Interestingly, very few scholars have asked who *owned* these books – despite interest in the cost of their production – and whether they were owned by individuals or communities. An exception to this is H.I. Bell and T.C. Skeat, *Fragments of an Unknown Gospel and Other Early Christian Papyri* (London: British Museum, 1935) p. 1, who pointed out that they could not be certain whether or not certain manuscripts 'were used by, and very likely written for, a Christian owner or community'.

[8] On the problem of the dating of Colossians, see V.P. Furnish, 'Colossians,

a concern of 'Paul' about his books and parchments (2 Timothy 4:13) presumably from sometime in the first-half of the second century.[9] The purpose of this paper is to 'fly a kite' and investigate whether in Luke 1:2 we have a reference to early Christian engagement with books. I want to argue that the essential basis of the usage of books, not to mention their availability for copying and dissemination, is some structure for keeping them safe from day to day when they were not being read in the community, and that in Luke 1:2 we may have the name which designated specific officers of the churches, 'the servants of the word' (ὑπηρέται τοῦ λόγου), whose task it was to preserve and guard each church's 'library'.[10]

LUKE 1:2 IN RECENT RESEARCH

Luke writes that he wants to produce in his book an 'orderly account' of 'the events ... just as they were handed on to us by those who from the beginning were eyewitnesses and servants (αὐτόπται καὶ ὑπηρέται) of the word.' The word 'eyewitnesses' has caught the attention of exegetes, while 'servants', the other term, has most commonly been seen as simply a clarification of their authority: they are ministers in the process of the *kerygma*. Those followers who were eyewitnesses from the beginning are indeed the servants of the word and, as such, it is what these eyewitnesses have handed on to writers such as Luke that forms the basis of his gospel.[11] At the core of the current lively debate over these 'eyewitnesses' (who are the focus of all attention) is whether or not they should be seen as simply firsthand observers of the events surrounding Jesus of Nazareth: they are the primary historical witnesses.[12] Their testimony builds the essential

---

Epistle to the' in D.N. Freedman (ed.), *The Anchor Bible Dictionary.* (New York NY: Anchor, 1992), I, pp. 1090–6 at pp. 1094–5.

[9] See T.C. Skeat, '"Especially the parchments": A note on 2 Timothy IV.13.' *JTS* ns 30 (1979) pp. 173–7. On the date of the Pastorals, see A. Yarbro Collins, 'The Female Body as Social Space in 1 Timothy' *NTS* 57 (2011) pp. 155–75.

[10] The first person to suggest some link between ὑπηρέται and a church's 'library' was J.N. Collins, 'Re-thinking "Eyewitnesses" in the Light of 'Servants of the Word' (Luke 1:2)' *ExpT* 121 (2010) pp. 447–52, at p. 452.

[11] See R. Bauckham, *Jesus and the Eyewitnesses: The Gospels as Eyewitness Testimony* (Grand Rapids MI: Eerdmans, 2006). This work has generated a large body of discussion; see, for example, J.C.S. Redman, 'How accurate are eyewitnesses? Bauckham and the eyewitnesses in the light of psychological research' *JBL* 129 (2010) pp. 177–97.

[12] Bauckham, *Jesus and the Eyewitnesses*, p. 117.

4   THOMAS O'LOUGHLIN

bridge between 'the Jesus of history' and 'the Christ of faith'; so it is
appropriate that Luke should designate them as 'the servants of the word'.
As such, the 'eyewitnesses' and the 'servants' are clearly one group.[13]

The rationale for Bauckham's position on the identity of the two
groups may be new, but the conclusion is not. Michael Goulder sees both
groups as Luke's 'tradents' and notes:

> The Greek requires a single group with a double function: those like
> Peter, who both companied with the Lord through the ministry, and
> witnessed to the fact thereafter in preaching.[14]

On this reading it is useless to imagine that there can be any specific group
of ὑπηρέται because it is but an aspect of being the living link from Luke's
time back to the events. Moreover, these 'ministers of the word' have a
distinct theological identity:

> The Gospel ... fulfils the word of God in the Old Testament, and it was
> handed down to the present Church by men who saw it all from the
> beginning, and also preached it. 'Ministers of the word' may include an
> element of seeing the events as fulfilments as well as proclaiming them
> as facts: only so, in Luke's understanding, do they become 'the word (of
> God)'.[15]

Thus Goulder arrives at what has been the most widespread view of the
passage: these servants/ministers are to be seen in terms of a ministry of
preaching, and this ministry in the church is the sort of high status activity
imagined in such passages as the Great Commission of Matthew 28:19.
They are 'servants' of the church in a manner analogous to that of Paul and
Barnabas taking the gospel into new situations, or, for that matter, later
clerical preachers who viewed themselves as 'ministers of the gospel'.

---

[13] Bauckham, *Jesus and the Eyewitnesses*, p. 122.

[14] M.D. Goulder, *Luke. A New Paradigm.* (Sheffield: Sheffield Academic Press,
1989), p. 201.

[15] Goulder, *Luke*, p. 201; J.A. Fitzmyer, *The Gospel according to Luke I-IX* (New
York NY: Doubleday, 1981), p. 294 is explicit that γένομενοι should be rendered
'becoming' which then is both the basis and conclusion of his argument; most
interpreters and translators have opted for the simpler solution of rendering it as
'being' (but Bauckham does consider the possibility that 'the eyewitnesses' later on
became 'the servants of the word').

A slightly more nuanced position can be found in Joseph Fitzmyer's commentary which acknowledges that 'the Greek of this phrase is not easily translated' and that the 'problem lies in whether Luke is referring here to one or to two groups ... who shaped the early tradition.'[16] In contrast to those who think that two groups are mentioned, Fitzmyer believes that the key lay in the 'single art[icle] *hoi* which governs the whole construction'. From this base he held that one should understand the sentence as 'the 'eyewitnesses' of [Jesus'] ministry ... who eventually became the 'ministers of the word'.'[17] While he acknowledged theat 'Luke is distancing himself from the ministry of Jesus by two layers of tradition', Fitzmyer is clear that what is involved is a single body of people, and their service is to be understood in evangelical terms: they preached God's word.

This consensus that 'eyewitnesses' and 'servants of the word' are identical (both as human beings and with regard to task) has recently been challenged by John N. Collins, who responding to Bauckham,[18] argues that this 'commonly accepted understanding, ... can now be seen as a misconception'.[19] His argument begins by noting that:

> ... of the 57 instances [in the *Thesaurus Linguae Graecae*] of *autopt-* prior to 100 CE, 54 instances occur in context with some form of *gignesthai* ... Exactly the same pattern repeats in 200 instances (over and above citations of Luke's phrase in Christian writers) over the next 400 years. On the other hand, no instance of such a pairing (other than at Luke 1:2) occurs in the case of the Greek servant word (*hypéret-*).[20]

Collins having thus dismissed the notion of some historical progression (implicitly replying to Fitzmyer), now thinks of a single group of human beings but with two functions: they have the twin tasks of eyewitnessing the word (Collins points out that 'eyewitness' has no forensic connotation in Greek; so perhaps a better rendering of his meaning would be 'being observers') and being servants of the word:

---

[16] Fitzmyer, *The Gospel according to Luke I-IX*, p. 294.

[17] Fitzmyer, *The Gospel according to Luke I-IX*, p. 294; who based his conclusion on the work of R.J. Dillon, *From Eyewitnesses to Ministers of the Word* (Rome: Pontifical Biblical Institute, 1978), pp. 269–72.

[18] Collins writes: 'Bauckham (p. 122) agrees, as perhaps most do, that the two designations apply to one group of people.' ('Re-thinking "Eyewitnesses"', p. 450).

[19] Collins, 'Re-thinking "Eyewitnesses"', p. 450.

[20] Collins, 'Re-thinking "Eyewitnesses"', p. 450.

So we have an eyewitnessing function 'of the word' as well as a distinct function of being servant 'of the word'.[21]

Collins also makes another significant observation: Luke's 'focus in his preface is upon a literary tradition'. While Luke's gospel was written in an oral environment,[22] Luke is concerned with earlier written materials, i.e. books, and the place they hold in the communities' memory.[23] This allows Collins to note that the moment of writing narratives is one event, but there is a subsequent reception and use of those books in the communities: here lies the role of the αὐτόπται καὶ ὑπηρέται γενόμενοι τοῦ λόγου in that they receive and read the narratives aloud in the community.[24]

This view is considerably different to that of earlier writers, and indeed Bauckham, in that we are now dealing with a group of functionaries in the churches, who are not only after the historical time of the events surrounding Jesus but also of the time when these events appeared as narratives in writing (a time which for Luke must be after the time of Mark, since we can be certain that Mark's narrative is one of those accounts). So, for Collins, these officials of the community, with the double name, are 'responsible for the library of the community' and, more significantly, for:

> receiving and authenticating documents of the tradition. They are highly literate and have received their appointments from the community.[25]

As such they fulfil a role of being guarantors of the assurance (ἀσφάλεια) of the treatises (λόγοι) with which Theophilus has been instructed (Luke

---

[21] Collins, 'Re-thinking "Eyewitnesses"', p. 450.

[22] Although Luke was concerned with books, he was dealing with them in an oral environment in which the book is more akin to a modern recording of a voice speaking, than a book as we conceive it which communicates from mind to mind without sounds being heard; see P.J. Achtemeier, '*Omne verbum sonat*: The New Testament and the Oral Environment of Late Western Antiquity' *JBL* 109 (1990) pp. 3–27.

[23] This significant observation picks up a theme that was common in older scholarship that emphasised the place of the book, as such, in Luke's thinking (e.g. E.J. Goodspeed, 'Some Greek Notes – I. Was Theophilus Luke's Publisher?' *JBL* 73 (1954) p. 84); and for a more recent view of the matter, see L. Alexander, 'Ancient Book Production and the Circulation of the Gospels' in R. Bauckham (ed.), *The Gospels for All Christians*, pp. 71–105, at pp. 103–5.

[24] Collins, 'Re-thinking "Eyewitnesses"', p. 451.

[25] Collins, 'Re-thinking "Eyewitnesses"', p. 452.

1:4).[26] So both Collins and Bauckham agree that this single group has the task of being 'specially authorised guarantors of the traditions':[27] they are the representative and responsible tradents. Yet while Collins begins with the assertion of two tasks, these are not clearly delimitated in his article and seem to be indistinguishable in practice.

ANOTHER FORMULATION OF THE EVIDENCE

Collins' work marks a definite advance on earlier exegesis in that (1) it clarifies the focus of Luke on *the written materials* already in existence at his time, and (2) proposes a distinction, at least conceptually, between αὐτόπται and ὑπηρέται. However, with regard to the latter point Collins does not draw out how these 'dual functions' are actually different in the life of the community. Being 'a witness and a servant of the word' seems to amount to belonging to the same group and doing the same thing: 'as well as handling the material [i.e. the books], they also taught it'.[28] So is this simply a hendiadys?[29]

Against this suggestion is the clear point that 'being observers'/ 'eyewitnessing', or even reading the word is distinct from being 'servants of the word' when we note that this servant-word, ὑπηρέτ-, is usually linked not with a notion of 'minister' (in the modern sense of a 'minister of religion') but that of a minor practical functionary.[30] The ὑπηρέται, Collins has shown elsewhere,[31] were functionaries that dealt with practical matters of commerce; they are the clerks and officials that put into effect the instructions of others who are their superiors. They are, by analogy, those one meets when one goes to a modern office with a query rather than those

---

[26] Collins' translation is worth noting: 'that you [Theophilus] may learn to have a deeper appreciation of the treatises about which you have been instructed' ('Re-thinking "Eyewitnesses"', pp. 452).

[27] Collins quoting Bauckham.

[28] Collins, 'Re-thinking "Eyewitnesses"', p. 452.

[29] So thought B. Gerhardsson, *Memory and Manuscript* (Lund: Gleerup, 1961) pp. 234–5, who compared it to another, 'service and apostleship', in Acts 1:25; we should add the references to 'bishops and deacons' in Philippians 1:1 and *Didache* 15.1.

[30] Collins, 'Re-thinking "Eyewitnesses"', p. 451, points out that '*hypéretés* is, in fact, a term with a well established place in bureaucratic usage for minor officials.'

[31] J.J. Collins, *Diakonia: Re-interpreting the Ancient Sources.* (Oxford: Oxford UP, 1990), pp. 83, 94, 125, 153, 166–7, 174, 183, 314, and 320.

'in charge' or those ministers that one sees in the pulpit. This notion of
ὑπηρέτης referring to a functionary assisting someone else is consistent
with its use in Jewish writings be they prior to or roughly contemporaneous
with Luke (e.g. Josephus).[32] Moreover, when we look at its usage in the
New Testament two points stand out. First, ὑπηρέτης designates *lesser*
officials, usually within some power pyramid. A clear case of this is
Matthew 5:25 where 'the judge hands over to the guard' (μήποτέ σε
παραδῷ ὁ ἀντίδικος τῷ κριτῇ καὶ ὁ κριτὴς τῷ ὑπηρέτῃ) and where the
story's rhetoric assumes that one knows that one is descending from the
judge to the ὑπηρέτης and thence to prison. This would be true whether
the usage is 'factual' (e.g. Mark 14:54) or 'imaginary' (e.g. John 18:36 – the
angelic army are Jesus' operatives, not his equals).[33] Second, there is no
specifically cultic or religious range to the word. One might argue that 1
Corinthians 4:1 (where Paul, Apollos and Cephas are to be thought of as ὡς
ὑπηρέτας Χριστοῦ) is an exception, but this fails to see the point Paul is
making: these named people, himself included, are to be seen as lesser
officials carrying out the work of the Christ, and they should be seen as
functionaries for him despite being designated 'apostles'. Equally, when in
Acts 26:16 Paul is appointed to be a ὑπηρέτης καὶ μάρτυς of Jesus, the
point of the story is to express the fact that Paul is the functionary of Jesus
in what he does.

So the notion that αὐτόπται and ὑπηρέται form a hendiadys does not
take account of the lowliness of ὑπηρέται, while, if it is the case that the
αὐτόπται have some specific function in the churches of being the
performers or guarantors 'of the word', then it is most unlikely that they
would also be the ὑπηρέται. The implication seems clear: not only do these
officials belong to the time between the arrival of written accounts of Jesus
and Luke's time, but they are two distinct groups in the church. Read in this
way there was not one group in the communities,[34] but those who
witnessed to the orderly accounts in the churches – presumably with high

---

[32] See K.H. Rengsdorf, 'ὑπηρέτης κτλ.' in G. Kittel and G. Friedrich, *Theological Dictionary of the New Testament* (Grand Rapids MI: Eerdmans, 1972), VIII, pp. 530–9.

[33] See also Matt. 26:58; Mark 14:65; John 7:32 and 45; 18:3 and 12; 19:6; Acts 5:22 and 26. This point was also made by Rengsdorf in *Theological Dictionary of the New Testament*, VIII, pp. 539–42.

[34] We might recall that both αὐτόπται and ὑπηρέται were the same individuals was the one element common to the positions of Rengsdorf (p. 543), Fitzmyer, Goulder, Bauckham, and Collins.

literary skills (as Collins suggests) and who gave voice to those texts by reading them aloud – and a group of *lesser* officers (ὑπηρέται) who were more concerned with the practicalities of having 'orderly narratives' in the community, kept them safe, brought them out at their gatherings, and made sure that they were preserved. Both together were needed to allow for the word to be heard in the churches, and to ensure that these accounts, such as Mark (and Q, if that was some sort of written document), were available to someone like Luke who was about to write his own orderly account.

We noted earlier that if ὑπηρέται was to be rendered as 'ministers'[35] then we tend to think of someone like 'the minister in the pulpit'; whereas it would be better to think in terms of them being 'office assistants'. Now I would like to refine the simile: if the αὐτόπται are the lectors to the community and had some significant function such as selecting what was read, then ὑπηρέται should be imagined as similar to those lesser officers in a community, perhaps called 'sacristans' or 'vergers', who look after the practicalities of the cult.

However, before exploring this further, I want to express my debt to Collins' article. It is there that the notion that the αὐτόπται and ὑπηρέται are officers within the Christian community, and that Luke is familiar with them as such, is first made. However, for both Collins and Bauckham these αὐτόπται have an authorizing, and guaranteeing function. Collins thinks of them as 'authenticating documents of the tradition'. This notion seems a little wide of the mark: we have no evidence whatsoever of any system of these tasks; and if there were such a system then the tasks of those who were later arguing for a 'canon' would have been much easier.[36] In fact, our evidence points overwhelmingly towards the conclusion that there was nothing like a system of 'authorization' in the early communities.[37]

---

[35] So Douay-Rheims, Authorised Version, and RSV; following the usage of the Vulgate: *ministri*.

[36] Both Bauckham and Collins (despite his warning note) seem to have exported the forensic overtones of 'eyewitness' in our usage into Greek; moreover, Collins earlier in his article dwells on the question of authority as exercised by the Vatican's doctrinal watchdogs (under a variety of names) and seems to have imagined that there was a similar concern for 'authorised' texts in the early churches.

[37] See W. Bauer (trans. R.A. Kraft and G. Krodel), *Orthodoxy and Heresy in Earliest Christianity*. (Philadelphia PA: Fortress Press, 1961) [English translation of *Rechtgläubigkeit und Ketzerei in ältesten Christentum*, Tübingen: Mohr, 1934].

Ὑπηρέται: A JOB SPECIFICATION?

At this point we should turn our attention to other references to a ὑπηρέτης found in Luke. The first occurs in Luke's depiction of Jesus going to the synagogue in Nazareth. When he stood up to read, he was given (by whom it is not stated, but presumably this was the same person to whom Jesus returned the scroll)[38] the scroll of Isaiah. He read, rolled up the scroll again, gave it back to the attendant (τῷ ὑπηρέτῃ),[39] and sat down (4:20). Commentators usually point out that this assistant was but one of a range of synagogue officials mentioned by Luke: there are also the ἀρχισυνάγωγος (8:49 and 13:14) and πρεσβύτεροι (7:3).[40] That the ὑπηρέτης was the lesser official, dealing with the liturgical practicalities would fit what we know of the word's range of meanings from elsewhere. This has led Fitzmyer to see this person as 'the *hazzan*' and describe him as 'a sort of sacristan or sexton'; while Rengsdorf has noted that there is a burial plaque to one Flavios Julianos, a ὑπηρέτης, who was apparently a synagogue official.

However, if we shift our attention from the scene in the story to that of its narration we have, very probably, a scene with which Luke's audience were themselves familiar. The prophets were being read in their assembly and there too the gospel was being proclaimed sometimes by an evangelist, but probably more often by someone else – we might adopt Collins' suggestion of the literate αὐτόπται – giving sound to marks on papyrus. That person had to be provided with the book, and the book had to be preserved afterwards. The ὑπηρέτης of the story set in Nazareth is a reflection of the tasks performed by the ὑπηρέτης in the Christian community. If that is the case, then the similarity of scene would be theologically significant within Luke's view of history: the risen Christ is imagined to be present in that community hearing the story just as he was recalled as being present in the Nazareth synagogue.

That ὑπηρέτης was a specifically Christian term for Luke is supported by his non-use of the term in 12:58. While Matthew (5:25) reads ὁ κριτὴς

---

[38] A point made by Rengsdorf in *Theological Dictionary of the New Testament*, VIII, p. 540, n. 80.

[39] 'Attendant' is found in RSV and NRSV; older translations echo the Vulgate's use of *minister*.

[40] Rengsdorf, *Theological Dictionary of the New Testament*, VIII, p. 540, n. 80; and Fitzmyer, *The Gospel according to Luke I-IX*, p. 533.

τῷ ὑπηρέτῃ, Luke has ὁ κριτής σε παραδώσει τῷ πράκτορι. This change to a word, otherwise not attested in early Christian literature, may indicate an unwillingness in Luke to have any in his audience hearing, in a parable on repentance, the equivalent of 'and the judge hand you over to the sacristan' – a fate that does not inspire urgency.

The other occurrence of a ὑπηρέτης is in Acts at 13:5 where a certain John was the 'assistant' to Barnabas and Saul in Cyprus.[41] Only one thing is clear from the text: this assistant is not placed on the same level those who have been 'sent out by the Holy Spirit' (13:4). How John assisted Barnabas and Saul is not mentioned – and he is often assumed to have, in Jefford's words, 'served as a recorder, catechist, and travel attendant'. But since he is not sent 'by the Spirit' it seems implicit in Luke's account that he dealt with practical matters, and as such was more likely the 'travel attendant' rather than a 'catechist'. Many years ago, B.T. Holmes took up this question in detail and studied all the then known mentions on papyrus of such a ὑπηρέτης.[42] This reveals that these were minor officials, but also (or at least for those who left a trace on papyrus) that they were minor bureaucratic officials carrying out the sort of tasks we today might link with term 'office assistants' or, more quaintly, 'clerks'. This reveals, first and foremost, that for Luke there seems to be no notion of a ὑπηρέτης being some sort of preacher/teacher in the churches, and also that he would expect them to be the sort of people who could read in order to keep track of books, make lists, and perform all the other office skills that a group which uses writings in its corporate life needed.

So how should we imagine them? Assuming that by the time Luke wrote there was already a separation of the churches from the synagogues, then the Jesus-followers were gathering in private houses (Acts 2:42 or 20:8), and we should not imagine these are large spaces, for their regular meetings.[43] To this gathering would have to be brought the books they

---

[41] Usually identified as 'John Mark' on the basis that the reference to 'John' at 13:5 refers back six sentences to the 'John, whose other name was Mark' at 12:25. This John is also linked to others with the names 'John' or 'Mark' with varying degrees of certainty; see C.N. Jefford, 'Mark, John' in D.N. Freedman (ed.), *The Anchor Bible Dictionary.* (New York NY: Doubleday, 1992), IV, pp. 557–8.

[42] B.T. Holmes, 'Luke's Description of John Mark' *JBL* 54 (1935) pp. 63–72 – this work has still not been bettered; the most recent study of the term ὑπηρέτης (Collins' *Diakonia*) does not, however, use this invaluable article.

[43] See B.S. Billings, 'From House Church to Tenement Church: Domestic

would use by someone who had a means of caring for the books in his home. The alternative is that the same house was the regular location, and the books were held there, and that there was suitable storage in that house. Either way, someone must have had responsibility for the books, with the task of making sure that they were kept safe – assuming that the outlay and so the ownership of the codices was a community matter – and that the specific book needed for a meeting was at hand.

We know that these communities were in contact with each other through a network of travelling disciples – designated by a number of names such as 'teachers', 'prophets', 'evangelists' – for we glimpse them in many writings, such as Acts, and have regulations regarding them in the *Didache*.[44] When one of these arrived he may have had his own book with him – the codex is a book for travellers after all – but he might need to use one of the community's books or to make use in his teaching of some other texts. If the traveller brought with him a text unknown in that community, there might then be the need to arrange to have a copy made for the community; and if the traveller were only staying for the short period, three days, envisaged by the *Didache* (11:5), then this would require familiarity with the processes of copying or knowing how to arrange to have a copy made in the near future whose exemplar would be supplied from elsewhere. By the same token, if another church wanted a copy of something in the care of the ὑπηρέτης, then this would bring its own problems. Making sure that the copy was made, that the original was returned, the copy safely dispatched, and the finances of the whole affair accounted for: such office-based skills were not least among those of the ὑπηρέται noted by Holmes in his 1935 study. And, of course, books wear out and become damaged and so there was need to find replacements: were they being read, for

Space and the Development of Early Urban Christianity – the Example of Ephesus.' *JTS* ns 62 (2011) pp. 541–69, who challenges the assumptions of many earlier writers who imagined large palatial edifices as the location of 'house churches'. Moreover, Billings makes the point (p. 543) that the writings which constitute the New Testament are 'arguably the best primary source for non-elite populations that has survived antiquity'; and I would consequently argue that the ὑπηρέται are just such non-elite officials.

[44] On this network see T. O'Loughlin, *The Didache: A Window on the Earliest Christians* (London: SPCK, 2010), pp. 105–28; on the practicalities of the network, see Thompson, 'The Holy Internet'; and on the problems of such inter-church travellers, see A. Milavec, 'Distinguishing True from False Prophets: the Protective Wisdom of the *Didache*.' *JECS* 2 (1994) pp. 117–36.

example, at *symposia* (the scene usually imagined today for early Christian gatherings[45]) where just one spill could render pages illegible? The layers of redaction we find in the text of Mark would provide supporting evidence for many such renewals.[46] Given the special skills involved in book-related work, I imagine that when the need for such a person arose in a church, if there was a ὑπηρέτης, who already possessed them and had the bureaucratic leaning for keeping track of lists, accounts, and money, that individual would have been selected and could then be known as their ὑπηρέτης τοῦ λόγου.

In short, the ὑπηρέτης kept the codices safely, made them available to those who taught, organised the copying of books and was probably the 'contact person' in a church when book production was taking place for another community. In this last task they were, in effect, acting as publishers. Today we would find their analogue in institutional librarians charged to ensure the availability of the books and databases needed for that institution's work.

So for how many books would they have been responsible? If we take 90–110 CE as roughly the period when Luke was active, then there would possibly have been at least two accounts of Jesus in most communities (Mark and Q) and Luke himself suggests more than two accounts by his reference to πολλοί (Luke 1:1). There was, almost certainly, some collection of letters – its extent in any church at that date cannot be known – but we might think of that as being the ancestor to P46. We can also assume a collection of other shorter texts – other letters, or the *Didache* in some form, or some written sermons – which might have been bundled into a single codex. When we actually look at our evidence for such early combinations of texts – 2 Corinthians being an ideal example[47] – then we may indeed be observing the work not of theologically sophisticated

---

[45] See D.E. Smith, *From Symposium to Eucharist: The Banquet in the Early Christian World* (Minneapolis MN: Fortress, 2003); and for its appropriateness of a *symposium*-setting to Luke, see his 'Table Fellowship as a Literary Motif in the Gospel of Luke.' *JBL* 106 (1987) pp. 613–6; and P.-B. Smit, 'A Symposiastic Background to James?' *NTS* 58 (2011) pp. 105–22.

[46] See H. Koester, *From Jesus to the Gospels: Interpreting the New Testament in its Context.* (Minneapolis MN: Fortress, 2007), pp. 39–53.

[47] See H.D. Betz, *2 Corinthians 8 and 9* (Philadelphia PA: Fortress, 1985); we might also think of the various attempts to explain the development of the Pauline corpus as a corpus of letters.

preachers or those who might attract the title of αὐτόπται or προφῆται, but of the keepers of the codices who were pressed by practical considerations of convenience in storing texts in determining what was bound with what. An average collection of half-a-dozen 'Christian' books would not be surprising, but that is little more than a guess. However, the largest part of the library – in both the number of texts as well as in awkwardness for storage – and its most valuable asset must surely have been 'the scriptures' (i.e. those texts we now group under the heading of 'the Septuagint'). Given the importance attached to them by Luke (e.g. in the Emmaus story at Luke 24:27, 32 and 45) and the way he imagines them being used by Peter and Paul (Acts 2:14–36; 17:2 and 11; 18:24 and 28), we must assume that having a copy of 'the scriptures' was a *desideratum* of each community. This is paralleled in the writing of the other evangelists. In the time of Paul, the need would have been supplied in the synagogue; but by the end of the century – with groups gradually separating into different religions, and an increasing division upon linguistic lines – if a church wished to read 'the scriptures' (and all the evidence points to the fact that they did), then they had to have them for themselves.[48] Obtaining and maintaining such a collection may have been the most demanding task facing the ὑπηρέται. Moreover, if we think of them having to look after both 'the scriptures' and the new texts of their own movement, then the designation ὑπηρέται τοῦ λόγου makes all the more sense. In this case, 'the word' would not simply refer to the Christian message – as most commentators on Luke assume – but to 'the word of God' implying the whole event of revelation to Israel as recorded in books.[49]

CONCLUSION

One could find support for this understanding of ὑπηρέται by following the uses of the term in second-century Christian writings, especially those of Ignatius of Antioch, and this has been done by Holmes, Rengsdorf, and Collins.[50] I do not want to follow this route for two reasons. First, if one

---

[48] The references to 'the reading of prophets' in Justin (*First Apology*, 67) or the second-century papyrus fragments of codices containing Old Testament texts would be certain evidence for this concern albeit from a generation later than Luke.

[49] Such an understanding of 'the word of God' would be consistent with Luke's use of the term in Luke 5:1, 8:11, 13, 15, 21; and 11:28, and with Acts 4:31 and 6:2,4, and 7.

[50] Collins did this in his book *Diakonia* and his references to the matter on pp.

accepts this paper's proposal for the task of the ὑπηρέται, then that conditions one's expectations from other references to 'minor officials'; it is simpler to note that these references do not contradict what I have argued here. Second, each of the scholars just mentioned worked on the assumption that Ignatius wrote in roughly the same period as Luke – both reflecting the church in the last decade of the first century and the first years of the second. However, if we accept the later dating for Ignatius, as I believe we must, then that evidence is much more problematic.[51] Ignatius would not be simply a generation later than Luke, but reflect a situation where many developments regarding the Christian self-identity, views of the status of Christian texts, and structures within the churches had taken place. Consequently, a study of ὑπηρέτ- in Ignatius or the *Letter of Barnabas* is today a study in its own right.

Whether one accepts my proposal or not, some things are certain from the very survival of those first-century documents that have come down to us. First, there was some kind of preservation system for books. Second, there was attention to, and mechanisms for, the copying and diffusion of those books. Third, there were structures that allowed texts to circulate independently of travelling performers – because texts have survived (such as Paul's letter to Philemon) which were never intended as performances. Considering these facts we recognise that it is most unlikely they would have come about without attention from those in the community with a specific set of skills, quite apart from literacy. These skills were present in the churches – though probably not ubiquitous or else we might not have lost so much – and the term by which Luke knew them was ὑπηρέται τοῦ λόγου, a group which for him were distinct from αὐτόπται. In performing these mundane but most necessary tasks, these sacristan/librarian-figures deserve, in retrospect, the respect given to them when we view them as 'ministers of the word'.

---

240 and 330 are particularly important in showing that there is no contradiction with what I have argued here.

[51] See T.D. Barnes, 'The Date of Ignatius.' *ExpT* 120 (2008) pp. 119–30 who shows that it must date from the 140s at the earliest.

2. THE GOSPEL OF JOHN AND ITS ORIGINAL READERS

HANS FÖRSTER
IN CO-OPERATION WITH ULRIKE SWOBODA

INTRODUCTION

The Gospel of John is not an easy text to assign to a specific group of intended readers. Some words are explained in full, which might therefore hint at a group not familiar with Jewish terminology or customs. For example, names and even the theological title Messiah are translated (e.g. Σιλωάμ in 9:7; Μεσσίας in 1:41, Μεσσίας in 4:25) and certain activities take place 'according to the custom of the Jews' (e.g. καθὼς ἔθος ἐστὶν τοῖς Ἰουδαίοις in 19:40; compare also John 2:6). These observations have often been used to argue that the addressees were from a non-Jewish community.[1] Other things from a similar context, however, which might be thought to need an explanation are not explained. This leads to the conclusion that the implied author has an expectation of a model-reader who is familiar with certain terms but not others.[2] This assumed knowledge

---

[1] Cf. for example Udo Schnelle, *Das Evangelium nach Johannes*, 3rd edn. (ThHKNT 4. Leipzig: Evangelische Verlagsanstalt, 2004), p. 8 n. 39, 64.

[2] On potential readers of John, see Gerald L. Borchert, *John 1-11* (The New American Commentary 25A. Nashville TN: Broadman & Holman, 1996), p. 51 and Richard A. Culpepper, *Anatomy of the Fourth Gospel. A Study in Literary Design* (Philadelphia PA: Fortress, 1983), p. 212; the latter should be read with Staley's caution in mind that 'Culpepper is primarily indebted to Prince, Rabbinowitz, and Iser for his description of the "readers" in the Fourth Gospel. But because he does not clarify the differences or overlapping areas of their respective theories, his own discussion of the narratee becomes quite confused.' (Jeffrey L. Staley, *The Print's*

has in consequence led to problems in the ancient translations of some passages, where the references were no longer understood. It seems possible to show that even early translators of the Gospel of John were in some cases lacking specific knowledge which the original addressees were assumed to possess. The aim of this research project is therefore to collect those instances where the special knowledge assumed of the intended readers seems to have resulted in inaccuracies or problems in either the Latin or the Coptic tradition of John's Gospel. Furthermore, if it is possible to demonstrate that there are some areas of knowledge which are more prone to be lacking from the translations, this might give additional insight into the question of the original addressees of this narrative, whose identity is still a puzzle.[3]

THE CURRENT STATE OF RESEARCH

For a long time the addressees of John's Gospel were supposed to have come from a mostly non-Jewish environment. Wellhausen argued forcefully – focussing especially on the occurrence of the Greek word ἀποσυνάγωγος, whose three occurrences in the New Testament are all within this Gospel (John 9:22; 12:42 and 16:2) – that the group which is addressed by the author of the Gospel of John has already fully broken with the synagogue.[4] In the scholarly literature of the last two decades, a tendency to a new or at least a newly accented interpretation can be observed. The argument found in Wellhausen's publications is taken into consideration by Hengel and Schnelle[5] who argue that the addressees are

---

First Kiss. A Rhetorical Investigation of the Implied Reader in the Fourth Gospel. SBLDS 82. Atlanta: Scholars Press, 1988, p. 43.)

  [3] Cf. Francis J. Moloney, *The Gospel of John.* (Sacra Pagina 4. Collegeville MN: Liturgical Press, 1998), p. 16.

  [4] Julius Wellhausen, *Evangelienkommentare. Mit einer Einleitung von Martin Hengel.* (Berlin et al.: de Gruyter, 1987), p. 127.

  [5] Schnelle, *Evangelium*, p. 8: 'Beeinflußt und geprägt wurde die überwiegend heidenchristliche Gemeinde des Evangelisten im Verlauf ihrer Geschichte durch die Auseinandersetzung mit Anhängern Johannes d. Täufers, den Juden und doketischen Irrlehrern innerhalb der joh. Schule.' Cf. also ibid. 9: 'Zweifellos gab es in der Geschichte der joh. Schule Auseinandersetzungen mit der jüdischen Umwelt, die sich auch in den Texten des Johannesevangeliums als einer Vita Jesu niederschlugen (vgl. z. B. Joh. 5; 9; 16,1–4; 19,38). Bestimmend für die aktuelle Situation der joh. Schule z. Z. der Abfassung des Johannesevangeliums ist diese Auseinandersetzung aber nicht mehr.'

mostly of Hellenistic (i.e. non-Jewish) origin.[6] These authors, however, dedicate extensive passages to the question of the relationship of the Gospel of John to Judaism. Hengel also brings the old age of the author into consideration, drawing attention to the late date of the composition of this Gospel. His conclusion is that the Johannine community has already distanced itself from the synagogue.[7]

A contrasting argument can be found in the publications of Wengst, who argues that the author of this Gospel focusses on a Jewish audience who found themselves in a minority position compared with other Jews in their immediate environment.[8] For Wengst, the question of the exclusion from the synagogues, and therefore the use of the Greek word ἀποσυνάγωγος, is a discussion taking place during the composition of the Gospel.[9] This is directly opposed to the way in which scholars like Schnelle interpret the situation but is, however, supported by Ashton.[10] The fear of the parents of the man born blind (John 9:22) to express an opinion concerning Jesus and his mission is seen by Wengst as exactly the situation in which the addressees of John's Gospel find themselves: were they to confess they would be denied community with their fellow Jews.[11] Needless to say, the hypothesis proposed by Wengst attracted criticism. Hengel's critique focusses on the reconstruction of the historical situation in which the Gospel had been composed, and argues that ἀποσυνάγωγος in John 16:2 is a reminiscence of an earlier time when the separation had already taken place.[12] This hypothesis of a strongly Hellenistic environment,

---

[6] Martin Hengel, *Die johanneische Frage. Ein Lösungsversuch. Mit einem Beitrag zur Apokalypse von Jörg Frey* (WUNT 67. Tübingen: Mohr, 1993), p. 300; Schnelle, *Evangelium*, pp. 8–9.

[7] Hengel, *Johanneische Frage*, p. 298: '... daß der Alte Johannes, seine Schule und die sie umgebenden kleinasiatischen Gemeinden sich schon längst von der Synagoge getrennt haben. Die 'Ausstoßung' bzw. Trennung liegt lange zurück, und sie hat sich vermutlich auf unterschiedliche Weise und sukzessive vollzogen.'

[8] Klaus Wengst, *Das Johannesevangelium*, 2nd edn. (ThKNT 4.1. Stuttgart: Kohlhammer, 2004), p. 30.

[9] Wengst, *Johannesevangelium*, p. 27.

[10] Schnelle, *Evangelium*, pp. 9–10, contrasted with John Ashton, *Understanding the Fourth Gospel*. 2nd edn. (Oxford: Oxford UP, 2008), p. 111.

[11] Wengst, *Johannesevangelium*, pp. 26–7.

[12] Hengel, *Johanneische Frage*, pp. 291–3; see also Keith Hopkins, 'Christian Number and its Implications.' *JECS* 6 (1998) pp. 185–226.

however, made it necessary to 'reclaim' the Gospel of John as a text which
is deeply rooted in 'Scripture' (in this context denoting the Septuagint as
well as the Hebrew Bible).[13] This is one of the reasons why scholars caution
against the overinterpretation of the word ἀποσυνάγωγος.[14] One possible
solution would be to explain the difficulties (and inconsistencies)
throughout the Gospel as evidence for the widely-held hypothesis of an
evolution of the Johannine community.[15]

In summary, it is obvious that the text of John's Gospel can be (and
has been) used to support different interpretations of the addressees and
the historical situation of the time when this Gospel was written. These
proposed settings can be mutually exclusive. What is more, no agreement
has been reached as to the interpretation of the data. One could even argue
that some of the scholars try to pacify both parties in the discussion, which
leads to contradictory theories and in consequence to the suggestion that
the question is in need of further research.[16]

---

[13] For the sources of the Gospel, see Ruben Zimmermann, 'Jesus im Bild
Gottes. Anspielungen auf das Alte Testament im Johannesevangelium am Beispiel
der Hirtenbildfelder in Joh 10.' In: Frey and Schnelle (eds), *Kontexte des
Johannesevangeliums. Das vierte Evangelium in religions- und traditionsgeschichtlicher
Perspektive.* (WUNT 175. Tübingen: Mohr Siebeck, 2004), pp. 81–116, especially p.
86: 'Die konkreten Zitate zeigen, daß Johannes die LXX gekannt hat, aber ebenso
'eine intime Bekanntschaft mit dem hebräischen Text' zu erkennen gibt. Er benutzt
also die LXX und/oder den MT als Quelle.'

[14] E.g. Philippe Roulet and Ulrich Ruegg, 'Etude de Jean 6. La narration et
l'histoire de la redaction' in Kaestli, Poffet and Zumstein (eds), *La Communauté
Johannique et son Histoire. La trajectoire de l'évangile de Jean aux deux premiers siècles.*
(Genève: Labor et Fides, 1990), p. 244.

[15] E.g. Raymond E. Brown, *Ringen um die Gemeinde. Der Weg der Kirche nach den
Johanneischen Schriften.* (Salzburg: Müller, 1982), p. 22.

[16] One example of such contradiction is Michael Theobald, *Das Evangelium nach
Johannes. Kapitel 1-12.* 4th edn. (Regensburger Neues Testament. Regensburg: Pustet,
2009), p. 69, who sees the Gospel of John as 'Katalysator ... im ungeklärten
Trennungsprozess von Kirche und Synagoge, von dem man ja noch nicht wusste,
wohin er führen sollte ...' but states on p. 154 that: 'Nimmt man die stereotype
Rede von Festen der Juden hinzu (2,13; 5,1; 6,4; 7,2; 11, 55; 19,42; vgl. auch 2,4) –
in der Regel Wallfahrtsfeste, zu denen viele Juden aus der Diaspora nach Jerusalem
kamen –, dann wird die Entgrenzung des Terminus hin zu einer gewöhnlichen
Bezeichnung für die Mitglieder der synagogalen Religionsgemeinschaft insgesamt
deutlich. Der so gebrauchte Terminus gibt – wie z.B. in 1 Makk, wo er im Mund

The Method: Combination of Textual Criticism and Collocation Analysis

The intention of this project is to combine two methods in order to achieve a better understanding of the addressees of John's Gospel. The first method to be used may be called collocation analysis, while the second is textual criticism. In this context, collocation means the occurrence of one sort of term in close proximity to another which might convey specific information.[17] If this information is different from the information conveyed by a term which – on principle – belongs to a similar group and is collocated with different terms in a statistically significant way, this is of importance for the identification of the intended reader of the text since it presupposes a special knowledge in certain areas. In other words, collocations in the Firthian sense, who spoke of 'an order of mutual expectancy', can be interpreted as empirical statements about the predictability of word combinations.[18] Any disruption of this predictability in certain groups of words is therefore highly significant.

Example: The Treatment of Jewish Feasts

Different Jewish celebrations are collocated with information concerning time and/or place (e.g. John 2:13; 6:4; 11:55). On the other hand, the names of places – which, by collocation, are part of the information conveyed about the celebrations – are very often translated or explained (e.g. John 5:2 or 19:17). This combination leads to the somewhat contradictory conclusion that the reader seems to be expected to know and to understand how the Jewish liturgical year functions and the meaning and content of the different feasts, but is not expected to understand the meaning of certain

---

von Nicht-Juden begegnet, während die Juden selbst von Israel sprechen (anders in 2 Makk) – die Außenperspektive wieder (vgl. auch oben S. 66f.).'

[17] See Matthew B. O'Donnell, *Corpus Linguistics & the Greek of the New Testament*. (New Testament Monographs 6. Sheffield: Phoenix, 2005), pp. 331–6; Maria Iliescu, 'Kollokationen in den romanischen Sprachen' in Dietrich, *Lexikalische Semantik und Korpuslinguistik* (Tübingen: Narr, 2006), pp. 189–208.

[18] John R. Firth, 'A Synopsis of Linguistic Theory 1930–1955' in *Studies in Linguistic Analysis*. (Special vol. of the Philological Society. Oxford: Blackwell, 1962) pp. 1–32: 'Collocations of a given word are statements of the habitual or customary places of that word in collocational order but not in any other contextual order and emphatically not in any grammatical order. The collocation of a word or a 'piece' is not to be regarded as a mere juxtaposition, it is an order of mutual expectancy' (pp. 12–13).

Hebrew terms for places (or even persons; e.g. John 1:42). This in principle, would point to a very specific group of readers which knew the Jewish liturgy but not Hebrew.[19] As for the specific feasts mentioned, it is noteworthy that the Dedication of the Temple and Tabernacles only occur in John, whereas Pesach appears in all four Gospels. However, neither the meaning of the names of these feasts nor any indication of the content is given in John, not even for the transliterated Pesach which all three other Gospels implicitly or explicitly explain as the feast of 'unleavened bread.'[20]

It seems that the meaning of the feasts mentioned in the Gospel of John was not always grasped by the translators. In John 10:22, the Dedication of the Temple is treated differently in Latin and Sahidic traditions. The Sahidic translates ἐγκαίνια correctly as ϫⲓ ⲁⲉⲓⲕ, which may be translated literally as 'to receive consecration'. This circumlocution is required because a direct equivalent obviously did not exist in Sahidic. The *Vulgate* of the New Testament, which seems to be more literal than the *Vetus Latina*, has a transliteration of this Greek word, as do certain *Vetus Latina* manuscripts.[21] In contrast to the Sahidic version, the word is here treated as a name.[22] The most probable interpretation of this is that the Greek word was not understood by some of the Latin translators. Jerome chooses a transliteration rather than an idiomatic translation, one of the characteristics of his translation of the Gospel of John which Burton would characterise as 'merely competent'.[23] However, Jerome's practice could pose problems for those not familiar with the content of the transliterated word

---

[19] Cf. however, Raymond E. Brown, *The Gospel According to John (I-XII)*. (Anchor Bible Commentary 29. New York: Doubleday, 1966), p. lxxiv: '[I]t is not impossible that the first edition of John was directed to the Palestinian scene and the subsequent edition(s) adapted for an audience living outside Palestine. Nor, since we believe that the Gospel was also directed to Gentiles, is it impossible that some of these explanations were included for Gentile readers.'

[20] Matthew 26:17; Mark 14:1 and 12; Luke 22:1 and 7.

[21] On the literalism of the Vulgate, see Philip Burton, *The Old Latin Gospels. A Study of their Texts and Language*. (Oxford: Oxford UP, 2000), p. 192; Rebecca R. Harrison, "Jerome's Revision of the Gospels." (Unpublished doctoral dissertation, University of Pennsylvania, 1986), p. 16.

[22] Cf. Franz Wutz, *Onomastica Sacra. Untersuchungen zum Liber Interpretationis Nominum Hebraicorum des Hl. Hieronymus. 1. Hälfte Quellen und System der Onomastika.* (Leipzig: J. C. Hinrichs'sche Buchhandlung, 1914), p. 413.

[23] Burton, *Old Latin Gospels*, p. 199.

because they did not possess the same linguistic expertise as Jerome which would have enabled them to understand a Greek word in a Latin text. This impression is strengthened by the fact that there is high variation in the spelling of this 'name' (for example *enkennia, enchenia, incenia, inchenia* and so on).[24] The Latin word *dedicatio* is, however, the technical term used in the Latin translation of the Old Testament for ἐγκαίνια. This shows that the translators of John had problems with the 'name' – or rather with a Greek word which they perceived to be a name. Since the first translations into Latin were probably made in the latter part of the second century, this shows that even by this time the term was not understood by the rather well trained specialists translating the Gospel. The reader, of course, had similar problems with newly created names derived from a foreign language or a new meaning added to a commonly known word. Jerome's practice of calquing carries with it the risk of mistranslation and/or misunderstanding.[25] Some Old Latin manuscripts use *dedicatio* as equivalent of the Greek term, translating in accordance with the Latin version of the Old Testament (cf. also *renouatum est* for ἐνεκαινίσθη at 1 Macc. 4:54).

We may therefore observe that the term used in the Greek text of John 10:22 to denote the feast of the Dedication of the Temple might be one which might require explanation even for a reader of the original. The confusion of the trained second-century Latin translators indicates that this word and its meaning in the given context might not be common knowledge, but rather a special knowledge. However, as no explanation is given, the writer of the Gospel clearly expects the reader to know what he describes. This corresponds to the treatment of Jewish feasts in John in general: an understanding of the feast is presupposed among the intended readers but not knowledge of the geography of the Holy Land or of Hebrew. In addition, the feast is used to locate the time of year at which an event occurred, in this case winter. This appears to contradict the commonly-held opinion concerning John 10:22, that it indicates a community of readers which is not Jewish. Culpepper, for example, comments: 'A Jewish reader would hardly need to be told when the festival was celebrated, since it occurs at the same time every year.'[26] The lack of

---

[24] For the fluctuations of proper nouns, see Harrison, "Jerome's Revision", p. 159.

[25] On calques (or 'loan translations'), see Burton, *Old Latin Gospels*, p. 195.

[26] Culpepper, *Fourth Gospel*, pp. 220–1.

explanation of the name of the feast, however, suggests that the readers may have been Jewish.

The same conclusion may be drawn from the treatment of the feast of Tabernacles in John 7:2. All Latin and Coptic traditions simply transliterate the Greek term. The Latin translators of the Old Testament used *tabernacula* – the plural of *tabernaculum* – to translate σκηνοπηγία.[27] In a similar way, one might suggest that the transliteration in the New Testament of the word for 'unleavened bread' (*azymos*) is a further example of this phenomenon. Here, however, there is an important difference in that this is also transliterated in the Latin version of the Old Testament, and the combination *panis azymus* becomes a technical term for unleavened bread.[28] A comparable development may be seen in *encenia*, the word used in John 10:22 instead of the Latin term *dedicatio*. By the time of Egeria, this has become a fixed term for the dedication of a church: it seems most likely that she knew this word from her versions of the Bible.[29] Church Fathers such as Isidore of Seville and Augustine even explain the word in John from its Greek origins.[30]

CONCLUSION

The results of this first application of a combination of textual criticism and collocation analysis are promising. The Gospel of John provides less explanation of the Jewish feast Pesach than the other canonical Gospels. At the same time, it mentions more feasts than the other Gospels. The names of these feasts seem already to have been problematic for the translators of

---

[27] See further Wutz, *Onomastica Sacra*, p. 431.

[28] See Georgij Avvakumov, *Die Entstehung des Unionsgedankens. Die lateinische Theologie des Hochmittelalters* (Veröffentlichungen des Grabmann-Institutes 47. Berlin: Akademischer Verlag, 2002), p. 35.

[29] Egeria, *Itinerarium* 48.1f., 49.1ff. See further Antonius A. R. Bastiaensen, *Observations sur le vocabulaire liturgique dans l'intinérarie d'Égérie.* (Academisch Proefschrift. Nijmegen/Utrecht: Dekker, 1962), pp. 119–121.

[30] Isidore of Seville, *De officiis ecclesiasticis* 1.36.1; Augustine, *In evangelium Johannis tractatus* 48.2: *Encaenia festivitas erat dedicationis templi. Graece enim* καινόν *dicitur novum. Quandocumque novum aliquid fuerit dedicatum, Encaenia vocantur.* Nonetheless, in the prayer over the dedication of a church the word is also glossed with a Latin explanation: *Praesta quaesumus Domine, ut haec basilica, cuius hodie nunciamus incenia, quae tua dedicatione subsistit solemnis, tua semper fiat habitatione praeclara.* (Benedictio ecclesiae novae; cod. Vindob. theol. 277; *PL* 138, col. 1040a).

the second and third centuries. Therefore, caution must be adopted in using the mention of these feasts as an indication that the intended readership of the Gospel was not Jewish. It is also possible, if not probable, that the mention of the feasts was intended as a way of measuring time, with the reader being expected to connect the feasts with the different times of the year. This, however, would point to a model-reader quite familiar with Jewish life (or rather with the Jewish structuring of the year) while it seems quite obvious that the reader is not assumed to know the geography of the Holy Land or Jerusalem. At this stage of the research, however, it is not yet possible to propose sound conclusions on the basis of these preliminary results.

3. THE EUSEBIAN CANONS: THEIR IMPLICATIONS AND POTENTIAL

SATOSHI TODA

PROLOGUE

The purpose of this paper is to examine the implications of the so-called Eusebian (Evangelical) Canons and to see the potential of this interpretative device for New Testament studies, including the textual criticism of the Gospels. A question should be posed at the outset as to what has been regarded as the merit of the Eusebian Canons. It was once thought that Ammonius, whose name is mentioned in Eusebius' *Letter to Carpianus*,[1] is the one who introduced the division of sections into the four Gospels: 355 sections for Matthew, 233 for Mark, 342 for Luke, and 232 for John.[2] Now,

---

[1] The Greek text is in NA28, pp. 89*–90*. Its English translation can be found in H.H. Oliver, 'The Epistle of Eusebius to Carpianus. Textual Tradition and Translation.' *NovT* 3 (1959) pp. 144–5.

[2] These four figures amount to 1162, the very figure which is mentioned in Epiphanius, *Ancoratus*, 50.6 = K. Holl, ed., *Epiphanius (Ancoratus und Panarion). Bd. 1: Ancoratus und Panarion haer. 1–33* (GCS 25. Leipzig: J.C. Hinrichs, 1915), p. 60. It is probable that this division into 1162 sections was made by Eusebius himself (see also E. Nestle, *Einführung in das Griechische Neue Testament*, 3rd edn. (Göttingen: Vandenhoeck & Ruprecht, 1909), p. 64.

In passing I add that G.H. Gwilliam, 'The Ammonian Sections, Eusebian Canons, and Harmonizing Tables in the Syriac Tetraevangelium' *Studia biblica et ecclesiastica*, vol. 2, (Oxford: Clarendon, 1890), pp. 241–72 discusses the division into sections introduced in Syriac manuscripts of the Gospels, and argues that the sections of this Syriac division are more numerous than that introduced by Eusebius himself (426 for Matthew, 290 for Mark, 402 for Luke, and 271 for John; 1389 in total), and that this more minute division does not derive from Eusebius

27

however, it is Eusebius that is considered the person in question.[3] The *Letter to Carpianus* suggests that, in Ammonius' harmonization, on the one hand, only the text of Matthew could be read continuously, whereas the text of the other three Gospels was cut into pieces and each piece was placed in a column parallel to the relevant passage of Matthew. The Eusebian Canons, on the other, allow the text of each Gospel to be read continuously, and enable comparison of different Gospels by means of separate canon tables. This was considered a great merit of the Eusebian Canons. However, is this the only merit? This is the question which will be discussed in this paper.

EARLIER STUDIES

So far the Eusebian Canons have been studied mainly from the viewpoint of art history,[4] and little attention has been paid to their content.[5] A number of dictionary entries may be briefly mentioned.[6] The most voluminous work

---

himself, but should be considered an invention of later Syriac tradition of Gospel manuscripts (at p. 253). It is this (Syriac) division into sections that is dealt with in A. Vaccari, 'Le sezioni evangeliche di Eusebio e il Diatessaron di Taziano nella letteratura siriaca' *Rivista degli studi orientali* 32 (1957), pp. 433–52. This Syriac division into sections is printed in the margin in P.E. Pusey & G.H. Gwilliam (eds), *Tetraeuangelium sanctum juxta simplicem Syrorum versionem* (Oxford: Clarendon, 1901).

[3] See e.g. Nestle, 'Evangeliensynopse' (see note 13 below), p. 41.

[4] For example, in J. Leroy, 'Nouveaux témoins des Canons d'Eusèbe illustrés selon la tradition syriaque' *Cahiers archéologiques* 9 (1957) pp. 117–40 and id., 'Recherches sur la tradition iconographique des Canons d'Eusèbe en Ethiopie' *Cahiers archéologiques* 12 (1962) pp. 173–204, the Eusebian Canons are treated solely from the viewpoint of the history of illuminated manuscripts (Syriac and Ethiopic respectively).

[5] Here I mention two articles which will not be touched upon later in this paper. S. Grébaut, 'Les dix canons d'Eusèbe et d'Ammonius d'après le ms. éthiopien n° 3 de M. E. Delorme' *Revue de l'Orient chrétien* 18 (1913) pp. 314–7 publishes simply the passages which Grébaut found in the aforementioned Ethiopic manuscript and which are related to the Eusebian Canons (Ethiopic texts as well as their translation in French), and does not contain any discussion. A. Penna, 'Il De consensu evangelistarum ed i Canoni Eusebiani' *Biblica* 36 (1955) pp. 1–19 argues that it is unlikely that Augustine, when composing *De consensu evangelistarum*, consulted the Eusebian Canons.

[6] These include J. van den Gheyn, art. 'Eusèbe', in *Dictionnaire de la Bible*, vol. 2.2 (Paris: Letouzey et Ané, 1899), 2051–6 (mentions the Canons at 2051–2); A. Penna, art. 'Eusebio di Cesarea' in *Enciclopedia cattolica*, vol. 5 (Città del Vaticano, s.d. (1950?)), 851–4 (mentions the Canons at 852); G. Ladocsi, art. 'Eusebian Canons',

hitherto published concerning the Eusebian Canons is that of Nordenfalk.[7] Although it is a work of art history, in the introduction (pp. 45–54) the author discusses the content of the Canons. He argues, for example, that the canon tables do not enumerate all the possible combinations and that the combinations 'Sections common to Mark, Luke and John' and 'Sections common to Mark and John' are lacking. Nordenfalk simply describes this lack, and it seems as if he suggests that it thereby reveals the imperfection of Eusebius' analysis of the Gospels.[8]

Concerning the way Eusebius compiled the canon tables, Nordenfalk points out that, like Ammonius, Eusebius' work is first and foremost based upon Matthew, and that as a second term of comparison he uses not Mark but Luke.[9] This observation is correct, as the combination 'Sections common to Matthew, Luke and John', which is Canon III, precedes Canon IV ('Sections common to Matthew, Mark and John'), and that the combination 'Sections common to Matthew and Luke', which is Canon V, precedes Canon VI ('Sections common to Matthew and Mark').[10]

As for the date of compilation of the Canons, Nordenfalk argues that it is later than Eusebius' ordination as bishop of Caesarea in 314 (*terminus post quem*) and earlier than 331 (*terminus ante quem*) when the Roman emperor Constantine ordered him fifty copies of the Bible (Gospels). Nordenfalk's arguments are not decisive, however. There is no reason to fix the *terminus post quem* as the time of Eusebius' consecration; it can be earlier or later. As for the *terminus ante quem*, Nordenfalk's view is based on the supposition

---

in: A. di Berardino (ed.), *Encyclopedia of the Early Church*, vol. 1 (New York: Oxford University Press, 1992), p. 298; Anon., art. 'Eusebian Canons and Sections', in: F.L. Cross & E.A. Livingstone (eds), *The Oxford Dictionary of the Christian Church*, 3rd edn (Oxford: Oxford UP, 2005), p. 577. H. Leclercq, art. 'Canons d'Eusèbe', in *Dictionnaire d'archéologie chrétienne et de liturgie*, vol. 2.2 (Paris: Letouzey et Ané, 1910), 1950–4 discusses solely the aspects pertaining to art history.

[7] C. Nordenfalk, *Die spätantiken Kanontafeln*, 2 vols. (Göteborg: Oscar Isacsons, 1938).

[8] Nordenfalk, *Kanontafeln*, Textband, p. 48. This lack is also mentioned in Nestle, *Einführung*, pp. 64–5, without presenting any interpretation.

[9] Nordenfalk, *loc. cit.*

[10] It should be added that Eusebius knew the normal order of the four Gospels, i.e., Matthew, Mark, Luke, John; this is clear from the fact that Canon X (*proprie*) is arranged along this order. It appears that Luke is used as a second term simply because Luke contains many more episodes than Mark.

that Codex Sinaiticus (GA 01, ‭א‬) is among the aforementioned copies ordered by Constantine, but this is far from certain.

Nordenfalk came back to the subject in an article published almost 50 years after the appearance of his monograph.[11] In this article he mainly discusses the textual problems of the Canons. For example, he points out that, in the Stuttgart Vulgate the canon tables of the (Latin) Eusebian Canons are also critically edited,[12] whereas in Nestle–Aland only the beginning of each section of the four Gospels was checked throughout.[13] The canon tables themselves have never been an object of a critical edition.[14]

A recent article of Thomas O'Loughlin[15] deals with much wider subjects than this paper, but it does not put the Canons themselves to detailed scrutiny, the very thing that I intend to present in this paper. Another difference is that O'Loughlin thinks that the Eusebian 'Apparatus' (according to his terminology) was compiled at the end of the third century,[16] which differs from my view, as will be explained later.

ANALYSES

After reviewing earlier studies, some observations will be presented so as to show the implications of the Eusebian Canons. Materials are taken from the narrative of the Passion. Roman numerals always refer to the numbers of the Canons.

---

[11] C. Nordenfalk, 'The Eusebian Canon-Tables. Some Textual Problems.' *JTS* ns 35 (1984) pp. 96–104.

[12] R. Weber, R. Gryson et al. (eds), *Biblia sacra iuxta vulgatam versionem*, 5th edn, (Stuttgart: Deutsche Bibelgesellschaft, 2007), includes on pp. 1515–26 the critically edited Latin canon tables as well as Jerome's letter to Pope Damasus which serves as an introduction to the Canons.

[13] This check was made by E. Nestle, 'Die Eusebianische Evangeliensynopse', *Neue Kirchliche Zeitschrift* 19 (1908) pp. 40–51, 93–114, 219–232, and the result was incorporated for the first time in the seventh edition of Nestle's *Novum Testamentum Graece*.

[14] Nordenfalk, 'Textual Problems', p. 96. I understand that a critical edition of the Greek Eusebian Canons is now in preparation by Prof. Martin Wallraff (Basel).

[15] T. O'Loughlin, 'Harmonizing the Truth: Eusebius and the Problem of the Four Gospels.' *Traditio* 65 (2010) pp. 1–29.

[16] *Ibid.*, 1.

A. Problems Related to the Combinations of the Canon Tables

First of all, what does it mean that the Canon-tables have only ten canons, whereas the number of all the mathematically possible combinations is still greater?[17] As mentioned above, the combinations which do not exist in the canon tables are 'Sections common to Mark, Luke and John' and 'Sections common to Mark and John'. The latter means that, according to Eusebius, no section is common to Mark and John; in other words, since John was generally considered to be the last of the four Gospels to be written, this lack implies that, according to the Eusebian Canons, the author of John never consulted Mark when composing his Gospel. To the best of my knowledge, such an interpretation has never yet been presented concerning the relationship between Mark and John. So the problem is whether it is tenable or not.

Before trying to answer this question, we need to know the level of detail of the analysis on the basis of which Eusebius introduced the division into sections in John; in other words, we need to know how meticulous he was in compiling his Canons. Taking the narrative of the Passion as example, we see that many sections of John belong to Canon X (*in quo Ioh. proprie*; *Sondergut* in German). However, with remarkable attention to detail, Eusebius lists sections of John which can also be found in other Gospels. The following example from Chapter 15 of John will illustrate the point:

X Ioh 138 = John 15:17-19

III Ioh 139 = John 15:20a ʻοὐκ ἔστιν <u>δοῦλος</u> μείζων τοῦ <u>κυρίου</u> <u>αὐτοῦ</u>ʼ; cf. Matt. 10:24 ʻοὐκ ἔστιν μαθητὴς ὑπὲρ τὸν διδάσκαλον οὐδὲ <u>δοῦλος</u> ὑπὲρ τὸν <u>κύριον αὐτοῦ</u>ʼ; Luke 6:40

X Ioh 140 = John 15:20b

I Ioh 141 = John 15:21a ʻἀλλὰ ταῦτα πάντα ποιήσουσιν εἰς ὑμᾶς <u>διὰ</u> <u>τὸ ὄνομά μου</u>ʼ; cf. Matt, 24:9 ʻἔσεσθε μισούμενοι ὑπὸ πάντων τῶν ἐθνῶν <u>διὰ τὸ ὄνομά μου</u>ʼ; Mark 13:9; Luke 21:12

III Ioh 142 = John 15:21b ʻὅτι οὐκ οἴδασιν τὸν πέμψαντά με'; cf. Matt. 11:27b ʻκαὶ οὐδεὶς ἐπιγινώσκει τὸν υἱὸν εἰ μὴ ὁ πατήρ, οὐδὲ

---

[17] The number of all the mathematically possible combinations is 15, that is: 1 <four out of four> + 4 <three out of four> + 6 <two out of four> + 4 <one out of four> + 1 <none out of four>, but the last case <none out of four> is meaningless in our context. However, since Eusebius calls all the four cases of <one out of four> 'Canon X (*proprie*)', according to Eusebius' counting all the possible combinations amount to 12.

τὸν πατέρα τις ἐπιγινώσκει εἰ μὴ ὁ υἱὸς καὶ ᾧ ἐὰν βούληται ὁ υἱὸς ἀποκαλύψαι'; Luke 10,22

X Ioh 143 = John 15:22

I Ioh 144 = John 15:23 'ὁ ἐμὲ μισῶν καὶ τὸν πατέρα μου μισεῖ'; cf. Matt. 10:40 'ὁ δεχόμενος ὑμᾶς ἐμὲ δέχεται, καὶ ὁ ἐμὲ δεχόμενος δέχεται τὸν ἀποστείλαντά με'; Mark 9:37b; Luke 10:16

In the cases of Ioh 139 and 141, verbal coincidences can be seen between John and the other Gospels (the underlined expressions). However, in Ioh 142 and 144, the coincidences are not verbal but relate to the content; for Ioh 144 in particular, the resemblance can be identified only after some mental exercise. This being so, one may suppose that, generally speaking, Eusebius' analysis of the Gospels, which led to the classification of sections into various Canons, was quite thorough and minute.

In their lack of the aforementioned two combinations, the Eusebian Canons seem to indicate, at least *de facto*, that the author of John did not need Mark when composing his Gospel. Is this correct or not? In his *Ecclesiastical History* Eusebius explicitly says that the three Gospels (i.e., Matthew, Mark and Luke) 'were distributed to all including himself [i.e., John]', and that John 'welcomed them [i.e., the other three Gospels] and testified to their truth but said that there was only lacking to the narrative the account of what was done by Christ at first and at the beginning of the preaching.'[18] This demonstrates Eusebius' understanding that John consulted Mark, in apparent contradiction to the canon tables. However, since the implication of the absence of the combination 'Sections common to Mark and John' is also crystal-clear, I think it is better to understand a change in Eusebius' conception of the relationship between the Gospels. As Books 1 to 7 of the *Ecclesiastical History* were written early in his career (probably at the end of the third century, and in any case before the Great Persecution), this implies that the Canons were compiled later.

The next step is to ask whether there is any section common to Mark and John or not. I do not pretend to have made as thorough an investigation as Eusebius himself, but I have found two passages which seem to be common only to Mark and John.

---

[18] Eusebius, *Historia Ecclesiastica* III.24.7. The translation is by Kirsopp Lake in the Loeb Classical Library.

(1) **I Mc 64 = I Ioh 49**
Mark 6:37 καὶ λέγουσιν αὐτῷ, ἀπελθόντες ἀγοράσωμεν <u>δηναρίων</u>
<u>διακοσίων ἄρτους</u> καὶ δώσομεν αὐτοῖς φαγεῖν;
John 6:7 ἀπεκρίθη αὐτῷ [ὁ] Φίλιππος, <u>διακοσίων δηναρίων ἄρτοι</u>
οὐκ ἀρκοῦσιν αὐτοῖς ἵνα ἕκαστος βραχύ [τι] λάβῃ.

(2) **I Mc 158 = I.IV Ioh 98**
Mark 14:5 ἠδύνατο γὰρ τοῦτο τὸ μύρον πραθῆναι ἐπάνω <u>δηναρίων</u>
<u>τριακοσίων</u> καὶ δοθῆναι τοῖς πτωχοῖς·
John 12:5 διὰ τί τοῦτο τὸ μύρον οὐκ ἐπράθη <u>τριακοσίων δηναρίων</u>
καὶ ἐδόθη πτωχοῖς;

The underlined expressions are only present in Mark and John. It is therefore not quite correct to think that the author of John did not need Mark *de facto* when composing his Gospel. However, it should be immediately added that this possibility should not be dismissed outright, because the fact that both Mark and John have these expressions ('bread of two hundred denarii' or 'three hundred denarii') may be sheer coincidence. Furthermore, as the thoroughness of Eusebius' analysis has been demonstrated above, the number of passages common only to Mark and John is very few. In this context it would be useful to remember that the number of Greek papyri attesting each Gospel suggests (if not demonstrates) that in antiquity the diffusion of the Gospel of Mark was rather limited compared with the other Gospels.[19]

I therefore argue that suggesting the possibility that the author of John did not need Mark when composing his Gospel is, in itself, a contribution the Eusebian Canons can make to the study of the Gospels and one which should be seriously considered.

B. Implications for the Textual Criticism of the Gospels

It is of course not at all new to take the Canons into consideration for the textual criticism of the Gospels; for instance, the materials analyzed in the volume of the *Biblia Patristica* dedicated to Eusebius of Caesarea include the *canones euangeliorum*. However, since Eusebius was, after Origen, one of the most eminent biblical scholars of the time, the significance of his testimony on the Gospels is especially valuable. Whereas many of the important

---

[19] For instance, NA28 p. 62* mentions 24 papyri for Matthew, 3 for Mark, 10 for Luke, 30 for John.

Greek New Testament manuscripts are dated to the fourth or fifth century, Eusebius died around 340. The testimony of the Eusebian Canons thus antedates many, if not most, of the major manuscript witnesses. Of course Eusebius' biblical scholarship is different from that of the 21st century, but as far as textual criticism is concerned he is someone who should be taken into account.[20] One example of this is that the 233 sections for Mark imply that Eusebius' copy of this Gospel ended at Mark 16:8.

In my view, Eusebius' testimony becomes very important in cases where passages mentioned in the Eusebian Canons are relegated into the *apparatus criticus* in today's textual criticism. In the following three instances, it should be surmised each time that the Eusebian Canons are always on the side of the addition.

(1) **VIII Mc 216** = Mark 15:28
καὶ ἐπληρώθη ἡ γραφὴ ἡ λέγουσα· καὶ μετὰ ἀνόμων ἐλογίσθη.
And the scripture was fulfilled which says, 'He was reckoned with the transgressors'. (Revised Standard Version)
om. ℵ A B C D Ψ 2427 *pc* k sy^s sa bo^pt
add. L Θ 083. 0250 *f*^1.13 33 𝔐 lat sy^p.h (bo^pt); Eus

It cannot be denied that in this case the absence of this verse is probably to be preferred, in favour of which Bruce Metzger observes that 'It is understandable that the sentence may have been added from Luke 22:37 in the margin, whence it came into the text itself.'[21] However, his reasoning is unconvincing in that it does not explain why the verse was interpolated in precisely this place in Mark. In the same passage, Metzger argues that 'it is also significant that Mark very seldom expressly quotes the Old Testament.' This is not correct as far as the narrative of the Passion in Mark is concerned, because in Mark 14:49, Jesus says:

ἀλλ' ἵνα πληρωθῶσιν αἱ γραφαί.
But let the scriptures be fulfilled.

Perhaps it is precisely to this verse, Mark 14:49, that Mark 15:28 corresponds. Furthermore, Metzger explains his view by saying 'there is no

---

[20] This view is also expressed e.g. in W. Thiele, 'Beobachtungen zu den eusebianischen Sektionen und Kanones der Evangelien.' *ZNW* 72 (1981) pp. 100–1.

[21] B.M. Metzger, *A Textual Commentary on the Greek New Testament,* 2nd edn, (Stuttgart: Deutsche Bibelgesellschaft, 1994) p. 99.

reason why, if the sentence were present originally, it should have been deleted', but in my view there are ample reasons why early (and even earliest) copyists wanted to eliminate Mark 15:28, the verse which condemns Jesus as one of the transgressors. The explanation of Metzger is far from persuasive.

(2) **X Lc 283** = Luke 22:43–44
ὤφθη δὲ αὐτῷ ἄγγελος ἀπ' οὐρανοῦ ἐνισχύων αὐτόν. καὶ γενόμενος ἐν ἀγωνίᾳ ἐκτενέστερον προσηύχετο· καὶ ἐγένετο ὁ ἱδρὼς αὐτοῦ ὡσεὶ θρόμβοι αἵματος καταβαίνοντες ἐπὶ τὴν γῆν.
And there appeared to him an angel from heaven, strengthening him. And being in an agony he prayed more earnestly; and his sweat became like great drops of blood falling down upon the ground.
om. 𝔓⁷⁵ ℵ¹ A B N T W 579. 1071*. / 844 *pc* f sy* sa bo*ᵖᵗ*; Hier*ᵐˢˢ* (*f*¹³ *om. hic et pon. p.* Mt 26,39)
add. (*pt. c. obel.*) ℵ*·²* D L Θ Ψ 0171 *f*¹ 𝔐 lat sy*ᶜ·ᵖ·ʰ* bo*ᵖᵗ*; Ju Ir Hipp Eus Hier*ᵐˢˢ*

(3) **II Lc 309** = Luke 23:17
ἀνάγκην δὲ εἶχεν ἀπολύειν αὐτοῖς κατὰ ἑορτὴν ἕνα.
Now he was obliged to release one man to them at the festival.
om. 𝔓⁷⁵ A B K L T 070. 892*ᵗˣᵗ*. 1241 *pc* a vg*ᵐˢ* sa bo*ᵖᵗ*
add. ℵ (D sy*ˢ·ᶜ* add. p. 19) W (Θ Ψ) *f*¹·¹³ (892) 𝔐 lat sy*ᵖ·ʰ* (bo*ᵖᵗ*)

These two verses are presented simply as examples of the cases in which, with the testimony of the Canons in favour of the addition of each verse, the balance of manuscript witnesses changes slightly, though not dramatically.

(4) **X Lc 320** = Luke 23:34a
ὁ δὲ Ἰησοῦς ἔλεγεν, Πάτερ, ἄφες αὐτοῖς, οὐ γὰρ οἴδασιν τί ποιοῦσιν.
And Jesus said, 'Father, forgive them; for they know not what they do.'
om. 𝔓⁷⁵ ℵ¹ B D* W Θ 070. 579. 1241 *pc* a sy* sa bo*ᵖᵗ*
add. ℵ*·²* (A) C D² L Ψ 0250 *f*¹·⁽¹³⁾ 33 𝔐 lat sy*ᶜ·ᵖ·ʰ* (bo*ᵖᵗ*); (Ir*ˡᵃᵗ*)

In the case of this extremely famous passage, the testimony of the Canons is again in favour of the addition of the verse; taking this into consideration, the weight of manuscript witnesses on each side (omission or addition) is more or less balanced. Metzger argues that its absence 'can scarcely be explained as a deliberate excision by copyists who, considering the fall of Jerusalem to be proof that God had not forgiven the Jews, could not allow it to appear that the prayer of Jesus had remained unanswered'.[22] However, in my view, early users may well have wished to eliminate this verse because of its content (Jesus forgiving the Jews): Christians of antiquity considered the Jews responsible for the death of Christ, a sentiment which is concretized in the ominous Greek term χριστόκτονος. Furthermore, this verse is in complete accord with Luke's overall tendency to depict Jesus as forgiving (Peter, one of the co-crucified robbers, etc.), and it also resounds with the act of forgiving performed by Stephen in another document written by Luke (Acts 7:60). Despite the generally-accepted opinion among New Testament textual critics, the possibility that this verse originally belongs to Luke should be seriously reconsidered.

C. Potential of the Canons as a tool for analysis of the Gospels

Another aspect in which the Eusebian Canons turn out to be useful is illustrated by the following table:

Mt 274	=Lc 260	=Mc 156	=Ioh 20	I
Mt 274	=Lc 260	=Mc 156	=Ioh 48	I
Mt 274	=Lc 260	=Mc 156	=Ioh 96	I
	Lc 262		=Ioh 113	IX
	Lc 262		=Ioh 124	IX
Mt 275		=Mc 157		VI
Mt 276	=Lc 74	=Mc 158	=Ioh 98	I
Mt 277		=Mc 159	=Ioh 98	IV
Mt 278	=Lc 263	=Mc 160		II
	Lc 264			X
Mt 279		=Mc 161	=Ioh 72	IV
Mt 279		=Mc 161	=Ioh 121	IV
Mt 280	=Lc 269	=Mc 162	=Ioh 122	I
			Ioh 123	X
Mt 281	=Lc 268	=Mc 163		II
Mt 282		=Mc 164		VI
Mt 283				X
Mt 284	=Lc 266	=Mc 165	=Ioh 55	I
Mt 284	=Lc 266	=Mc 165	=Ioh 63	I
Mt 284	=Lc 266	=Mc 165	=Ioh 65	I

---

[22] *Ibid.*, p. 154.

Mt 284	=Lc 266	=Mc 165	=Ioh 67	I
Mt 285	=Lc 265	=Mc 166		II
Mt 285	=Lc 267	=Mc 166		II
Mt 286		=Mc 167		VI
Mt 287		=Mc 168	=Ioh 152	IV
Mt 288		=Mc 169		VI
	Lc 273			X
	Lc 274		=Ioh 227	IX
	Lc 274		=Ioh 229	IX
	Lc 274		=Ioh 231	IX
Mt 289	=Lc 275	=Mc 170	=Ioh 126	I
	Lc 276			X
Mt 290		=Mc 171		VI
	Lc 278			X
Mt 291	=Lc 279	=Mc 172	=Ioh 156	I
			Ioh 157	X
Mt 292		=Mc 173		VI
Mt 293		=Mc 174	=Ioh 107	IV
Mt 294	=Lc 281	=Mc 175	=Ioh 161	I
Mt 295	=Lc 282	=Mc 176	=Ioh 42	I
Mt 295	=Lc 282	=Mc 176	=Ioh 57	I
Mt 296	=Lc 280	=Mc 177		II
	Lc 283			X
Mt 296	=Lc 284	=Mc 177		II
Mt 297		=Mc 178	=Ioh 70	IV
Mt 298		=Mc 179		VI
Mt 299		=Mc 180	=Ioh 103	IV
Mt 300	=Lc 285	=Mc 181	=Ioh 79	I
Mt 300	=Lc 285	=Mc 181	=Ioh 158	I
Mt 301	=Lc 286	=Mc 182		II
Mt 302	=Lc 287	=Mc 183	=Ioh 160	I
	Lc 288			X
Mt 303				X
Mt 304	=Lc 289	=Mc 184	=Ioh 170	I
			Ioh 171	X
Mt 305		=Mc 185		VI
		Mc 186		X
Mt 306	=Lc 290	=Mc 187	=Ioh 162	I
			Ioh 163	X
Mt 306	=Lc 290	=Mc 187	=Ioh 174	I

Mt 307		=Mc 188	=Ioh 164	IV
			Ioh 165	X
Mt 308	=Lc 305	=Mc 189		II
	Lc 306			X
Mt 309		=Mc 190		VI
Mt 310	=Lc 297	=Mc 191	=Ioh 69	I
	Lc 298			X
Mt 311		=Mc 192		VI
Mt 312	=Lc 299	=Mc 193		II
Mt 313	=Lc 294	=Mc 194	=Ioh 172	I
			Ioh 173	X
Mt 314	=Lc 291	=Mc 195	=Ioh 166	I
			Ioh 167	X
Mt 314	=Lc 291	=Mc 195	=Ioh 168	I
			Ioh 169	X
Mt 315	=Lc 292	=Mc 196	=Ioh 175	I
Mt 316	=Lc 293	=Mc 197		II
Mt 317	=Lc 295	=Mc 198		II
	Lc 296			X
Mt 318	=Lc 300	=Mc 199	=Ioh 176	I
Mt 319				X
	Lc 301			X
			Ioh 177	X
Mt 320	=Lc 302	=Mc 200	=Ioh 178	I
			Ioh 179	X
Mt 320	=Lc 302	=Mc 200	=Ioh 180	I
			Ioh 181	X
	Lc 303		=Ioh 182	IX
	Lc 303		=Ioh 186	IX
	Lc 303		=Ioh 190	IX
	Lc 304			X
	Lc 307		=Ioh 182	IX
	Lc 307		=Ioh 186	IX
	Lc 307		=Ioh 190	IX
	Lc 308			X
			Ioh 191	X
Mt 321		=Mc 201	=Ioh 192	IV
			Ioh 193	X
Mt 322	=Lc 309	=Mc 202		II
Mt 323		=Mc 203	=Ioh 183	IV

Mt	Lc	Mc	Ioh	
Mt 324				X
Mt 325	=Lc 310	=Mc 204	=Ioh 184	I
Mt 326	=Lc 311	=Mc 205	=Ioh 188	I
			Ioh 189	X
	Lc 312		=Ioh 182	IX
	Lc 312		=Ioh 186	IX
	Lc 312		=Ioh 190	IX
Mt 326	=Lc 313	=Mc 205	=Ioh 194	I
			Ioh 195	X
Mt 327				X
Mt 328	=Lc 314	=Mc 206	=Ioh 196	I
Mt 329		=Mc 207	=Ioh 185	IV
Mt 329		=Mc 207	=Ioh 187	IV
Mt 330		=Mc 208		VI
Mt 331	=Lc 315	=Mc 209	=Ioh 197	I
	Lc 316			X
Mt 332	=Lc 318	=Mc 210	=Ioh 197	I
Mt 333		=Mc 211	=Ioh 203	IV
Mt 334	=Lc 321	=Mc 212	=Ioh 201	I
		Mc 213		X
			Ioh 202	X
Mt 335	=Lc 324	=Mc 214	=Ioh 199	I
			Ioh 200	X
Mt 336	=Lc 317	=Mc 215	=Ioh 198	I
Mt 336	=Lc 319	=Mc 215	=Ioh 198	I
	Lc 320			X
	Lc 277	=Mc 216		VIII
Mt 337		=Mc 217		VI
Mt 338	=Lc 322	=Mc 218		II
Mt 339	=Lc 325	=Mc 219		II
	Lc 326			X
Mt 340	=Lc 327	=Mc 220		II
Mt 341		=Mc 221		VI
Mt 342	=Lc 323	=Mc 222		II
Mt 343	=Lc 329	=Mc 223	=Ioh 204	I
Mt 344	=Lc 328	=Mc 224		II
Mt 345				X
			Ioh 205	X
Mt 346	=Lc 330	=Mc 225		II
Mt 347		=Mc 226		VI

Mt	Lc	Mc	Ioh	
	Lc 331			X
Mt 348	=Lc 332	=Mc 227	=Ioh 206	I
			Ioh 207	X
Mt 349	=Lc 333	=Mc 228	=Ioh 208	I
Mt 350		=Mc 229		VI
	Lc 334			X
Mt 351				X
	Lc 335	=Mc 230		VIII
Mt 352	=Lc 336	=Mc 231	=Ioh 209	I
			Ioh 210	X
Mt 352	=Lc 336	=Mc 231	=Ioh 211	I
Mt 353	=Lc 337	=Mc 232		II
Mt 354	=Lc 338	=Mc 233		II
			Ioh 212	X
Mt 355				X
	Lc 339			X
	Lc 340		=Ioh 213	IX
			Ioh 214	X
			Ioh 216	X
	Lc 340		=Ioh 217	IX
			Ioh 218	X
	Lc 341		=Ioh 221	IX
	Lc 341		=Ioh 223	IX
			Ioh 224	X
	Lc 341		=Ioh 225	IX
			Ioh 226	X
	Lc 342			X

This table, which is limited to the narrative of the Passion, shows the parallelism of the Gospels according to the classification into the Canons. It is arranged in ascending order of the Matthean section number. However, it may be immediately noticed that the column of Mark is also in strictly ascending order: when we leave the *Sondergut* of Matthew and Mark aside, the coincidence between Matthew and Mark is perfect. Thus, as far as the narrative of the Passion is concerned, Matthew and Mark are in perfect parallelism. If we take this into consideration when examining the notorious Synoptic problem, we have to conclude that there is a direct relationship between Matthew and Mark. Any other explanation would fail to explain this perfect coincidence.

Normally the problem of priority among the Gospels, especially the Synoptic Gospels, is discussed with the three Gospels taken into account simultaneously; however, the Eusebian Canons seem to suggest that the relationship between Matthew and Mark can, and perhaps should, be considered by itself. Further analyses may also be possible using the Canons in a similar way. Nonetheless, although I have suggested above that Eusebius' analysis of the Gospels is quite thorough, that does not mean that his Canons are without error. If we in the twenty-first century wish to have such an interpretative device as the Eusebian Canons, we will be able to have much more sophisticated, much more text-oriented and thus much more correct Canon Tables.

D. Interpretation of the Gospels as reflected in the Canons

Lastly, Eusebius' interpretation of the Gospels is reflected in his Canons. The following six examples are again taken from the narrative of the Passion.

(1) I Mt 274 = Lc 260 = Mc 156 = Ioh 20 + 48 + 96
These sections, mentioned in Canon I, are concerned with the Passover, and this Canon shows that only John mentions this Jewish festival thrice. This difference, which is concerned with how many times the Passover happened during the time of Jesus' public ministry, is very well known and its significance is not limited to simple verbal comparisons. One may therefore say that the Eusebian Canons do not consist simply of verbal comparisons. It should be added that Eusebius himself apparently thought that the difference can be solved through harmonization: according to the Ecclesiastical History (*H.E.* III 24.8), the three (Synoptic) Gospels narrate Jesus' activity during the single year after the imprisonment of John the Baptist, whereas John also recounts Jesus' activity also before the Baptist's imprisonment.

(2) I Mt 284 = Lc 266 = Mc 165 = Ioh 55 + 63 + 65 + 67
These sections of the Synoptic Gospels, mentioned in Canon I, all describe the so-called institution of the Lord's Supper. It is very interesting to see that Eusebius puts sections from John 6 in parallel, which are not a description of the Last Supper at all. By this parallelism, Eusebius seems to suggest that in John there is no passage which can be regarded as describing the institution of the Lord's Supper.

(3) IV Mt 299 = Mc 180 = Ioh 103

Among these sections, mentioned in Canon IV, Ioh 103 says: 'The hour has come for the Son of Man to be glorified'. Putting this passage in parallel with the two sections of Matthew and Mark, both of which show Jesus saying: 'The hour is at hand, and the Son of Man is betrayed into the hands of sinners' (Matthew 26:45; Mark 14:41 is verbally almost the same), Eusebius seems to present an exegesis according to which it is a glorification for the Son of Man to be handed to sinners.

(4) IX Lc 303 = Ioh 182 = Ioh 186 = Ioh 190
    IX Lc 307 = Ioh 182 = Ioh 186 = Ioh 190
    IX Lc 312 = Ioh 182 = Ioh 186 = Ioh 190

In this strange presentation of the sections mentioned in Canon IX which describe Pilate's arguing for Jesus' innocence, the same passages of John are repeated three times. Eusebius' point appears to be that in Luke as well as in John Pilate argued for Jesus' innocence, but he was not concerned which section of Luke corresponds specifically to which section of John.

(5) II Mt 338 = Lc 322 = Mc 218

These sections, mentioned in Canon II, are more concretely Matthew 27:41–43, Luke 23:35 and Mark 15:31–32a. However, Matthew 27:43 runs as follows: 'He trusts in God; let God deliver him now, if he desires him; for he said, 'I am the Son of God.'', i.e., it comprises the citation of Psalm 22:9 and the expression 'for he said, 'I am the Son of God.'', neither of which can be found in Lc 322 and Mc 218. Thus Matthew 27:43 should be classified into Canon X. This is one of the examples of the imperfection of Eusebius' analysis, in which Eusebius' division into sections is insufficiently analytic; perhaps others of this kind may be found.

(6) II Mt 353 = Lc 337 = Mc 232
    II Mt 354 = Lc 338 = Mc 233

This example shows, conversely, a case in which Eusebius' division into sections is excessively analytic. Since both sections are consecutive in each Gospel and since they are both classified as Canon II, there should be no reason to divide them into two; in other words, Mt 353+354, Lc 337+338, and Mc 232+233 can be a single section. On a closer look, however, Mc 233, which is the last section of Mark and which states that the women who came to the tomb of Jesus fled and 'said nothing to any one, for they were afraid', cannot be put in parallel with the other sections (Mt 354 and Lc 338). This implies that Mc 233 should be classified as Canon X (Sondergut).

This may be taken as another example of the imperfection of Eusebius' analysis, although it is not impossible to think that Eusebius expressly divides these sections in this way.

EPILOGUE

In this paper various implications of the Eusebian Canons have been examined. The analysis has been limited to the Passion narratives, and it is likely that an extension of this 'interpretative device of the Gospels' to the other sections will result in similar insights into third-century text and exegesis.

4. DONKEYS OR SHOULDERS? AUGUSTINE AS A TEXTUAL CRITIC OF THE OLD AND NEW TESTAMENTS

REBEKKA SCHIRNER

When we think about the early history of biblical translation from Hebrew into Greek, the versions of the Septuagint, of Aquila, Symmachus and Theodotion, as well as Origen's Hexapla come into our mind. When it comes to Latin translations of the Greek text, however, the situation is much more complicated: usually, the beginning of Latin translation activity is dated to the time of the Church Fathers Tertullian or Cyprian, that is to the end of the second or the first half of the third century. But, in contrast with the development of the Greek translations of the Hebrew source text, we find no mention of an outstanding personality connected with the early Latin translations before Jerome's translational endeavours. In addition, opinions widely differ on the question as to whether there was originally one single translation of each book (or rather group of books) of the Bible which then underwent modifications and alterations by later editors, leading to a variety of versions, or whether different translations emerged simultaneously at different places from the outset.[1]

---

[1] For recent discussions of this topic see Eva Schulz-Flügel, 'The Latin Old Testament Tradition' in Magne Sæbø (ed.), *Hebrew Bible/Old Testament. The History of Its Interpretation. Vol. I. From the Beginnings to the Middle Ages (Until 1300). Part 1. Antiquity.* (Göttingen: Vandenhoeck & Ruprecht, 1996), pp. 642–62, here p. 646; Pierre-Maurice Bogaert, 'La Bible latine des origines au moyen âge. Aperçu historique, état des questions' *Revue théologique de Louvain* 19 (1988) pp. 137–159, here p. 146; Benjamin Kedar, 'The Latin Translations' in Martin Jan Mulder and Harry Sysling (eds), *Mikra, Text, Translation, Reading and Interpretation of the Hebrew*

What is important, however, is the fact that Latin Church Fathers such as Jerome or Augustine quite often speak of a multitude or variety of different Latin translations.[2] An important passage, regularly quoted in discussions of the history of Latin translations in general, is found in the second book of Augustine's *De doctrina christiana*, written around 396/7. In this work, he formulates a system of rules of how to interpret Holy Scripture correctly and how to convey this message rhetorically. In this section, he bears witness to an uncountable multitude of different Latin translations by stating that in the early times of Christianity everyone who had a basic knowledge of Greek undertook the task of translating the Bible from Greek into Latin.[3] This passage is by no means an exceptional statement: in a considerable number of passages throughout his works, Augustine not only comments on variant readings of biblical verses in a normative or descriptive way, but also mentions their consequences for exegetical and pastoral concerns as well as for anti-heretical disputes. In these instances, he indeed exhibits a degree of awareness of manuscripts as historical artefacts as well as philological sensitivity to various readings.

Usually, Augustine regards the existence of varying Latin translations as a helpful instrument for his exegesis of the relevant biblical verses, as can be seen in the context of the passage of *De doctrina christiana* mentioned above.[4] At first, however, Augustine gives the impression here that he is

---

Bible in Ancient Judaism and Early Christianity (Philadelphia PA: Fortress, 1988), pp. 299–338, here p. 300f.

[2] For Jerome, see, for example, *Prol. in Evang.*: *Si enim latinis exemplaribus fides est adhibenda, respondeant quibus; tot sunt paene quot codices. Sin autem veritas est quaerenda de pluribus, cur non ad graecam originem revertentes ea quae vel a vitiosis interpretibus male edita vel a praesumptoribus inperitis emendata perversius vel a librariis dormitantibus aut addita sunt aut mutata corrigimus?* (R. Weber, R. Gryson et al. (eds), *Biblia sacra iuxta vulgatam versionem.* 5th edn. (Stuttgart: Deutsche Bibelgesellschaft, 2007)).

[3] Augustine, *De doctrina christiana* 2.XI.16 [CCSL 32, p. 42 ll. 21–6]: *Qui enim scripturas ex hebraea in graecam uerterunt, numerari possunt, latini autem interpretes nullo modo. Vt enim cuique primis fidei temporibus in manus uenit codex graecus et aliquantum facultatis sibi utriusque linguae habere uidebatur, ausus est interpretari.*

[4] There are, however, two important exceptions to this general attitude, which can be explained by their special context: In two of his letters to the Church Father Jerome (*Epistulae* 71 and 82), Augustine complains about the multitude and variety of Latin versions, as well as about the incompetence of the Latin translators in general. This situation, in his opinion, is unbearable, as it renders every single Latin translation a potentially faulty one. But, since these lamentations are voiced in order

very displeased with the diversity of Latin renderings: he stresses the necessity of looking into the texts of the source language, as the variety and multitude of Latin versions render every single one of them doubtful due to the fact that even those with rudimentary linguistic proficiency translated biblical texts.[5] Later on, he emphasizes that the diversity of translations is to be seen as useful and not problematic, since it can provide a better understanding of the text and clarify obscure passages.[6] Hence, it is not surprising that a remarkable number of passages can be found throughout Augustine's works – especially in his commentary on the Psalms – where he uses differing translations for his exegesis by either interpreting them differently or establishing a single semantic concept by a combination of the various meanings. This kind of approach may be illustrated by one such example where Augustine himself explicitly refers to the benefit that could be gained from looking into various versions.

In his homily on Psalm 70, which was preached between the years 412 and 415, Augustine first quotes Psalm 70:15 as follows: *Quoniam non cognoui negotiationes* ('as I have known nothing of trade activities').[7] There is no explicit reference to codices at this point. Later, he raises the question as to

---

to convince Jerome of the necessity to produce a Latin translation on the base of the Greek Septuagint text, it seems safe to assume that they do not reflect Augustine's genuine opinion on this topic, which is usually much milder. (*Epistula* 71.6 [CSEL 34.2, p. 254 l. 11 – p. 255 l. 1]: *ac per hoc plurimum profueris, si eam scripturam Graecam, quam septuaginta operati sunt, Latinae ueritati reddideris quae in diuersis codicibus ita uaria est, ut tolerari uix possit, et ita suspecta, ne in Graeco aliud inueniatur, ut inde aliquid proferre aut probare dubitemus.* and *Epistula* 82.35 [CSEL 34.2, p. 386 ll. 11–3]: *Ideo autem desidero interpretationem tuam de septuaginta, ut et tanta Latinorum interpretum, qui qualescumque hoc ausi sunt, quantum possumus, inperitia careamus* [...]).

[5] Augustine, *De doctrina christiana* 2.XI.16 [CCSL 32, p. 42 ll. 2–6, 18–23]: *Et latinae quidem linguae homines, quos nunc instruendos suscepimus, duabus aliis ad scripturarum diuinarum cognitionem opus habent, hebraea scilicet et graeca, ut ad exemplaria praecedentia recurratur, si quam dubitationem attulerit latinorum interpretum infinita uarietas.* [...] *Sed non propter haec pauca,* [...] *sed propter diuersitates, ut dictum est, interpretum illarum linguarum est cognitio necessaria. Qui enim scripturas ex hebraea in graecam uerterunt, numerari possunt, latini autem interpretes nullo modo.*

[6] Augustine, *De doctrina christiana* 2.XII.17 [CCSL 32, p. 42 ll. 1–4]: *Quae quidem res plus adiuuit intellegentiam quam impediuit, si modo legentes non sint neglegentes. Nam nonnullas obscuriores sententias plurium codicum saepe manifestauit inspectio* [...]. Augustine illustrates this assessment subsequently by citing two different versions of Isaiah 58:7 which, in his opinion, explain each other.

[7] All translations are mine.

what kind of trade is referred to here and, within this context, he also discusses the nature of the traders.[8] After a rather long discussion of this topic, he addresses the variant manuscript readings for this verse, *negotiationem* ('trade') and *litteraturam* ('literature, written text'), which are obviously not equivalent.[9] Interestingly, in contrast to the version he first cited he now gives the noun *negotiatio* in the accusative singular form (instead of accusative plural) without commenting on this slight difference.

Augustine then acknowledges the problem of interpretation which arises from the divergent meanings but, nevertheless, he asserts (by formulating some kind of general rule) that a diversity of translations might be seen as a means to discover the underlying sense of a verse.[10] He subsequently offers a rather complicated exegesis of the noun *litteraturam* in the context of the relevant verse, also taking into consideration his previous discussion of the wording *non cognoui negotiationes*.

Kamesar aptly referred to this way of dealing with variants, which is also found in the writings of the Greek Church Father Origen, as exegetical maximalism.[11] This general openness of Augustine towards different versions has often been interpreted as a lack of philological or text-critical skills or an inadequate command of the Greek language, which, as Marrou insinuated, could be evaluated as some kind of intellectual decline, paralleled by the political decline of the Roman Empire in the fourth and fifth centuries.[12] While this tendency in Augustine is undeniable, I

---

[8] Augustine, *Enarrationes in Psalmos* 70.1.17 [CCSL 39, p. 954 ll. 1–3]: *Quoniam non cognoui negotiationes* [Ps. 70:15]. *Ideo, inquit, tota die salutem tuam, quoniam non cognoui negotiationes. Quae sunt istae negotiationes?*

[9] Augustine, *Enarrationes in Psalmos* 70.1.19 [CCSL 39, p. 956 ll. 1–3]: *Sed est in quibusdam exemplaribus: Quoniam non cognoui litteraturam. Vbi alii codices habent negotiationem, ibi alii: litteraturam* [...]. This variety within the Latin tradition, however, seems to be due to the different readings γραμματείας and πραγματείας in the Greek Septuagint.

[10] Augustine, *Enarrationes in Psalmos* 70.1.19 [CCSL 39, p. 956 ll. 3–5]: [...] *quomodo concordent, inuenire difficile est; et tamen interpretum diuersitas forte sensum ostendit, non errorem inducit.*

[11] Adam Kamesar, *Jerome, Greek Scholarship, and the Hebrew Bible: A Study of the Quaestiones Hebraicae in Genesim* (Oxford: Oxford UP, 1993), pp. 19, 27.

[12] Henri-Irénée Marrou, *Saint Augustin et la fin de la culture antique*, 4th edn. (Paris: Boccard, 1958). The question of Augustine's knowledge of Greek is highly debated. For a discussion of this issue see, for example, Gerard J. M. Bartelink, 'Die

nevertheless want to take a stand for his abilities as a textual critic. It has to be noted at this point that, despite Amy Donaldson's discussion of a number of passages where Augustine deals with variant readings in the New Testament,[13] normally only a rather small and non-representative sample of passages is mentioned in accounts of Augustine's attitude towards textual variants in biblical verses.[14] The resulting conclusions are therefore more negative than they need or ought to be, even though Augustine himself never claims to be a philologist or text-critic. To anticipate the conclusion of this paper, and also some of the results of my doctoral research,[15] I believe that Augustine is able not only to comment on different translations, but also to decide on the basis of a recognisable set of principles which one of them should be preferred. That is to say that he has at his command a set of philological, or rather text-critical, principles for evaluating textual variants. Nevertheless, he commonly does not see the need for an evaluation that would either lead to the exclusion of or

---

Beeinflussung Augustins durch die griechischen Patres' in J. den Boeft and J. van Oort (eds), *Augustiniana Traiectina, Communications présentées au Colloque International d'Utrecht. 13-14 novembre 1986* (Paris: Études Augustiniennes, 1987), pp. 9–24 or the comprehensive presentation of Pierre Courcelle, *Les Lettres Grecques en Occident, de Macrobe à Cassiodore* (Paris: Boccard, 1948), pp. 137–209.

[13] Amy M. Donaldson, 'Explicit References to New Testament Variant Readings among Greek and Latin Church Fathers' (Ph.D. diss., University of Notre Dame, 2009), especially pp. 167–80, http://etd.nd.edu/ETD-db/theses/available/etd-12112009-152813/.

[14] Among more recent works, see Raymond F. Collins, 'Augustine of Hippo – Precursor of Modern Biblical Scholarship' *Louvain Studies* 12 (1987) pp. 131–51, here pp. 137–43; Michael Fiedrowicz, *Psalmus Vox Totius Christi. Studien zu Augustins »Enarrationes in Psalmos«* (Freiburg in Breisgau: Herder, 1997), pp. 61–7; Eva Schulz–Flügel, 'Augustins textkritische Beschäftigung mit dem Bibeltext', in Volker Henning Drecoll (ed.), *Augustin Handbuch* (Tübingen: Mohr Siebeck, 2007), pp. 237–41; H.A.G. Houghton, *Augustine's Text of John: Patristic Citations and Latin Gospel Manuscripts* (Oxford: Oxford UP, 2008), pp. 5–21 and 78–84.

[15] Rebekka Schirner, *Inspice diligenter codices. Philologisch Studien zu Augustins Umgang mit Bibelhandschriften und -übersetzungen* (Millennium Studien: Berlin, De Gruyter, 2014). In this study, I examine Augustine's general attitude towards and use of biblical manuscripts and translations from a philological point of view by looking at passages where he either explicitly refers to variant readings (of the text of the Old and New Testament respectively) or where he gives more general instructions of how to deal with these sources.

preference for one version, since this could mean a limitation of the content of the respective biblical verse and thus of the word of God.[16]

In the following argumentation, I would like to present a selection of passages where Augustine applies principles which – on a basic level – are also relevant with regard to the methods of modern textual criticism, such as the consideration of the number or age of manuscripts containing a certain reading. By employing these principles, he favours one reading over the other or, more importantly, even rules out a reading which he may ascribe to an error or misunderstanding of either the translator or the scribe, or even to an intentional alteration. In this context, I am also going to address the question of the role played by the application of text-critical principles in Augustine's use of biblical manuscripts.[17]

The importance of the use of accurate Latin copies containing correct translations of the Bible for exegetical purposes, in Augustine's opinion, can be deduced from another passage of the second book of *De doctrina christiana*. According to Augustine, this ideal can be obtained by corrections based on comparison with better copies containing the same type of translation or by resorting to manuscripts of the source language.[18] At the beginning of the third book of the same work, he again stresses the necessity of working with corrected manuscripts when attempting the exegesis of biblical texts.[19] Thus he defines textual criticism (or rather

---

[16] Of all the opinions on this topic, the view held by Fiedrowicz, *Vox*, p. 66 is the closest to my own argument (see also Schulz-Flügel, 'Bibeltext' and Donaldson, *References*, pp. 179f.).

[17] In this paper, passages of the Old and New Testaments are analyzed in the same way, in spite of the methodological difficulty that in the former the Greek text (which is the only source language explicitly mentioned by Augustine, as he knew no Hebrew) is just a translation, whereas it is the original text in the case of the New Testament.

[18] Augustine, *De doctrina christiana* 2.XIV.21–XV.22 [CCSL 32, p. 47 ll. 20–5.3]: *Plurimum hic quoque adiuuat interpretum numerositas conlatis codicibus inspecta atque discussa. Tantum absit falsitas; nam codicibus emendandis primitus debet inuigilare solertia eorum, qui scripturas diuinas nosse desiderant, ut emendatis non emendati cedant ex uno dumtaxat interpretationis genere uenientes.* [...] *Et latinis quibuslibet emendandis graeci adhibeantur* [...].

[19] Augustine, *De doctrina christiana* 3.I.1 [CCSL 32, p.77 ll. 1–9]: *Homo timens deum uoluntatem eius in scripturis sanctis diligenter inquirit. Et ne amet certamina pietate mansuetus; praemunitus etiam scientia linguarum, ne in uerbis locutionibusque ignotis haereat, praemunitus etiam cognitione quarundam rerum necessariarum, ne uim naturamue earum, quae propter*

criticism of translations, since Augustine usually works with biblical translations even though he sometimes resorts to the Greek text, especially in his later works) as a basic step towards the interpretation of biblical texts itself.

It is therefore not surprising that Augustine, in the eleventh book of his work against the Manichaean Faustus (*Contra Faustum Manichaeum*), written approximately between 400 and 405, establishes a catalogue of criteria to evaluate copies and their texts or rather translations. In this book, he deals primarily with the eclectic attitude of the Manichaeans towards the Bible. According to Augustine, they arbitrarily condemn exactly those passages of the Holy Scripture which are not in accordance with their belief system by pointing to seemingly contradictory passages which, in their opinion, bear witness to alterations of the biblical text. Within the context of a discussion of two verses of the Apostle Paul which seem to contradict each other (Romans 1:3 and 2 Corinthians 5:16f.), the Church Father presents his model for verifying verses and passages of the Bible that seem to be spurious or interpolated, describing precisely the kinds of authority and arguments to which the Manichaeans cannot resort to substantiate their statements. Thus if someone asked them to prove their assertions regarding the authenticity of biblical verses, they would not be able to revert to manuscripts of higher quality (*non confugias ad exemplaria ueriora*) or to a majority of copies (*uel plurium codicum*) or to older ones (*uel antiquorum*) or to those containing the respective passage in the source language (*uel linguae praecedentis, unde hoc in aliam linguam interpretatum est*) in order to prove that the condemned text had indeed been tampered with.[20] In the following, he adds the provenance of a manuscript as another principle that should be considered (*uel ex aliarum regionum codicibus, unde ipsa doctrina commeauit, nostra dubitatio diiudicaretur*) and, by repeating the criteria listed previously, establishes a kind of hierarchy in applying these principles by mentioning the use of manuscripts of the source language as a last resort after taking into consideration origin, number, and age of the respective copies (*et si*

---

similitudinem adhibentur, ignoret, adiuuante etiam codicum ueritate, quam sollers emendationis diligentia procurauit, ueniat ita instructus ad ambigua scripturarum discutienda atque soluenda.

[20] Augustine, *Contra Faustum* 11.2 [CSEL 25.1, p. 315 ll. 6–11]: *ubi cum ex aduerso audieris, 'proba', non confugias ad exemplaria ueriora uel plurium codicum uel antiquorum uel linguae praecedentis, unde hoc in aliam linguam interpretatum est, sed dicas: inde probo hoc illius esse, illud non esse, quia hoc pro me sonat, illud contra me.*

adhuc esset incerta uarietas, praecedens lingua, unde illud interpretatum est, consuleretur).[21]

Does Augustine himself apply these criteria in order to evaluate different Latin versions of biblical verses? There is, indeed, a considerable number of passages where this is the case. For example, let us consider a short passage of his commentary on the Lord's Sermon on the Mount (*De sermone domini in monte*), written about the year 393. After quoting the verse Matthew 6:4 (*Et pater tuus, qui videt in abscondito, reddet tibi*, 'and your father, who sees in secret, will give you in return'), Augustine mentions that many Latin manuscripts (*multa Latina exemplaria*) add the adverb *palam* ('openly') at the end of this verse.[22] In this context, Augustine also emphasises the anteriority of the Greek manuscripts (*priora sunt*), and as these do not in general support the version containing the adverb, he explicitly states that there is nothing further to discuss.[23] In this instance, then, the criteria of source language and age override the multitude of Latin codices.

A passage where the number of manuscripts plays a decisive role in Augustine's treatment of different readings is found in one of his treatises on the Gospel of John (*In Iohannis evangelium tractatus* 120), dating to about 419. Here, he cites John 20:2 (*Tulerunt dominum de monumento*, 'they carried the Lord from the grave') and afterwards asserts that even some Greek codices (*nonnulli codices etiam graeci*) add (the equivalent of) the Latin possessive adjective *meum* (*Tulerunt dominum meum*, 'they carried my Lord'), implying that there is also a variation within the Latin tradition. That Augustine sympathises with this version can be seen by the additional benefit he deduces from the possessive adjective for his exegesis of this verse: in his opinion, the addition of this word expresses the love and

---

[21] Augustine, *Contra Faustum* 11.2 [CSEL 25.1, p. 315 l. 25 – p. 316 l. 6]: *itaque si de fide exemplarium quaestio uerteretur, sicut in nonnullis, quae et paucae sunt et sacrarum litterarum studiosis notissimae sententiarum uarietates, uel ex aliarum regionum codicibus, unde ipsa doctrina commeauit, nostra dubitatio diiudicaretur, uel si ibi quoque codices uariarent, plures paucioribus aut uetustiores recentioribus praeferrentur: et si adhuc esset incerta uarietas, praecedens lingua, unde illud interpretatum est, consuleretur.*

[22] Augustine, *De sermone Domini in monte* 2.2.9 [CCSL 35, p. 100 ll. 217–8]: *Multa Latina exemplaria sic habent: Et pater tuus, qui uidet in abscondito, reddet tibi palam* [Matt. 6:4].

[23] Augustine, *De sermone Domini in monte* 2.2.9 [CCSL 35, p. 100 ll. 218–20]: *Sed quia in Graecis, quae priora sunt, non inuenimus palam, non putauimus hinc esse aliquid disserendum.*

emotion that is shown to Jesus.[24] Nevertheless, he closes the discussion by stating that the majority of (probably Greek and Latin) manuscripts does not support this reading; in this context, the adversative conjunction *sed* suggests that this version is not to be preferred.[25]

Let us now take a look at a passage of Augustine's commentary on Psalm 67 (*Enarratio in Psalmum* 67), dictated in the year 415, where he assesses a variation concerning the Old Testament text. At the beginning of paragraph 41, the Church Father discusses the correct division of two verses (Psalm 67:32 and 33), for which the manuscripts display different results: in one version (only implicitly identified as a manuscript reading) the wording *Deo regna terrae* is placed at the end of the previous verse, while in the other one the noun *Deo* appears at the end of one verse and the combination *regna terrae* at the beginning of the subsequent one. In short, the first version reads *Aethiopia praeueniet manus eius Deo regna terrae* and *Cantate Deo, psallite Domino*, while the second version has *Aethiopia praeueniet manus eius Deo* and *Regna terrae cantate Deo, psallite Domino*. I will pass over the interpretational difficulties raised by these different versions, which also depend on the referent of the pronoun *eius*,[26] as they are not relevant to my main argument.

Augustine offers two reasons why the second way of dividing the two verses should be preferred. First, he claims that this latter version is contained in not only the majority of Latin but also of Greek copies (*plures autem codices latini, et maxime graeci*) – indicating that there is also a variation within the Greek tradition. Secondly, he describes the authority of these manuscripts as remarkable (*auctoritate digniorum*).[27] The criteria leading to this

---

[24] Augustine, *In Iohannis Evangelium tractatus* 120.6 [CCSL 36, p. 663 ll. 10–2]: *Nonnulli codices etiam graeci habent: Tulerunt dominum meum* [John 20:2], *quod uideri dictum potest propensiore caritatis uel famulatus affectu* [...].

[25] Augustine, *In Iohannis Evangelium tractatus* 120.6 [CCSL 36, p. 663 ll. 12–3]: [...] *sed hoc in pluribus codicibus quos in promtu habuimus, non inuenimus.*

[26] In the preferred version, the pronoun *eius* is interpreted as if the reflexive pronoun *suas* was found in the Latin verse. Augustine explains this mode of interpretation by referring to the Greek text which is ambiguous with regard to the reflexivity of the pronoun.

[27] Augustine, *Enarrationes in Psalmos* 67.41 [CCSL 39, p. 898 ll. 1–8]: *Plures autem codices latini, et maxime graeci ita distinctos uersus habent, ut non sit in eis unus uersiculus Deo regna terrae* [Ps. 67:32f.], *sed Deo in fine sit uersus superioris, atque ita dicatur: Aethiopia praeueniet manus eius Deo, ac deinde sequatur in alio uersu: Regna terrae, cantate Deo, psallite*

evaluation and to the preference for one verse division are thus the multitude (or rather majority) of manuscripts and their authority, as well as the fact that it is corroborated by Greek codices. Furthermore, his preferred version is indeed the one on whose basis the following detailed exegesis of this passage is undertaken.

But the application of the criteria mentioned above sometimes not only leads to a preference for one reading, but – more radically – also results in the rejection of a version that is ascribed to a faulty manuscript, a translation error or even a deliberate alteration. An example can be found in Augustine's Letter 265 written about 408/9. This is addressed to an otherwise unknown Seleuciana, who contacted the Church Father with some questions regarding the doctrine of a certain follower of Novatian who claimed that the Apostle Peter had not been baptized. Answering this assertion, Augustine cites Acts 1:5 in order to show that the apostles (and therefore Peter as well) had already been baptized with water but not yet with the Holy Spirit at the time when Peter denied Jesus. As a general remark, and to avoid a misunderstanding of this verse, he refers to a noteworthy textual variation: while in some manuscripts the reading *incipietis baptizari* ('you will begin to be baptized') is found, others have the version *baptizabimini* ('you will be baptized'), which, in his opinion, makes no difference.[28] But the Church Father subsequently also mentions two other renderings – *baptizabitis* and *incipietis baptizare* ('you will baptize' and 'you will begin to baptize' respectively) – displaying an active instead of a passive phrasing. By implicitly resorting to the Greek source text, which reveals the Latin copies containing these versions as faulty, he is able to reject these renderings.[29] In this passage, however, Augustine only speaks of erroneous manuscripts (*mendosi*), but – unlike his approach in the texts I am about to present – he does not attempt to trace back the faulty readings to their source (i.e. a translation error, an intentional alteration, an error made by negligent copyists, etc.).

Domino. Qua distinctione, multorum codicum et auctoritate digniorum consonantia, sine dubio praeferenda, fides commendari mihi uidetur, quae opera praecedit [...].

[28] Augustine, *Epistula* 265.3 [CSEL 57, p. 640 ll. 9–11]: *aliqui autem codices habent: Vos autem spiritu sancto incipietis baptizari; sed siue dicatur 'baptizabimini' siue dicatur 'incipietis baptizari', ad rem nihil interest.*

[29] Augustine, *Epistula* 265.3 [CSEL 57, p. 640 ll. 12–4]: *nam in quibuscumque codicibus inueniuntur 'baptizabitis' aut 'incipietis baptizare', mendosi sunt, qui ex Graecis facillime conuincuntur.*

In contrast, in his commentary on Psalm 105:38, dictated about 419, Augustine confirms a reading in his Latin manuscript, which seems to be due to a scribal error, by referring to the underlying Greek. After quoting this verse (*Et interfecta est terra in sanguinibus*, 'and the land was killed by bloodshed'), he mentions that some people might trace the wording *interfecta* back to a mistake of the scribe (*putaremus enim scriptoris errorem*) and therefore recommend that the similar sounding participle *infecta* ('defiled') should be read instead.[30] Augustine does not further comment on this assumption, but it is obvious that the participle *infecta* referring to the noun *terra* in connection with the prepositional phrase *in sanguinibus* (that is: 'the land is defiled with blood') makes for a more obvious meaning and interpretation of the verse than the version that offers the reading *interfecta* ('killed'). The absence of a scribal error, however, is attested by Augustine's reference to Greek codices: *interfecta est terra in sanguinibus inspectis graecis codicibus uideremus*. He goes on to refer to the divine inspiration which has led to the translation of the Bible into many languages, and later explains the peculiar expression *interfecta est terra* by pointing to the use of a rhetorical device.[31]

A translational error is addressed by Augustine in his work *De opere monachorum*, written about the year 400, in which he sums up the duties of monks, alluding, amongst other things, to sayings of the Apostle Paul. Having quoted 1 Corinthians 9:1–5, where Paul claims certain rights for himself, the Church Father points to a misunderstanding by some translators who have rendered the underlying polysemic Greek noun (γυνή, not quoted by Augustine) in 1 Cor. 9:5 (*numquid non habemus licentiam sororem mulierem circumducendi sicut et ceteri apostoli et fratres domini et Cephas?* 'Are we not allowed to bring along a sister, a woman, like the other apostles and brothers of the Lord and Cephas?') exactly the wrong way by putting the word *uxor* ('wife') instead of *mulier* ('woman'). From this wrong meaning it could be derived that the apostle postulates the privilege of marriage, but

---

[30] Augustine, *Enarrationes in Psalmos* 105.31 [CCSL 40, p. 1564 ll. 1–3]: *Sed quid est quod sequitur? Et interfecta est terra in sanguinibus* [Ps. 105:38]. *Putaremus enim scriptoris errorem, eumque diceremus pro eo quod est infecta fecisse interfecta* […].

[31] Augustine, *Enarrationes in Psalmos* 105.31 [CCSL 40, p. 1564 l. 4 – p. 1565 l. 11]: […] *nisi haberemus beneficium Dei, qui scripturas suas in multis linguis esse uoluit; atque ita esse scriptum: Interfecta est terra in sanguinibus inspectis graecis codicibus uideremus. Quid est ergo: Interfecta est terra, nisi hoc referatur ad homines qui habitabant in terra, tropica locutione, qua significatur per id quod continet, id quod continetur, sicut dicimus malam domum, in qua mali habitant, et bonam in qua boni?*

the Church Father does not address this problem explicitly. According to him, the correct meaning in this verse is clearly indicated by the context. In addition, he refers to the authority of a group of translators who have rendered the Greek word adequately.[32] Hence in this passage Augustine evaluates the Latin variants by referring to their translators; his final judgement is based on the meaning of the verse and its general context. To sum up: in this example, the Church Father chooses between two theoretically acceptable translations of a semantically ambiguous term by taking into account the context of the relevant biblical verse.

A passage where Augustine mentions the problem of ambiguous Greek words explicitly is found in the second book of his work *De doctrina christiana*. Here he states that ambiguous terms in a source language pose significant problems for translators, as they can quite easily choose the wrong counterpart in the target language.[33] As an example, Augustine quotes Romans 3:15 according to a false translation (*Acuti pedes eorum ad effundendum sanguinem*, 'their feet are peaked to shed blood') and then explains that the Greek adjective ὀξύς – which can be either translated with the Latin word *acutus* ('peaked') or *uelox* ('quick') – has simply been rendered the wrong way in this translation.[34] As a consequence, Augustine proposes that the copies containing the word *acuti* instead of *ueloces* are to be corrected.[35]

---

[32] Augustine, *De opere monachorum* 5 [CSEL 41, p. 538 ll. 10–2, p. 539 ll. 3–13]: *numquid non habemus licentiam sororem mulierem circumducendi sicut et ceteri apostoli et fratres domini et Cephas?* [1 Cor. 9:5] […] *hoc quidam non intellegentes non 'sororem mulierem', cum ille diceret: numquid non habemus potestatem sororem mulierem circumducendi? sed 'uxorem' interpretati sunt. fefellit eos uerbi graeci ambiguitas, quod et uxor et mulier eodem uerbo graece dicitur. quamquam hoc ita posuerit apostolus, ut falli non debuerint, quia neque 'mulierem' tantummodo ait, sed 'sororem mulierem' neque 'ducendi', sed 'circumducendi'. uerumtamen alios interpretes non fefellit haec ambiguitas et 'mulierem', non 'uxorem' interpretati sunt.*

[33] Augustine, *De doctrina christiana* 2.XII.18 [CCSL 32, p. 44 ll. 33–5]: *Et ex ambiguo linguae praecedentis plerumque interpres fallitur, cui non bene nota sententia est, et eam significationem transfert, quae a sensu scriptoris penitus aliena est […].*

[34] Augustine, *De doctrina christiana* 2.XII.18 [CCSL 32, p. 44 ll. 36–40]: […] *sicut quidam codices habent: Acuti pedes eorum ad effundendum sanguinem;* ὀξύς *enim et acutum apud Graecos et uelocem significat. Ille ergo uidit sententiam, qui transtulit: Veloces pedes eorum ad effundendum sanguinem; ille autem alius ancipiti signo in aliam partem raptus errauit.*

[35] Augustine, *De doctrina christiana* 2.XII.18 [CCSL 32, p. 44 ll. 40–3]: *Et talia quidem non obscura, sed falsa sunt. Quorum alia conditio est; non enim intellegendos, sed*

There are also a few special instances where Augustine attributes completely different Latin versions to a variation within the Greek text, resulting from the phonetic and graphic similarities between two words which have been confounded by copyists. In these cases, he is eager to accept and to comment on both variants, sometimes suggesting a slight preference for one of the versions because of its meaning and context. A very interesting example for this phenomenon is found in the sixth book of his writing *Questions on the Heptateuch* (*Quaestiones in Heptateuchum*, written about 419), where he discusses difficulties regarding the understanding of certain passages from the first seven books of the Old Testament. The paragraph we are interested in deals with two differing versions of Joshua 9:4, part of the story of the Gibeonites who were afraid that they would be attacked by Joshua and thus came to him in order to form an alliance, pretending to have travelled a long way from a faraway country. Augustine first quotes this verse as follows: *et accipientes saccos ueteres super humeros suos* ('and they put old bags on their shoulders') and subsequently points to a variation within the Greek and Latin tradition: instead of the noun *humeros* ('shoulders'), some manuscripts, which Augustine later declares as the more trustworthy (*ueraciores*) ones, have the reading *asinos* ('donkeys').[36]

He then traces these variant readings *humeros* and *asinos* back to the Greek words ὤμων and ὄνων, explaining the diversity within the Latin tradition by errors that have already arisen within Greek manuscripts due to phonetic similarities.[37] Augustine seems to accept both readings but he nevertheless indicates a preference for ὄνων/*asinos*, which is the version already designated as the reading of the *codices ueraciores*, because of the context itself: in his opinion, it is more plausible that the Gibeonites would

---

emendandos tales codices potius praecipiendum est.

[36] Augustine, *Quaestiones in Heptateuchum* 6.12 [CCSL 33, p. 319 ll. 282–9]: *Quod Gabaonitae uenerunt ad Iesum cum uetustis panibus et saccis, ut putarentur, sicut finxerant, de terra uenisse longinqua, quo eis parceretur – constitutum enim erat a domino, ne alicui terras illas inhabitanti parcerent, quo ingrediebantur – nonnulli codices et graeci et latini habent: et accipientes saccos ueteres super humeros suos [Ios. 9:4]; alii uero, qui ueraciores uidentur, non habent: super humeros, sed: super asinos suos.*

[37] Augustine, *Quaestiones in Heptateuchum* 6.12 [CCSL 33, p. 319 ll. 289–93]: *Similitudo enim uerbi in graeca lingua mendositatem facilem fecit et ideo latina quoque exemplaria uariata sunt;* ὤμων *quippe et* ὄνων *non multum ab inuicem dissonant, quorum prius humerorum nomen est, posterius asinorum.*

have carried their bagagge with the help of donkeys than on their bare
shoulders.[38]

Moreover, a mix-up of Greek nouns on the part of the translators is
addressed by Augustine in the fourth book of his *Quaestiones in Heptateuchum*.
Here, he draws attention to two different versions of Numbers 16:30: *in
uisione ostendet dominus* ('the Lord will show by his appearance') vs. *in hiatu
ostendet dominus* ('the Lord will show by an opening/chasm'). In this verse,
Moses announces the destiny of Korah and his followers who revolted
against him. Augustine traces the second rendering (*hiatu*, 'opening') back to
a confusion that has occurred in the process of translating the Greek: He
assumes that the translators have mistaken the actual Greek word φάσματι,
which is correctly rendered by the Latin noun *uisione*, for the similar
sounding and looking word χάσματι, which is the Greek counterpart of the
Latin word *hiatu*.[39] Having identified the Latin version *hiatu* with a
translation error, he rejects this variant and explains the meaning of the
noun *uisione* in the context of the biblical passage: he states that it is used
precisely in the sense of the Latin noun *manifestatione*, which means
'revelation', and not in order to express the concept of an illusion.[40]
Interestingly, the Church Father subsequently mentions that some
translators have nevertheless used the word *phantasmate* (which conveys
exactly the concept of a vision of something which is not actually there) in
their Latin translation.[41] He disapproves of this rendering, pointing to the

---

[38] Augustine, *Quaestiones in Heptateuchum* 6.12 [CCSL 33, p. 319 l. 293 – p. 320 l.
297]: *Ideo est autem de asinis credibilius, quoniam se a sua gente longinqua missos esse dixerunt:
unde adparet eos fuisse legatos et ideo magis in asinis quam in humeris necessaria portare potuisse,
quia nec multi esse poterant et non solum saccos sed etiam utres eos portasse scriptura
commemorat.*

[39] Augustine, *Quaestiones in Heptateuchum* 4.28 [CCSL 33, p. 251 ll. 641–4]: *Quod
ait Moyses de Core et Abiron et Dathan: in uisione ostendet dominus et aperiens terra os suum
absorbebit eos* [Num. 16:30], *quidam interpretati sunt: in hiatu ostendet dominus* [Num.
16:30]. *Credo putantes dictum* χάσματι, *quod graece positum est* φάσματι [...].

[40] Augustine, *Quaestiones in Heptateuchum* 4.28 [CCSL 33, p. 251 ll. 645–9]: [...]
*quod pro eo dictum est, ac si diceretur: in manifestatione, quod aperte oculis adparebit. Non enim
sic dictum est 'in uisione', quemadmodum solent dici uisiones siue somniorum siue quarumque in
extasi figurarum, sed, ut dixi, in manifestatione.*

[41] In Wevers's edition (John William Wevers, *Numeri*. (Septuaginta auctoritate
Societatis Scientiarum Gottingensis ed. 3.1, Göttingen: Vandenhoeck & Ruprecht,
1982)) the following variants are listed: φάσματι, χάσματι, φαντάσματι and

customary use of this noun in the Latin language which is opposed to his interpretation of this verse.[42]

Another kind of confusion on the part of the translators is brought up in a further passage of Augustine's *Quaestiones*. After quoting Genesis 47:31 according to a group of Latin manuscripts (*et adorauit super caput uirgae eius*, 'and he prayed on top of his stick'), he offers four variant readings primarily differing from the first one in the way the possessive relation is expressed.[43] By introducing these versions with the phrasing *nonnulli emendantes habent* ('some correcting copies have'), he seems to voice a preference at first, but then points to the mistake the editors or translators of these copies have made: Augustine explains that the Greek words expressing a reflexive and a non-reflexive possessive relation respectively, differ with regard to their breathings (and sometimes also with respect to an additional letter; that is: ἑαυτοῦ and αὐτοῦ).[44] This fact, Augustine claims, has been neglected and therefore has caused the faulty versions.[45] Hence, according to him, the translators or editors who meant to simplify the text by using the reflexive possessive adjective introduced an error into the text. In Augustine's subsequent comments, it becomes clear why the reading *suae* is more comprehensible: in this version, Jacob, an old man who declares his dying

---

σφάλματι. Therefore, the Latin rendering *in phantasmate* seems to have an equivalent within the Greek tradition of this verse, too.

[42] Augustine, *Quaestiones in Heptateuchum* 4.28 [CCSL 33, p. 251 ll. 649–52]: *Nonnulli autem aliud opinantes 'in phantasmate' interpretare uoluerunt: quod omnino sic abhorret a consuetudine locutionis nostrae, ut nusquam fere dicatur phantasma, nisi ubi falsitate uisorum sensus noster inluditur.*

[43] Other differences concern the choice of the preposition (*super* vs. *in*) and the noun which is accompanied by the genitive attribute *uirgae*. Augustine, *Quaestiones in Heptateuchum* 1.162 [CCSL 33, p. 63 ll. 2148–51]: *Quod habent latini codices: et adorauit super caput uirgae eius* [Gen. 47:31], *nonnulli emendantes habent: adorauit super caput uirgae suae, uel in capite uirgae suae siue in cacumen uel super cacumen.*

[44] Augustine's reference to accents here (*accentus dispares sunt*), obviously refers to the breathings rather than to the accentuation.

[45] Augustine, *Quaestiones in Heptateuchum* 1.162 [CCSL 33, p. 63 ll. 2151–6]: *Fallit eos enim graecum uerbum, quod eisdem litteris scribitur siue eius siue suae; sed accentus dispares sunt et ab eis qui ista nouerunt in codicibus non contemnuntur. Valent enim ad magnam discretionem; quamuis et unam plus litteram habere posset, si esset suae, ut non esset* αὐτοῦ, *sed* ἑαυτοῦ.

wish to his son Joseph, would be leaning on his own stick (*uirgae suae*) instead of that of his son (*uirgae eius*).[46]

Another passage which has been mentioned quite often in order to show that Augustine has some kind of ability as a textual critic, is found in his work on the harmony of the Gospels (*De consensu evangelistarum*), written about 404/5.[47] In this passage, Augustine prefers a so-called *lectio difficilior*: he accepts a reference to the prophet Jeremiah in Matthew 27:9 – *quod dictum est per Hieremiam prophetam* ('which was said by the prophet Jeremiah') – after a prophecy that is not found in this prophet but in Zechariah. At first, the Church Father mentions that not all manuscripts contain the name Jeremiah in this passage but that some copies only have the wording *per prophetam*. As the relevant prophecy is found precisely in the book of Zechariah, Augustine continues, one could assume that the manuscripts containing the shorter reading (*per prophetam*) are the correct ones, and that these copies are faulty which support the reading *per Hieremiam prophetam*.[48]

---

[46] Augustine, *Quaestiones in Heptateuchum* 1.162 [CCSL 33, p. 63 ll. 2156–62, 2166–70]: *Ac per hoc merito quaeritur quid sit quod dictum est. Nam facile intellegeretur senem, qui uirgam ferebat eo more, quo illa aetas baculum solet, ut se inclinauit ad deum adorandum, id utique fecerit super cacumen uirgae suae, quam sic ferebat, ut super eam caput inclinando adoraret deum. Quid est ergo: adorauit super cacumen uirgae eius* [Gen. 47:31], *id est filii sui Ioseph?* Augustine actually achieves some kind of solution to this problem of interpretation by turning to the Latin version of the Hebrew text with an indirect quotation: *Quamuis in hebraeo facillima huius quaestionis absolutio esse dicatur, ubi scriptum perhibent: et adorauit Israhel ad caput lecti* [Gen. 47:31], *in quo utique senex iacebat et sic positum habebat, ut in eo sine labore, quando uellet, oraret.*

[47] This example is mentioned, for instance, by Allen A. Gilmore, 'Augustine and the Critical Method', *Harvard Theological Review* 39.2 (1946): pp. 153–7 (here p. 154), Bruce M. Metzger, *The Text of the New Testament: Its Transmission, Corruption, and Restoration*, 2nd edn. (Oxford: Oxford UP, 1968), pp. 153f., Collins, 'Precursor', pp. 142f., Joseph G. Prior, *The Historical Critical Method in Catholic Exegesis* (Rome: Gregorian University Press, 2001), p. 68, and Donaldson, "References", pp. 177–80, 192.

[48] Augustine, *De consensu euangelistarum* 3.28–29 [CSEL 43, p. 304 ll. 6–20]: *tunc impletum est quod dictum est per Hieremiam prophetam dicentem: et acceperunt triginta argenteos pretium adpretiati. quem adpretiauerunt filii Israhel et dederunt eos in agrum figuli, sicut constituit mihi dominus* [Matt. 27:9f.]. *Si quis autem mouetur, quod hoc testimonium non inuenitur in scriptura Hieremiae prophetae, et ideo putat fidei euangelistae aliquid derogandum, primo nouerit non omnes codices euangeliorum habere, quod per Hieremiam dictum sit, sed tantummodo per prophetam. possemus ergo dicere his potius codicibus esse credendum, qui*

The decision in favour of the more difficult reading, however, is explained by pointing to the majority of Latin manuscripts as well as to the older Greek ones which also contain the name Jeremiah.[49]

Besides this evidence, Augustine also provides a reconstruction of the scribal intentions which supports a preference for the more difficult reading as well: he assumes that the prophet's name is more likely to have been erased from the original copies in order to avoid the problem that the prophecy is not found in Jeremiah, than to have been added to an otherwise comprehensible text.[50] It has to be admitted, however, that Augustine also offers two other ways of explaining the textual difficulties in Matthew 27:9 besides this rather philological approach in the subsequent paragraphs. First, he proposes a theological solution to the problem: as the prophets are all inspired by the same divine spirit, one could easily exchange their names, according to the logic that what was said by one of them was, in a way, also said by the others. The second theory assumes a conflation of passages found in the books of Zechariah and Jeremiah respectively.

In contrast with this, in his commentary on Psalm 108:21 (dictated about 419), Augustine attributes the existence of different Latin versions of this verse to an addition some people had made in their copies in order to provide a better interpretation. Quoting this verse (*Et tu, Domine, Domine fac mecum*, 'and you, Lord, Lord, do with me'), he states that some people have thought that the Latin noun *misericordiam* should be added for the interpretation of this verse and that some have indeed added it in their manuscripts (which then leads to the version: *Et tu, Domine, Domine fac mecum misericordiam*, 'and you, Lord, Lord, exercise mercy with me').[51] As the

---

Hieremiae nomen non habent. dictum est enim hoc per prophetam, sed Zachariam, unde putatur codices esse mendosos, qui habent nomen Hieremiae, quia uel Zachariae habere debuerunt uel nullius, sicut quidam, sed tamen per prophetam dicentem, qui utique intellegitur Zacharias.

[49] Augustine, *De consensu euangelistarum* 3.29 [CSEL 43, p. 304 l. 20 – p. 305 l. 4]: *sed utatur ista defensione cui placet; mihi autem cur non placeat, haec causa est, quia et plures codices habent Hieremiae nomen et qui diligentius in Graecis exemplaribus euangelium considerauerunt in antiquioribus Graecis ita se perhibent inuenisse.*

[50] Augustine, *De consensu euangelistarum* 3.29 [CSEL 43, p. 305 ll. 4–8]: *nulla fuit causa, cur adderetur hoc nomen, ut mendositas fieret; cur autem de nonnullis codicibus tolleretur, fuit utique causa, ut hoc audax imperitia faceret, cum turbaretur quaestione, quod hoc testimonium aput Hieremiam non inueniretur.*

[51] Augustine, *Enarrationes in Psalmos* 108.23 [CCSL 40, p. 1597 ll. 1–3]: *Et tu, Domine, Domine, fac mecum* [Ps. 108:21]. *Quidam subaudiendam putauerunt misericordiam, quidam uero et addiderunt* […].

more accurate, or rather more carefully-corrected copies (*emendatiores codices*) do not have this addition – thus Augustine assesses the quality of codices here[52] – he subsequently offers an exegesis of the shorter version, which, in his opinion, has the 'deeper meaning'.[53] Nevertheless, he does not exclude that some kind of merciful behaviour or action is expressed in this verse, especially as it continues with the wording: *quia suauis est misericordia tua* ('as your mercy is sweet'), but he does not support the addition of the noun.

A passage where the Church Father even gives consideration to an intentional alteration of the text is found in his unfinished work against Julian (*Contra Iulianum opus imperfectum*), which was written in the final years of Augustine's life and remained unfinished at his death in 430. In this writing, Augustine mainly tries to refute the arguments of Julian, Bishop of Eclanum and a follower of Pelagianism, concerning the doctrine of original sin and the question of the power of God's grace by quoting passages from Julian's work *Ad Florum* and responding to them.[54] In this context, he repudiates a reading of Romans 5:15, *Multo magis gratia dei et donum unius hominis Iesu Christi in plures abundavit* ('the grace of God and the gift of one human being, Jesus Christ, has been much more abundant for more people'), which Julian has used for his argumentation.[55] Augustine achieves this refutation by resorting to the Greek text. Julian himself cited this verse

[52] Augustine, *Enarrationes in Psalmos* 108.23 [CCSL 40, p. 1597 ll. 3–4]: [...] *sed emendatiores codices sic habent: Et tu, Domine, Domine, fac mecum, propter nomen tuum.*

[53] Augustine, *Enarrationes in Psalmos* 108.23 [CCSL 40, p. 1597 ll. 5–7]: *Vnde sensus altior non est praetermittendus, ita dixisse Filium Patri: Fac mecum, quia eadem sunt opera Patris et Filii.*

[54] *Ad Florum* was itself written as an answer to Augustine's work *De nuptiis et concupiscentia*, dealing mainly with the topics of concupiscence and original sin.

[55] Augustine, *Contra Iulianum opus imperfectum* 2.147 [CSEL 85.1, p. 269 ll. 1–7]: *Pervenire autem et ad innocentes gratiam Christi, ad quos Adae culpa non pervenit, propter quod vigilanter inculcavit: Multo magis gratia dei et donum unius hominis Iesu Christi in plures abundavit* [Rom. 5:15], *ut illa superior coaequatio eius aetatis, quae ratione utitur, in contrariis studiis indicet imitationem, haec autem in gratiae largitate praelatio consecratos et provectos approbet innocentes.* Throughout the second book of his unfinished work against Julian, Augustine quotes Julian's citation and exegesis of Romans 5:15 several times (*Contra Iulianum opus imperfectum* 2.69, 85, 96, 98f., 142, 205, 208) and refutes it. In *Contra Iulianum opus imperfectum* 2.206 [CSEL 85.1, p. 318 ll. 8–9] he refers to the Greek text again: *Non pronuntiat plures, sed multos. Graece locutus est, pollus dixit, non plistus; lege et tace.*

in order to illustrate that innocent newborn children are affected by God's grace but not by original sin, claiming that the Apostle Paul argues here that divine grace has an effect on more people than sin does. With this interpretation, Julian denies the whole concept of original sin, as it would pertain to everyone.[56] Augustine, however, counters this interpretation by pointing to Greek manuscripts. Instead of the word πλείστους which, according to Augustine, would be correctly translated by the word *plures* ('more people'), the Greek copies contain the reading πολλοὺς, which has to be rendered by the word *multos* ('many people') so that Julian's interpretation based on the term *plures* cannot stand. Interestingly, the Church Father does not only adduce the considerations that Julian could have used a faulty manuscript or could have been deceived by someone else's wrong judgement or his own mistaken memory, but also that he deliberately could have quoted an altered version (*ipse mentiris*); he even encourages him to look into the Greek text himself: *Graecum attende codicem et invenies pollus, non plistus.*[57]

Beyond these, there is another rather special group of passages where Augustine applies methods of textual criticism, or rather of criticism of translations, in a particular way. In his *Retractationes*, written about 427, a work in which he proposes corrections and modifications to his own writings, he sometimes rejects the wording of a biblical verse he quoted in an earlier work according to faulty manuscripts. He achieves this by resorting to better copies containing the same translation (implying that an error has been induced by scribal activities) or by referring to Greek codices. In the first book of his *Retractationes*, for example, he remarks that he cited the verse Wisdom of Solomon 8:7 in his early work *De moribus ecclesiae catholicae* according to an erroneous manuscript as follows: *Sobrietatem enim sapientia docet et iustitiam et uirtutem* ('as wisdom teaches modesty, justice and virtue'), while in the better copies of the same type of translation the wording *et sapientiam* (i.e. accusative instead of nominative, accompanied by

---

[56] Augustine, *Contra Iulianum opus imperfectum* 2.148 [CSEL 85.1, p. 271 ll. 19–24]: *Et quod superius dixisti vigilanter inculcasse apostolum: Multo magis gratia dei et donum unius hominis Iesu Christi in plures abundavit* [Rom. 5:15] *volens intellegi ideo plures dictos, quia pervenit gratia eius ad parvulos, ad quos imitatio primi hominis non pertinet* [...].

[57] Augustine, *Contra Iulianum opus imperfectum* 2.148 [CSEL 85.1, p. 271 ll. 24–7]: [...] *aut mendosus codex tibi mentitus est aut ipse mentiris aut ab aliquo falso sive fallente aut oblivione deceptus es. Non enim ait apostolus plures, sed multos. Graecum attende codicem et invenies pollus, non plistus.*

the conjunction *et*) is found.[58] Therefore the verse has to be read as 'as she teaches modesty, wisdom, justice and virtue' instead. Augustine corroborates this latter version by referring to Greek manuscripts which he claims he came across much later (*longe postea repperimus in codicibus Grecis*).[59] Interestingly, the Church Father does not withdraw the interpretation of the respective verse here which he gave in *De moribus* based on the incorrect reading, but even emphasizes that he has unfolded 'true things' (*res ueras*)[60] on the basis of his faulty codex.

Not quite as important, but nevertheless still relevant when asking about the application of some kind of critical method by Augustine, are instances where he resorts to the Greek text in order to exemplify the meaning of a Latin version which displays, for example, a difficult or obscure expression or a grammatical or semantic ambiguity. In these cases, Augustine is not dealing with variant readings but with Latin translations which pose difficulties for the understanding of a certain biblical verse. This approach is mentioned amongst others in his argumentation in the third book of *De doctrina christiana* where he talks about ways of treating ambiguities in the biblical text in general.[61]

Augustine's discussion of 1 Corinthians 15:31 provides an interesting example for this way of dealing with ambiguous Latin renderings:

---

[58] Augustine, *Retractationes* 1.7.3 [CCSL 57, p. 18 l. 25 – p. 19 l. 34]: *Similiter et paulo post testimonium posui de libro Sapientiae secundum codicem nostrum, in quo scriptum erat: Sobrietatem enim sapientia docet et iustitiam et uirtutem* [Sap. 8:7] [*De moribus* 1.27]. *Et secundum haec uerba disserui res quidem ueras, sed ex occasione mendositatis inuentas. Quid enim uerius quam quod sapientia doceat ueritatem contemplationis, quam nomine sobrietatis significatam putaui, et actionis probitatem, quam per duo alia intellegi uolui, per iustitiam atque uirtutem, cum codices eiusdem interpretationis ueriores habeant: Sobrietatem enim et sapientiam docet et iustitiam et uirtutem* [Sap. 8:7]?

[59] Augustine, *Retractationes* 1.7.3 [CCSL 57, p. 19 ll. 39–41]: *Has autem quattuor uirtutes in eodem libro Sapientiae suis nominibus appellatas, sicut a Grecis uocantur, longe postea repperimus in codicibus Grecis.*

[60] Augustine, *Retractationes* 1.7.3 [CCSL 57, p. 19 ll. 27–9]: *Et secundum haec uerba disserui res quidem ueras, sed ex occasione mendositatis inuentas.*

[61] Augustine, *De doctrina christiana* 3.IV.8 [CCSL 32, p. 82 ll. 17–22]: *Rarissime igitur et difficillime inueniri potest ambiguitas in propriis uerbis, quantum ad libros diuinarum scripturarum spectat, quam non aut circumstantia ipsa sermonis, qua cognoscitur scriptorum intentio, aut interpretum conlatio aut praecedentis linguae soluat inspectio.*

explanations of this verse are repeatedly found throughout his works.[62] Let us now take a closer look at one of these instances. In the discussion of Matthew 5:33–37 in his commentary on the Lord's Sermon on the Mount, which I have already mentioned, Augustine poses the question of how the rule of not swearing an oath is reconcilable with the behaviour of the Apostle Paul who sometimes swears by invoking God.[63] In this context, he quotes 1 Cor. 15:31 as an example of this practice (*Cotidie morior, per uestram gloriam*, 'I die every day by your glory') and points to the ambiguity of this verse. This arises from the Latin preposition *per,* which can either be used to express an instrumental relation or to introduce an oath. In order to prevent a wrong understanding of this verse, Augustine illustrates that the wording could also be interpreted to explain the reason for Paul's death and that a disambiguation and clarification could only be achieved by looking into the Greek source text itself. [64] By quoting the Greek version of the text (νὴ τὴν ὑμετέραν καύχησιν), he then shows that the preposition *per* is to be understood as an oath formula.[65]

Furthermore, passages where Augustine verifies two or three different Latin renderings with recourse to the underlying Greek text in a way also bear witness to the application of text-critical or rather philological principles. One short example for this kind of method should be sufficient here: in his treatises on the Gospel of John, Augustine mentions the existence of variant readings which are derived from the Latin verbs *clarificare* ('clarify') and *glorificare* ('glorify') respectively on several occasions. In these instances, he traces the versions back to the Greek text (the noun δόξα and the verb δοξάζειν respectively) in order to confirm both translation versions as adequate Latin renderings.[66]

---

[62] See *De doctrina christiana* 3.IV.8, *Epistula* 157.40, *Ad Galatas* 9, and *Sermo* 180.5.

[63] Augustine, *De sermone domini in monte* 1.17.51 [CCSL 35, p. 58 ll. 1240–2]: *Tamen propter contentiosos aut multum tardos, ne aliquid interesse quis putet, sciat etiam hoc modo iurasse apostolum dicentem: Cotidie morior, per uestram gloriam* [1 Cor. 15:31].

[64] Augustine, *De sermone domini in monte* 1.17.51 [CCSL 35, p. 58 ll. 1243–6]: *Quod ne quis existimet ita dictum, tamquam si diceretur: Vestra gloria me facit cotidie mori – sicut dicitur: Per illius magisterium doctus factus est; id est illius magisterio factum est, ut perfecte doceretur* […].

[65] Augustine, *De sermone domini in monte* 1.17.51 [CCSL 35, p. 58 ll. 1246–8]: […] *Graeca exemplaria diiudicant, in quibus scriptum est:* Νὴ τὴν ὑμετέραν καύχησιν, *quod nonnisi a iurante dicitur.*

[66] Augustine, *In Iohannis Euangelium tractatus* 82.1 [CCSL 36, p. 532 ll. 4–7]: *Siue*

In conclusion, even though Augustine is willing to accept and include in his exegesis different translations and variants, passages can nevertheless be found where he not only favours one version over the other but even refuses one reading. As has been demonstrated above, this is due to the application of philological principles, such as recourse to Greek manuscripts. Sometimes Augustine also considers the number or age of certain copies, while the context of a verse is of importance as well. Moreover, when we take a look at the passages where he rejects a version due to evidence for a mistake or forgery with regard to the respective reading, different categories of errors addressed by the Church Father can be accounted for, such as grammatical mistakes, translation errors caused by ambiguities of Greek words, scribal errors induced by a confusion of phonetically or graphically similar forms in Greek manuscripts, a mix-up on the part of the translators or omissions and additions; sometimes the accusation that a text has been deliberately quoted the wrong way also plays an important role.

To summarise, on occasion Augustine does not only address the existence of differing Latin renderings, but also evaluates them according to a set of philological principles. Nonetheless, for Augustine philology and textual criticism are not an end in themselves but are subordinated to the exegesis of the Bible.

---

glorificatus [John 15:8] *siue clarificatus dicatur, ex uno graeco uerbo utrumque translatum est, quod est* δοξάζειν, Δόξα *enim quae graece dicitur, latine gloria est;* 100.1 [p. 588 ll. 25–29]: *Verbum quippe graecum quod est* δοξάσει, *alius clarificabit* [John 16:14], *alius glorificabit* [John 16:14], *latini interpretes in sua quisque translatione posuerunt; quoniam ipsa quae graece dicitur* δόξα, *unde dictum est uerbum* δοξάσει, *et claritas interpretatur et gloria;* 105.3 [p. 605 ll. 21–3]: *Summa tunc Dei clarificatio, quia summa gloria, quae graece dicitur* δόξα. *Vnde dictum est* δόξασον, *quod latini quidam interpretati sunt: clarifica; quidam: glorifica* [John 17:1]. Cf. also *In Iohannis Euangelium tractatus* 104.3.

5. THE SOURCES FOR THE TEMPTATIONS EPISODE IN THE *PASCHALE CARMEN* OF SEDULIUS

OLIVER NORRIS

In the introduction to his 2013 translation and commentary of the *Paschale Carmen*, the first of its kind in English, Carl Springer poses a series of unanswered questions: 'Which version of the Bible did Sedulius use? Did he consult the Greek original? Did he use a version of the Vulgate or the *Itala* or both? Did he have some kind of harmony of the Gospels before him as he wrote, or did he rely on his memory, or use some combination of both? Upon what extra-biblical sources (e.g. apocryphal gospels, contemporary art, oral catechesis and preaching, or his own fertile imagination), might he have drawn?'[1] The present article aims to address some of these questions by focussing on one passage in particular, Sedulius's portrayal of the Temptations of Jesus.

The great Spanish grammarian Antonio Nebrija opened his sixteenth-century commentary on Sedulius by saying 'who Sedulius was, whence he came or when he flourished, things which we are wont to look for in other writers, I confess that as far as I can recall I have never read.'[2] Despite a recent flurry of studies on Sedulius, five hundred years have passed and we are little closer to knowing who he was. What little solid evidence we do have comes from manuscript subscriptions and a pair of dedicatory letters that preface Sedulius's two principal works, the *Paschale Carmen*, a 1753-line

---

[1] Carl Springer, *Sedulius, The Paschal Song and Hymns* (Atlanta GA: Society of Biblical Literature, 2013).

[2] Antonio de Nebrija [Aelius Antonius Nebrissensis], *Comentario al Carmen Paschale y a dos himnos de Sedulio*, (Longroño, 1509), Prologus pp. 5–7.

hexameter poem largely on the miracles of the Old Testament and the life of Jesus, and the *Paschale Opus*, a prose rewriting of the *Carmen*.

In the first letter Sedulius makes reference to Jerome's correspondence with Paula and Eustochium, providing a *terminus post quem* of around 390. A *terminus ante quem* is provided by a subscription found in the oldest Sedulian manuscript, the seventh-century Taurinensis (Turin, Biblioteca Nazionale Universitaria E.IV.42), stating that the Roman consul of 494, Turcius Rufius Apronianus Asterius, produced an edition of Sedulius.[3] A narrower time frame is accepted by the majority of scholars based on details found in a biographical notice present in several Sedulian manuscripts that describes Sedulius as flourishing during the time of the emperors Valentian and Theodosius the Younger (425–450).[4] The details of Sedulius's country of origin or the place where he wrote his works are even more obscure, with the biographical notice's description of him composing his works in Greece almost universally rejected on the basis that there would have been little demand for Latin works in Greece at the time;[5] instead Italy or Southern Gaul is generally accepted.[6]

Only three studies have ever tried to establish the biblical sources used by Sedulius when composing his two principal works, namely Mayr's 1916 dissertation, Moretti Pieri's 1969 study and Van der Laan's 1990 commentary on book four of the poem.[7] Of these, the most thorough was Moretti Pieri, who went a long way to identifying the different Gospel sources used by Sedulius. While she concluded that some passages were taken from the individual Gospels, for others she found that Sedulius had

---

[3] Springer, *Sedulius*, pp. xiv–xv.

[4] Some scholars have urged caution in accepting the biographical notice that largely appears an extrapolation of information found in Sedulius's prefatory letters to his patron Macedonius. For a discussion see Springer, *Sedulius*, p. xv.

[5] Roger Green, *Latin Epics of the New Testament: Juvencus, Sedulius, Arator* (Oxford: Oxford UP, 2006), pp. 139–40.

[6] The evidence is thin: for a summary see Springer, *Sedulius*, p. xvi, or the introduction to Daniel Deerberg, *Der Sturz des Judas: Kommentar (5,1-163) und Studien zur poetischen Erbauung bei Sedulius* (Münster: Aschendorff, 2011), pp. 13–15.

[7] Theodor Mayr, *Studien zu dem Paschale Carmen des christlichen Dichters Sedulius, Inaugural-Dissertation* (Augsburg: Pfeiffer, 1916); Giovanna Moretti Pieri, *Sulle fonti evangeliche di Sedulio* (Firenze: Leo S. Olschki, 1969); Paul W.A.Th. Van der Laan, 'Sedulius Carmen Paschale boek 4: inleiding, vertaling, commentaar.' (Dissertation, Leiden University, 1990).

clearly drawn on multiple Gospels to create an account that harmonised elements from the different Gospels.[8] The following passage, taken from book three, lines 103–111, illustrates the level of harmonisation present in parts of Sedulius's text, here for his account of the resuscitation of Jairus's daughter:[9]

Paschale Carmen, 3.103–11	Gospel Readings
Principis interea synagogae filia clauso	Lk. 8:41 *princeps synagogae erat*
Functa die superas moriens amiserat auras.	Mt. 9:18 *defuncta est* | Lk. 8:42 *moriebatur*
At genitor, cui finis edax spem prolis adultae	Lk. 8:41 *rogans*
Sustulerat, sanctos Domini lacrimansque gemensque.	Lk. 8:41 *cecidit ad pedes;* Mk. 5:22 *procidit ad pedes* | Mk. 5:23 *et deprecabatur eum*
Conruit ante pedes, uix uerba precantia fari	Lk. 8:42 *filia unica erat illi fere annorum duodecim*
Singultu quatiente ualens, 'miserere parentis	Mt. 9:18 *modo (defuncta est)*
Orbati, miserere senis, modo filia' dicens	
'Vnica uirgineis nec adhuc matura sub annis	
Occidit et misero patris mihi nomen ademit.'	

The passage is principally Lukan but contains notable Matthean and Markan details. For example, the fact that Jairus's daughter is already dead is present in Matthew alone, whereas the Markan and Lukan accounts state only that she is dying. On the other hand, the details that she is the only daughter of Jairus and that he is the chief of the synagogue are Lukan. Another element that suggests harmonisation is that, with the present participle *moriens*, Sedulius's account appears to draw on information in Luke that the girl was dying (*moriebatur*) despite describing her earlier as dead, *functa*. Such details reveal the harmoniser's desire to include details from all the accounts at the same time as maintaining the congruity of the narrative. While such passages reveal harmonisation of this kind, it is difficult to know whether our poet was responsible for the harmonisation or whether Sedulius based his account on an existing harmonised source. Moretti Pieri attempted to provide an answer to this question by comparing the harmonised passages in the *Paschale Carmen* with parallel passages drawn

---

[8] Moretti Pieri, *Fonti*, p. 242.

[9] Quotations, page and line numbers taken from Victoria Panagl's 2007 revision of Johannes Huemer's CSEL edition (Johannes Huemer (ed.), *Sedulii opera omnia. Editio altera supplementis aucta curante Victoria Panagl.* (CSEL 10. Vienna: Österreichische Akademie der Wissenschaften, 2007).

from Agostino Ciasca's 1888 edition of the Arabic Diatessaron and Ernest Ranke's 1868 edition of Victor of Capua's *Unum ex quattuor* found in the Codex Fuldensis.

Moretti Pieri's study concluded that there was a similarity between Sedulius's base text and that of the 'Syriac Diatessaron' as preserved by the Arabic Diatessaron that was difficult to attribute to coincidence alone.[10] However, subsequent scholars have been reluctant to follow her findings, which at times pay little attention to episode sequence.[11] This is especially the case in the Temptations episode, where Sedulius's text in the *Carmen* offers a totally different, Lukan sequence to the Matthean order found in the Arabic Diatessaron. It was on the basis of this that Van der Laan rejected Moretti Pieri's suggestion that the 'Syriac Diatessaron' was Sedulius's primary model.[12] To correct this, the current study will therefore pay greater attention to the episode sequence found in Sedulius's text. In addition, Moretti Pieri's study makes little attempt to explain how Sedulius might have obtained a harmonised text or to consider the variety of sources, written and oral, available to Sedulius, nor does she consider the existence of non-Diatessaronic harmonised passages that Sedulius could have used. Besides these issues, a large amount of recent research has improved our knowledge not only of Tatian's Diatessaron, but also of non-Tatianic Gospel harmonies and the Latin biblical tradition in general.[13] All these elements justify a review of her findings.

---

[10] Moretti Pieri, *Fonti*, p. 242.

[11] Green, *Latin Epics*, pp. 183–4; Van der Laan, 'Sedulius Carmen Paschale', p. 219.

[12] Van der Laan, 'Sedulius Carmen Paschale', p. 216: 'Het moge duidelijk zijn, dat juist de afwijkende volgorde ernstig afbreuk doet aan de veronderstelling, dat S. hier overeenstemt met het Syrische Diatessaron'.

[13] In particular, the work of Ulrich Schmid has shed much light on the Western Diatessaronic tradition both establishing once and for all the primacy of the *Unum ex quattuor* in the Medieval Latin Gospel harmony tradition as well as confirming the role of commentaries, glosses and scribal error in so-called diatessaronic readings, see Ulrich Schmid, *Unum ex quattuor: eine Geschichte der lateinischen Tatianüberlieferung* (AGLB 37. Freiburg im Breisgau: Herder, 2005); Ulrich Schmid, 'In Search of Tatian's Diatessaron in the West' *VC* 57.2 (2003) pp. 176–199. In addition, Philip Burton's study of the Old Latin Gospels has clarified much of the Old Latin tradition, see Philip H. Burton, *The Old Latin Gospels: A Study of their Texts and Language* (Oxford: Oxford UP, 2000).

The probable date of composition for Sedulius's works in the first half of the fifth century places them in the midst of a highly fluid era for biblical material, in which Old Latin versions of the Gospels co-existed alongside Jerome's revision of the Gospels (hereafter referred to as the Vulgate).[14] As such, changes can be observed in the use of biblical texts by patristic writers from this era. Augustine, for example, can be seen to change gradually the version of the Gospels that he uses from an Old Latin text to a Vulgate text after 403.[15] In such an environment, comparison of the *Carmen* and the *Opus Paschale* proves invaluable as the twin works offer an insight into the use of the Bible during this period. Since Sedulius re-wrote the poem as a prose work in order 'to add in the latter work that which had been left out in the former',[16] ensuring that he was 'changing neither the argument nor the order found in the *Carmen*',[17] he unwittingly created a perfect study in changing biblical usage whilst leaving most other variables constant.

In the current study the following method of enquiry was used. First, Sedulius's accounts of the Temptations in the *Opus* and the *Carmen* were examined and compared against the Old Latin codices and patristic citations in the *Vetus Latina Database* to establish whether their text type is Old Latin or Vulgate. Second, although it has already been stated that Sedulius follows a Lukan episode order, we established whether Sedulius's text type is also Lukan by way of lexical and structural analysis of the text, that is through comparison of Sedulius's word use and order with that of the Matthean and Lukan traditions. Finally, once Sedulius's text type had been fully established, it was compared against texts that bear witness to a similar text type as found in Sedulius.

---

[14] For details of the circulation of Vulgate, Old Latin and 'mixed texts', see the introduction to Burton, *Old Latin Gospels*, especially pp. 6–8.

[15] H.A.G. Houghton, *Augustine's Text of John: Patristic Citations and Latin Gospel Manuscripts*. (Oxford: Oxford UP, 2008), p. 13.

[16] Sedulius, *Epistola ad Macedonium II* (CSEL X, p. 173): *sed quae defuerant primis addita sunt secundis.*

[17] Sedulius, *Epistola ad Macedonium II* (CSEL X, p. 173): *nec impares argumento uel ordine, sed stilo uidentur et oratione dissimiles.*

Examining the Temptations episode in both the *Carmen* and the *Opus*,
it is quickly apparent that Sedulius used a Vulgate source for the latter, but
there is no evidence of such a source in the former work. It should be
added that this is not a general rule for Sedulius's use of biblical sources in
the *Paschale Opus*; indeed, as Van der Laan discovered in his 1990 study, Old
Latin readings occur both in the *Opus* and the *Carmen*, with no general
preference for the Vulgate text in the *Opus*.[18] However, at some points, in
particular the Nativity, the Baptism and the Temptations episodes, Sedulius
has replaced the paraphrased biblical text found in the Carmen by chunks
of biblical verses (sometimes up to 10 verses long) taken from the Vulgate,
as though he were 'weeding out' unwanted text from his poem and
replacing it with better stock.

In the Temptations passage as found in the *Opus*, the Vulgate character
of Sedulius is apparent from the presence of the following Vulgate
readings:[19]

> *Opus* 2.14 (p. 214:18) *et <u>accedens</u> ad eum temptator* (Mt. 4:3; *accedens* Vg, VL 9
> 11; *accessit* VL 1 3 4 5 6 12; προσελθὼν NA28)

> *Opus* 2.14 (p. 216:8–9) *in omni uerbo <u>quod procedit de ore Dei</u>* (Mt. 4:4; *in omni
> uerbo quod procedit de ore Dei* Vg, VL 9 11; *in o. u. D. q. p. de ore* VL 6; *o. u.
> procedenti ex ore Dei* VL 12; *in o. u. Dei* VL (3) 4 5; – VL 1; ἐπὶ παντὶ
> ῥήματι ἐκπορευομένῳ διὰ στόματος θεοῦ NA28).

> *Opus* 2.14 (p. 216:13–15) *et duxit illum diabolus … et ait <u>ei</u>* (Lk. 4:6; *ei* Vg;
> *ad eum* VL 5; *ad illum* VL 2 3 4 8 13; *illi* VL 11 14; καὶ εἶπεν αὐτῷ
> NA28).

---

[18] Van der Laan, 'Sedulius Carmen Paschale', p. 212.

[19] The only Old Latin manuscripts considered are those listed as such in
Bonatius Fischer, 'Der lateinische Text der Evangelien' in Roger Gryson and
Pierre-Maurice Bogaert (eds), *Recherches sur l'histoire de la Bible latine* (Louvain-la-
Neuve: Faculté de théologie, 1987), pp. 51–104. Manuscript numbers refer to
Roger Gryson, ed., *Altlateinische Handschriften/Manuscrits vieux latins. Répertoire
descriptif.* Mss 1-275. (Vetus Latina 1/2A. Freiburg: Herder, 1999), where the Gospel
manuscripts are numbered VL 1–49. For identification of Vulgate readings I follow
the rule of thumb in Burton, *Old Latin Gospels*, pp. 7–8: 'any reading found in a
known mixed text, agreeing with the Vulgate but not found outside the Vulgate and
the other mixed texts, may be attributed to Vulgate influence'.

Opus 2.14 (p. 216:17–8) *si adoraueris coram me* (Lk. 4:7; *si adoraueris coram me* Vg, VL 6; *si prostratus* (5: om. *prostratus*) *a. in conspectu meo* VL 2 5; *si procidens a. ante me* VL 3 4 8 13; *si procidens* (14: *procedens*) *a. me* VL 11 14; ἐὰν προσκυνήσῃς ἐνώπιον ἐμοῦ NA28).

Opus 2.14 (p. 217:10–12) *diabolus… statuit eum supra pinnaculum* templi (Mt. 4:5; *pinnaculum* Vg, VL 11; *pinnam* VL 3 4 5 6 9 12; *fastigium* VL 1; τὸ πτερύγιον NA28)[20]

Opus 2.14 (p. 217:14) *et in manibus tollent te* (Mt. 4:6; *et…tollent* Vg, VL 5 11; *ut…tollant* VL 1 3 4 6 9 12; καὶ ἐπὶ χειρῶν ἀροῦσίν σε NA28).

Of these six Vulgate readings, none are found in the *Carmen*, which on the contrary shows evidence of Old Latin readings at these points:

Carmen 2.177-80, *Insidiis temptator adit* (Mt. 4:3; *accessit* VL 1 3 4 5 6 12; *accedens* Vg, VL 9 11; προσελθών NA28).[21]

Carmen 2.185, *cuncto sermone Dei* (Mt. 4:4; *in omni uerbo Dei* VL (3) 4 5; *in o. u. quod procedit de ore Dei* Vg, VL 9 11; *in o. u. Dei quod p. de ore* VL 6; *o. u. procedenti ex ore Dei* VL 12; – VL 1; παντὶ ῥήματι ἐκπορευομένῳ διὰ στόματος θεοῦ NA28).[22]

Carmen 2.202, *supra fastigia templi* (Mt. 4:5; *fastigium* VL 1; *pinnam* VL 3 4 5 6 9 12; *pinnaculum* Vg, VL 11; τὸ πτερύγιον NA28).

---

[20] For details of Jerome's translation technique for τὸ πτερύγιον, see Burton, *Old Latin Gospels*, p. 195.

[21] Sedulius's text of the first temptation begins with *Insidiis temptator adit*, the tempter approached him with traps. Moretti Pieri, *Fonti*, p. 135, feels that this is drawn from the Vulgate text of Matthew 4:3, *accedens temptator*, seeing the replacement of the participial phrase by a finite verb as Sedulius's effort to render the passage more precise. Against this, however, stand the Old Latin sources, which all have *accessit*. Rather than an adaption of the Vulgate, it appears more likely that Sedulius was simply following the Old Latin version of Matthew 4:3.

[22] Moretti Pieri, *Fonti*, p. 136, suggests that Sedulius's *sed cuncto sermone Dei* is a rendering of the Vulgate text of Deuteronomy 8:3 as given at Matthew 4:3, *sed in omni uerbo quod procedit de ore Dei*. This again seems implausible; instead, it appears a verbatim adaptation of *sed omni uerbo Dei* found in the Lukan text and in three Old Latin witnesses to Matthew (VL (3) 4 5; note however that the reading in VL 3 is now too worn to be read).

Carmen 2.189, *si me* <u>*prostratus*</u> *adores* (Mt. 4:9; *si prostratus adoraueris me* VL 1; *si procidens* (3: *procedens*) *a. me* VL 3 4 6 12; *si cadens a. me* Vg, VL 5 9 11; ἐὰν πεσὼν προσκυνήσῃς μοι NA28).

Carmen 2.205, *Angelicis* <u>*subvectus eas ut*</u> *tutior ulnis,* (Mt. 4:6; *ut...tollant* VL 1 3 4 6 9 12; *et...tollent* Vg, VL 5 11; καὶ ἐπὶ χειρῶν ἀροῦσίν σε NA28).

Thus there are six places where Sedulius's *Opus* text agrees with the reading found in the Vulgate against the European and African Old Latin traditions and five places in the *Carmen* where the text agrees with the European or African Old Latin tradition against the Vulgate. In addition, one of the above readings (*Carmen* 2.189) shows agreement with the Matthean text in the *Carmen* but with the Lukan text in the *Opus*. This is not restricted to this reading alone; in fact, where Sedulius follows Luke for the second temptation in the *Opus*, there is little evidence that the text of the *Carmen* also follows Luke, as shown in the following table. Here, Sedulius's passage has been placed alongside the two codices representing the African Old Latin tradition, Codex Bobiensis for Matthew and Codex Palatinus for Luke, as these are the only manuscripts that feature *prostratus adoraueris*, a phrase rendered by Sedulius as *prostratus adores*. This is the only instance of *prostratus* in Sedulius's text and it does not appear to be a replacement for the un-metrical *procidens* found in the majority of Old Latin codices (which could be replaced by *cadens* in any case).[23]

---

[23] Moretti Pieri, *Fonti, p.* 139, attributes Sedulius's use of the word to personal choice, perhaps in order to add a 'classical note' to the passage. This appears unlikely given that the word is not part of the Sedulian lexicon.

Paschale Carmen 2.187–9	Codex Bobiensis (VL 1)	Codex Palatinus (VL 2)
	Mt. 4:8	Lk. 4:5
vv. 187-8	*iterum adsumpsit illum diabolus in*	*et inposuit illum secundo supra*
Cum Domino montana petit	*montem altum nimis et ostendit*	*montem ostendit illi omnia regna*
cunctasque per orbem /		*orbis terrae in pucto temporis*
Regnorum monstrauit opes:	*illi omnia regna huius mundi et*	Lk. 4:6
	claritatem illorum	*et dixit ad illum diavolus tibi dabo*
		potestatem istorum omnium et
vv. 188-9	Mt. 4:9	*claritatem illorum quia mihi tradita*
haec omnia, dicens, /	*et dixit illi haec omnia tibi dabo si*	*est et cui uolo do illa.*
Me tribuente feres, si me prostratus	*prostratus adoraueris me*	Lk. 4:7
adores		*tu ergo si prostratus adoraueris in*
		conspectu meo, erit tua omnes.

This comparison shows that if we judge Sedulius's textual source on lexical criteria alone this passage could have been taken either from Luke or Matthew; the few Matthean or Lukan specific words are hardly conclusive. *Cunctasque per orbem regnorum monstrauit opes* appears to be a closer rendering of the Lukan *ostendit illi omnia regna orbis* than the Matthean *et ostendit illi omnia regna huius mundi*. Hypallage sees the accusative *regna* become a genitive plural and while the genitive *orbis* is apparently rendered by *per orbem*, metrical considerations may lie behind Sedulius's choice of *per orbem* over *mundi*.[24] On the other hand, the second part appears more Matthean, in the omission of a prepositional phrase after *adoraueris*, which is found in all of the Lukan witnesses bar two (VL 11 14) against the use of *adoraueris* with a direct object, as found in all the Matthean codices, as well as in the rendering of *dixit* through *dicens*.[25]

---

[24] It is however possible that Sedulius has rendered *mundi*, the Matthean reading, by *per orbem*, as he does elsewhere in the *Carmen* to complete the end of the hexameter line (*Paschale Carmen* 3.287, *ut maior sit nostra fides, nunc esse per orbem*). For further discussion, see Moretti Pieri, *Fonti*, p. 137.

[25] Moretti Pieri, *Fonti*, p. 138, sees *me tribuente feres* as a rendering of the Lukan *tibi dabo … erunt tua*, on the basis that *feres* shifts the focus from the giver to the receiver, as does the Lukan *erunt tua* but not the Matthean *tibi dabo*. While this is possible, the Ovidian allusion (Met. 2.44–5: *quoduis pete munus ut illud / me tribuente feres*) rather muddies the water and weakens her hypothesis.

These lexical findings are supplemented by a structural analysis of the passage that strongly suggests that Sedulius used the Matthean passage. Drawing on a source that would have had no verse separation, the opening lines, *cum ... opes*, succinctly paraphrase the Matthean sentence in verse 4:8. Such faithfulness to the text is in accordance with the programme of 'departing only very slightly from the heavenly scriptures' that Sedulius outlines in his first prefatory letter to Macedonius.[26] On the other hand, there is nothing in Sedulius's text that replicates Luke 4:6, where the Devil states that he has been granted the power and glory of the kingdoms and he gives them to whomever he chooses. Furthermore, Sedulius's word order in 188–9 is Matthean, beginning with *haec omnia* and concluding with *si me prostratus adores*, whereas in Luke the word order is reversed.

Thus two preliminary conclusions can be made concerning the biblical sources Sedulius used for the Temptations episode: first, that he used a Vulgate source in the *Opus* but an Old Latin source in the *Carmen* and second, that the *Carmen* text type combines a predominantly Matthean text with a Lukan order. It is the view of Green that this order is due to Sedulius's habit of switching between Gospel passages as he likes, while Van der Laan maintains that it is part of Sedulius's creativity.[27] However, there does not appear to be any advantage for Sedulius in choosing the Lukan order over the Matthean order for a largely Matthean text. Furthermore, in the Temptations episode found in the *Opus*, Sedulius's use of the Vulgate passages is strikingly at odds with his promise to depart only very slightly from the biblical text: he starts with Matthew 4:1–4 for the first temptation, before switching to Luke 4:5–8 for the second temptation, then back to Matthew for the third temptation, but in the Lukan order so that the next passage is Matthew 4:5–7, before finally concluding with Matthew 4:11. On the contrary, it appears that the text structure found in the *Carmen* reflects the peculiar character of Sedulius's source text and is not the result of his own intervention. However, the distortion to the Matthean structure in the *Opus* betrays Sedulius's desire to keep to the order of the text found in the *Carmen*, according to his above-cited intention to change neither the order nor the argument found in the *Carmen* when composing the *Opus*. Still, this does not explain why Sedulius uses Luke at all in the *Opus*; this can only be because Sedulius believed his text to be Lukan due to episode order but recognised the Matthean character of the text at certain points and thus

---

[26] Sedulius, *Epistola ad Macedonium* I.6: *paululum ab scripturis celsioribus uacans.*
[27] Van der Laan, 'Sedulius Carmen Paschale', p. 219. Green, *Latin Epics*, p. 176.

chose to insert Matthean passages in the *Opus* for those sections that were undeniably Matthean.

Armed with knowledge of Sedulius's text type, we can proceed to examine potential models. First and foremost, a Matthean text in a Lukan order is not found in any Old Latin codex. While several of the Old Latin Lukan codices (VL 4 6 11 13 14) follow (or show evidence of having followed, as in VL 3) the Matthean order for the Temptations, no extant codex shows evidence of the contrary, as is found in Sedulius. However, outside of the codices, the Sedulian type text is found in three African sources: Augustine's fourth-century treatise *De uera religione*, the recently discovered *Sermo de honorandis uel contemnendis parentibus*,[28] and Latin Pseudo-John Chrysostom's Sermon 21, *De lapsu primi hominis*.[29] In addition, two Medieval Gospel harmonies, the Persian Diatessaron and the Pepysian Harmony, as well as part of the Armenian version of Ephrem's commentary on Tatian's Diatessaron bear witness to this order.

Concerning the African texts, both *De uera religione* and the Latin Chrysostom text interpret the Temptations scene in the light of 1 John 2:16 (*quoniam omne quod est in mundo concupiscentia carnis et concupiscentia oculorum est et superbia vitae quae non est ex Patre sed ex mundo est*). *De uera religione* is one of Augustine's earliest writings and it contains the entire Temptations episode in which he equates *desire of the flesh* with the first temptation, *desire of the eyes* (*curiositas*) with the third temptation (the Temple) and *worldly ambition* with the second temptation.[30] The very fact that Augustine altered the order of 1

---

[28] Augustine, *De uera religione* 38 (CCSL 32, ed. Klaus-Detlef Daur and Josef Martin, Turnhout: Brepols, 1962); Augustine, *De honorandis uel contemnendis parentibus* 8 (Sermo D13=159A) (*Augustin d'Hippone, Vingt-six sermons au peuple d'Afrique*, ed. François Dolbeau, Paris: Inst. des Études Augustiniennes, 2009).

[29] John Chrysostom, *Sermones XXXI collectionis Morin dictae (perperam olim Iohanni Mediocri episcopo Neapolitano ascripti)* (CPL 915; PL supplement, IV, 741–834). For the text's dating and African origin see F.J. Leroy, 'Compléments et retouches à la 3ᵉ édition de la Clavis Patrum Latinorum. L'homilétique africaine masquée sous le Chrysostomus Latinus, Sévérien de Céramussa et la catéchèse donatiste de Vienne' *Révue d'Histoire Ecclésiastique* 99.2 (2004) pp. 425–34.

[30] We can be sure that Augustine's source had the standard order for he quotes 1 John 2:16 correctly a few lines earlier in *De uera religione* 38: *concupiscentia carnis est et concupiscentia oculorum et ambitio saeculi*. Augustine again manipulates the order of 1 John 2:16 to intrepret the Temptations in Lukan order in his Exposition on Psalm 8:13 before using the verse a third time to interpret the Temptations at a much later

John 2:16 so that it conformed to his text of the Temptations suggests that the Lukan order is genuine and not a memory slip.

The 'Latin Chrysostom' is likely to date from the early fifth century.[31] It clearly bears some relationship with Augustine's text, although direct dependence can probably be ruled out as the order in which the verse from the epistle is applied to the Temptations is different: *worldly ambition* is equated with the Temple temptation, while the devil's offer of his kingdoms is equated with *desire of the eyes*. It offers a number of readings found in the European text type as it includes readings such as *uada retro Satanas* found in VL 3 6 and 9, and *pinnam* (VL 3 4 5 6 9 12) for *fastigium* (VL 1; CY, AU), as well as the Vulgate reading *omni uerbo quod procedit ex ore Dei* (Vg; VL 9 11) but it does preserve some specifically Old Latin African readings, such as *si prostratus adoraveris me* (VL 1; AU). Furthermore, it contains a number of unusual readings that can also be found in Sedulius's text, such as the repetition of *repulit … repellens* to describe the devil's unsuccessful temptation attempts, which is paralleled by Sedulius's *repulsus … hoste repulso* and, most significantly of all, the curious phrase uttered by the devil before the temptations: *Aut iste est ut primus homo, et decipio eum: aut si ipse est Christus confusus recedo*. This finds a very close parallel in Sedulius's comment concerning the devil's flight after the third temptation, *et ualidi confusus cuspide uerbi … fugit*.[32]

The third text, from the end of the fourth century, is one of the Mainz Sermons of Augustine recently discovered by Dolbeau. It contains too little text for meaningful comparison with Sedulius but it does repeat the pattern found in these two texts.[33] The Temptations episode is this time used as an example of how to adhere to the Law of the Scripture. It preserves a

---

date, with the same comparisons but this time in the Matthean order, in his commentary on the First Epistle of John, 2. Gryson's *Répertoire Général* gives 390 as a composition date (Roger Gryson, *Répertoire général des auteurs ecclésiastiques latins de l'antiquité et du haut moyen âge*. (Vetus Latina 1/1. Freiburg: Herder, 2007), p. 231). For discussion see the introduction of Daur's edition in CCSL 32.

[31] Leroy, 'Compléments et retouches'.

[32] Huemer's edition reads *confossus … cuspide uerbi*, but *confusus* is found in the Turin manuscript. Given the similarities between Sedulius's passage and the passage found in the Latin Chrysostom and Augustine's *Sermo* 159A, there is a strong argument for accepting the older reading.

[33] The sermon is dated to 397 in François Dolbeau, 'Les sermons de saint Augustin découverts à Mayence. Un premier bilan.' *Comptes rendus des séances de l'Académie des Inscriptions et Belles-Lettres* 137.1 (1993) pp. 135–71.

Matthean text, once again set in a Lukan order, but this time without mention of 1 John 2:16. However, Augustine's sermon does include much of the same vocabulary as the Latin Chrysostom: for example, after the devil is foiled in his second temptation, Augustine writes *At ubi uidit se ille callidus serpens bis numero ex lege repulsum.*[34] Before the devil is foiled for the final time, Augustine writes *Et hic ex eadem lege uulnerauit inimicum, prostrauit, confusum abire fecit.*[35]

These three African texts therefore provide the same version of the Temptations but used in quite different contexts: the first as an example of how to overcome worldly temptations (*De uera religione*); the second as a demonstration of how Jesus redeemed man from Original Sin (Latin Chrysostom); and finally as an example of how to overcome those who wish to remove the Christian from adherence to the Scriptures (Augustine's Mainz Sermon). However, the different context of the texts should not distract from the similarities in their wording and their proximity in date that suggests that we are dealing with a single tradition in two forms as a base text used in one of Augustine's treatises and as a base text for several homiletic texts.

While it is very possible that a Matthean text in Lukan order such as the one that appears to have existed in Africa around the close of the fourth century could be the same as the base text used by Sedulius, there are a number of obstacles to this theory. First, Sedulius's text is not exclusively Matthean, containing Lukan readings at at least two points: at line 175 Sedulius's *sacro spiramine plenum* (*Iesum*) is surely a poetic rendering of Luke 4:1, *Iesus autem plenus spritu sancto*, avoiding the troublesome cretic in *spiritu.*[36] Furthermore, at line 206, Sedulius's text reads *Angelicis subuectus eas ut tutior ulnis*, a rendering of Psalm 90:11–12 as found in Luke 4:10 that reads *angelis suis mandabit de te ut conseruent te.* In Matthew, the devil misquotes Psalm 90 and the second part of verse 11 is omitted, whereas it is partly included in Luke as well as in Sedulius's text. Since Augustine's text is entirely Matthean such a detail is absent, but Psalm 90:11–12 is quoted in its entirety in Latin Chrysostom: *ut custodiant te in omnibus viis tuis.*[37] It is therefore possible that the African text preserved the Lukan reading in some form.

---

[34] Augustine, *De honorandis uel contemnendis parentibus* (*Sermo* 159A), p. 8.
[35] *ibid.*
[36] For a fuller discussion, see Moretti Pieri, *Fonti*, p. 134.
[37] John Chrysostom, *Sermones XXXI collectionis Morin dictae*, 21, col. 794.

This Lukan reading is also found in the Persian Diatessaron, as is the reading taken from Luke 4:1. It is necessary therefore to compare the harmonised tradition of the temptations where it exists in the Lukan order along with the African text against Sedulius's text to determine which of these, if any, is a possible source for Sedulius's base text.

Concerning the harmonies and the text in Ephrem's commentary on the Diatessaron, the inclusion in Ephrem's discussion of the Temptations of three lemmas presenting a harmonised text of the Temptations in Lukan order (in addition to a principal passage that is in the Matthean order as found in most Diatessaronic witnesses) has elicited various explanations. Boismard sees it as proof of the existence of a non-Tatianic harmony, a theory that Petersen accepts only as a possibility, referring to the Liège Harmony that contains a Lukan text as part of the harmonised Temptations episode.[38] The key difference, however, is that the Liège Harmony maintains the *Matthean* order and Petersen does not explain why Ephrem makes reference to the same passage with two different episode orders. While the text in shortened lemma form is too brief for meaningful comparison with Sedulius's text, two Medieval harmonies, the Persian Diatessaron and the Pepysian Harmony possibly bear witness to the tradition found in Ephrem's commentary.

The Persian Diatessaron has been known for some time for its unusual structure, which bears little resemblance to any other Diatessaronic witness.[39] It is found in a single manuscript (Florence, Laurentian Lib. XVII (81)), published and translated into Italian by Giuseppe Messina in 1951.[40] According to Messina, it was translated from a Syrian *Vorlage* and possibly bears witness to two different harmonies.[41]

The Pepysian Harmony is extant in one manuscript, dated to 1400, and is probably an Old English translation of a French model.[42] It was long

---

[38] Marie-Emile Boismard, *Le diatessaron, de Tatien à Justin* (Paris: Librairie Lecoffre, J. Gabalda et Cie, 1992), pp. 95–100. William Lawrence Petersen, *Tatian's Diatessaron: Its Creation, Dissemination, Significance, and History in Scholarship* (Leiden: E.J. Brill, 1994), pp. 355–6.

[39] Bruce M. Metzger, *The Early Versions of the New Testament: Their Origin, Transmission, and Limitations* (Oxford: Clarendon Press, 1977).

[40] Giuseppe Messina, *Diatessaron Persiano: Introduzione, testo e traduzione* (Rome: Pontificio Istituto Biblico, 1951).

[41] *ibid.*, p. xxi.

[42] Margery Goates, *The Pepysian Gospel Harmony* (Millwood, NY: Kraus Reprint,

neglected as a Diatessaronic witness, until becoming the subject of a couple of relatively recent studies.[43] Any consideration of the Pepysian Harmony must take into account the apparent influence of medieval commentaries and biblical glosses in particular Petrus Comestor's *Historia Scholastica* and the *Glossa Ordinaria*. However, neither appears to have played any role in the Temptations episode.[44] Given the Pepysian Harmony's English provenance, it must also be considered alongside Clement of Llanthony's Harmony, a harmony that was purportedly the creation of the Bishop of Gloucester in the twelfth century.[45] Indeed, Clement's Harmony also contains a harmonised Temptations episode in the Lukan order, but is a much fuller harmony, sometimes repeating redundant verses, a feature not at all found in the Pepysian harmony. Given the thoroughness with which Clement has endeavoured to include details from both the Lukan and the Matthean accounts of the Temptations, it is rare that the account found in the Pepysian includes readings omitted in Clement's account. However, in the second temptation close analysis of the verses selected for harmonisation reveals a real disparity in two accounts, which would appear to rule out dependence of the Pepysian account on Clement's text for the Temptations episode.

1987 [original edition: *Early English Text Society*, No 157, 1922]), pp. xv–xviii. Despite Goates's argument for an Anglo-Norman model, the provenance of such a text could well have been England given the extent of Anglo-Norman book production in post-conquest England.

[43] Petersen, *Diatessaron*, p. 244. Studies of note include Boismard's above-cited study and J. Neville Birdsall, 'The Sources of the Pepysian Harmony and its Links with the Diatessaron', *NTS* 22.2 (1976) pp. 215–23.

[44] Birdsall, "The Sources of the Pepysian Harmony".

[45] No detailed study of Clement's Harmony has been undertaken, but Clement claims the work as his own in the preface found in many of the extant manuscripts. For a discussion of Clement's method, see J. Rendel Harris, 'The Gospel Harmony of Clement of Llanthony', *JBL* 43.3/4 (1924) pp. 349–62. As Clement's Harmony is still unpublished, the analysis of the current article is based on the text found in London, British Library, Royal 3.A.x.

Pepysian Harmony	Clement of Llanthony's Harmony
Mt. 4:8a	Mt. 4:8a
Lk. 4:5a	Lk. 4:5
Mt. 4:8b–c	Mt. 4:8b
Mt. 4:9a–b	Lk. 4:6
Lk. 4:8a	Lk. 4:7
Mt. 4.10b–d	Mt. 4:10

The Pepysian is largely a Matthean-based harmony for the Temptations episode, while Clement's Harmony is largely Lukan: the former contains no reference to Luke 4:6–7, while Clement's contains no reference to Mt 4:9. It is therefore difficult to see how the Pepysian could depend on Clement's Harmony. As a result, we have included the former in a comparison with Sedulius's text on the grounds that it could bear witness, albeit somewhat distantly, to a Latin tradition known to Sedulius. On the other hand, it has been assumed that Clement's Harmony is part of a separate twelfth-century harmony tradition that bears no witness to a Latin tradition dating to Antiquity.

These three traditions, the African text, the Persian Diatessaron's text and the Pepysian Harmony text have been compared with Sedulius's text for the Temptations in the following set of tables. Sedulius's *Carmen* text for the first temptation is laid out below in the first column, with the Pepysian Harmony and the Persian Diatessaron in the second and third columns. The African text is given in the last column, based on Augustine's text as taken from the *De uera religione*: where this is missing or differs from that found in the Latin Chrysostom, the reading in the latter has been given in square brackets.

First Temptation[46]

Paschale Carmen II	Pepysian Harmony, ch. 8	Persian Diatessaron, ch. 19	Augustine, De uera religione 38 [Chrysostom, De lapsu primi hominis]
v. 176 (Lk. 4:1) sacro Spiramine plenum (Iesum)	Lk 4:1 (?) Also suiþe as Jesus had esceyued witnesse of al þe Trinite at his baptiȝinge, Mk. 1:12 + Mt 4:1 so ledd hym þe Holy Gost, þat he was fro þe folk in desert forto be tempted of þe deuel Mk. 1:13 And whan he hadde ybe wiþ þe wilde sauage bestes	Lk. 4:1 Quando Gesù fu pieno di Sprito Sancto ritornò dal Giordano. Mk. 1:12 + Mt 4:1 Allora lo Spirito Santo portò Gesù nel deserto, affinchè il diavolo lo tentasse. ...	... ...
v. 175-6 (Mt 4:2) Inde quater denis iam noctibus atque diebus / Ieiunum dapibus,	Mt. 4:2a in fastynge fourty daies & fourty niȝttes, Mt. 4:2b þan bigan he forto haue hunger	Lk. 4:1 + Mt. 4:2a Quaranta giorni e quaranta notti Lk. 4:2 fu tentato dal diavolo, e in questi giorni non mangiò alcunchè	Mt. 4:2a [Nam cum ieiunaret quadraginta diebus et quadraginta noctibus] Mt. 4:2b [... cum esuriret]
v. 177 (Mt. 4:3a) ...Insidiis temptator adit	Mt. 4:3a And þo cam þe deuel to hym	Mt. 4:2a digiunò. Lk. 4:2	Mt. 4:3a [diabolus accessit tentare eum]
vv. 178-9 (Mt. 4:3b) Si filius, inquit, / Cerneris esse Dei,	Mt. 4:3b & seide: ȝif þou art Goddes son,	E quando questi giorni si compirono, Gesù ebbe fame Lk. 4:3	Mt. 4:3b [Si filius dei es] Mt. 4:3c
vv. 179-80 (Mt. 4:3) dic ut lapis iste repente / In panis uertatur opem	Mt. 4:3c þan make bred of þe stones þorouȝ þine owen word.	Il diavolo disse a Gesù: Se tu sei il Figlio di Dio, Mt. 4:3c dì che queste pietre divengano pane.	dic, inquit temptator [i. t. om.] lapidibus istis ut panes fiant [ut lapides isti panes fiant].
vv. 183-5 (Mt. 4:4) Hac ergo repulsus / Uoce prius hominem non solo uiuere pane/ Sed cuncto sermone Dei	Mt. 4:4 And Jesus ansuered hym & seide þat man ne l!ueþ nouȝth onelich in bred of bodilich sustenaunce, ac God may þorouȝ his comaundement holelich susteigne man	Mt. 4:4 Rispose Gesù e disse: è scritto che la vita dell'uomo non è solamente nel pane, ma nella parola di Dio, che esce dalla sua bocca.	Mt. 4:4 [Et ille ... repulit eum, dicens]: Non in pane solo [~ s. p.] uiuit homo, sed in omni uerbo [quod procedit ex ore] dei

[46] Editions of Goates and Messina have been used for the text of the Pepysian Harmony and the Persian Diatessaron respectively. For the Persian Diatessaron, I have reproduced the Italian translation of the Persian text in Messina's edition, but where necessary, the original Persian is referred to in the discussion below.

As shown above, Sedulius's text is principally Matthean, with the addition that Jesus was 'filled with the Holy Spirit'. This detail is not found in the African texts, which start at Mt 4:2, but it is found in the Persian Diatessaron, *Gesù fu pieno di Sprito Sancto,* and is a feature also found in the Arabic Diatessaron.[47] It is the inclusion of this element in the Arabic Diatessaron that appears central to Moretti Pieri's belief that Sedulius's text is based on the same tradition witnessed by the Arabic Diatessaron.[48] It is entirely absent from the Latin harmony tradition of the *unum ex quattuor,*[49] and appears absent from the Pepysian Harmony, although *esceyued witnesse of al þe Trinite* ('bore witness of all the Trinity') is possibly a rendering of *plenus spritu sancto.* This must be taken with some reserve, however, as the phrase could just as easily be an elaboration of the Matthean *post baptismum.* For the rest of the passage, the Pepysian Harmony is principally Matthean, although with the inclusion of Mark 1:13, that 'Jesus was with wild beasts', a feature not found in any of the other texts.[50] Otherwise, the Pepysian Harmony offers very close agreement with the text found in Sedulius; the Persian Diatessaron on the other hand shows a significantly greater dependence on Luke, in particular through the detail that Jesus was *tempted* for forty days (and forty nights) by the devil, as against he *fasted* for forty days and forty nights in the Matthean tradition and through the absence of the devil's approach to Jesus.[51] These two factors significantly reduce the likelihood of the Persian Diatessaron preserving the text used by Sedulius. Concerning the African text, the approach of the devil is rendered by the Latin Chrysostom as *diabolus accessit tentare*; this appears to be a flattening of the Matthean *temptator accessit* found in the Old Latin Matthean tradition.[52] The Latin Chrysostom also includes the text *ille repulit eum,* a reading paralleled in Sedulius's text by *hac … repulsus uoce.*

---

[47] Arabic Diatessaron 4.42-3, ed. Augustin-Sebastien Marmardji, *Diatessaron de Tatien: texte arabe établi, trad. en français, collationné avec les anciennes versions syriaques* (Beirut: Impr. Catholique, 1935).

[48] Moretti Pieri, *Fonti,* p. 206.

[49] Schmid, *Unum ex quattuor,* pp. 331–5.

[50] For the significance of the position of this verse in a Diatessaronic context, see Petersen, *Diatessaron,* p. 349.

[51] The Persian Harmony does mention forty nights in the desert, a Matthean detail, and that Jesus fasted but in a different position to Sedulius' text.

[52] For a summary of flattening see Houghton, *Augustine's Text of John,* pp. 68–70.

As established earlier in the analysis of Sedulius's *Carmen* text, Sedulius includes the shortened Old Latin rendering of Deuteronomy 8:3.[53] However, it is his use of *sermone* that is curious. There appears to be no metrical advantage of using the dactylic *sermone* over the spondaic *uerbo* at this point. Elsewhere in the *Carmen*, Sedulius shows a slight preference for *uerbum* in general, so it is possible that *sermone Dei* was the reading found in his base text.[54] The two African texts preserve *uerbo* and while Codex Bobiensis (VL 1) omits the second part of Deuteronomy 8:3 at Matthew 4:4, the writings of Cyprian provide us with a likely early African version of the line: *non in pane solo uiuit homo at in sermone Dei*.[55] If *sermone* was the reading found in Sedulius's text, we would have to accept that it departs from the tradition found in the African texts, but towards an earlier African tradition.

For the harmonies, the Pepysian presents a problem as it is quite difficult to detect the text that lies behind the elaborate phrase *ac God may porou3 his comaundement holelich susteigne man*, although there is possibly a liturgical influence at play.[56] The Persian Diatessaron follows the Peshitta text in the main, but it should be noted that, contrary to the Peshitta that follows the Greek text in placing the participial phrase ἐκπορευομένῳ διὰ στόματος before θεοῦ, the Persian Diatessaron places the words in a relative clause after the word for God as though the words are a latter addition to the original text. Since Classical Persian has a present participle form, like Syriac and Greek, there appears no logical reason for the use of the relative clause over the participial phrase, unless the words 'which come from his mouth' were added at a later stage in the Syriac *Vorlage* in order to bring the harmonised text into line with the Peshitta.[57]

---

[53] See note 23 above.

[54] *Sermo* is used thirteen times in the *Paschale Carmen*, *uerbum* nineteen times, see Manfred Wacht, *Concordantia in Sedulium* (Hildesheim: Olms-Weidmann, 1992) pp. 180 and 212.

[55] Cyprian, *Epistulae* 76.2. For the categorisation of *sermo* as an African translation for ὁ λόγος, see Burton, *Old Latin Gospels*, p. 18.

[56] The idea of *holy sustenance* probably comes from the liturgy. The Gregorian Sacramentary, 39 (PL 78, col. 59A) includes in the Lenten liturgy the words *spritualem habeamus alimoniam* immediately after Matthew 4:4. Also see Hilary of Poitiers, *Commentarius in Evangelium Matthaei* 3.3: *sed in Verbo Dei alimoniam aeternitatis esse sperandam*.

[57] This also appears the case in Codex Colbertinus (VL 6): *in omni uerbo Dei quod*

Second Temptation

Paschale Carmen II	Pepysian Harmony, ch. 8	Persian Diatessaron, ch. 19	Augustine, *De uera religione* 38 [Latin Chrysostom, *De lapsu primi hominis*]
v. 187 (Mt. 4:8a) Cum Domino montana petit (diabolus)	Mt. 4:8a After þat toke þe fende hym Lk. 4:5a & ledd hym Mt. 4:8b to an heiȝ mountayne,	Mt. 4:8 Il diavolo portò Gesù sulla cima di un monte alto	Mt. 4:8a–b [Secunda itidem tentatio oboritur, ita ut leuaret eum in montem excelsum ualde]
vv. 187–8 (Lk. 4:5b?) cunctasque per orbem / Regnorum monstrauit opes	Mt. 4:8c and schewed hym wodes & feldes & tounes & alle þe feire þinges of þis werlde, Mt. 4:9a	Lk. 4:5b e gli mostrò tutto il regno del mondo in poco tempo.	Mt. 4:8c omnia ergo mundi regna monstrata sunt [ostendens ei o. r. m.]
vv. 188–9 (Mt. 4:9a) haec omnia, dicens, / Me tribuente feres,	& hiȝth hym þat he wolde ȝiue hym all þat he seiȝ	Lk. 4:6a E disse il diavolo: questo potere del mondo e la sua gloria che tu vedi,	Mt. 4:9a et dictum est [ait ei] : [haec] omnia tibi dabo,
...	...	Lk. 4:6b tutto fu consegnato in mia mano, e lo dò a chiunque voglio.	...
v. 189 (Mt. 4:9b) si me prostratus adores	Mt. 4:9b wiþ þat he fel adoune & honoured hym.	Mt. 4:9b Tutto dò a te, se una volta mi adorerai.	Mt. 4:9b si prostratus adoraueris me.
v. 196 (Mt. 4:10a) Christus ad haec:	Lk. 4:8a Þo ansuered Jesus & seide:	Lk. 4:8a Gesù rispose e disse:	Mt. 4:10a cui responsum est [et ille repellens etiam istam tentationem, ait]
...	Mt. 4.10b 'Goo þou, Sathanas;	...	Mt. 4:10b [Vade retro satana,
vv. 196-7 (Mt. 4:10c-d) tantum Dominum scriptura Deumque / Iussit adorari et soli famularier uni	Mt. 4:10c for it is writen Mt. 4:10d þat man schal honoure & serue God onelich.'	Lk. 4:8b è scritto: Lk. 4:8c Adora solamente Dio, e servi solamente a lui.	Mt. 4:10c scriptum est:] Mt. 4:10d dominum deum tuum adorabis et illi soli seruies

procedit de ore.

The predominantly Matthean character of Sedulius's text for the second temptation has been discussed above; this is in contrast to the principally Lukan character displayed here in the Persian Diatessaron. Sedulius's text shows a very close correspondence to that found in the African texts, in particular through his use of *prostratus*, found in both African texts, but also in his use of *monstrauit*, equivalent to Augustine's *monstrata sunt*. Sedulius's preference for *monstrauit* instead of *ostendit* appears to be due to the desire to avoid the elision after *regnorum*, but its presence in Augustine's text does suggest that *monstrauit* could have occurred in Sedulius's base text. No codices in either tradition have the verb *monstrare* for *ostendere*, but *monstrare* does appear twice in Augustine's writings on this passage, once here and once in in the *De consensu evangelistarum*.[58] However, both passages contain the verb in a paraphrased setting and it would be rash to postulate anything more than a possible occurrence of *monstrare* as a variant in the African text.

Prostratus however is different: it is clearly an African reading, its use in Sedulius is unique and it should be considered a clear indicator of his textual source. The absence from the Persian Diatessaron of any form of Jesus's being asked to fall down or prostrate himself reduces the chances that the Persian Diatessaron preserves the same text type as Sedulius. The Pepysian Harmony appears to render *cadens* with the words *fel adoune*, in which case we would have to postulate a Vulgatisation of the Latin *Vorlage* that is the ultimate source of the Pepysian Harmony if we are to accept that this text preserves the same text type as Sedulius. It is clear that the number of variables that are brought into play in such a hypothesis is too great to offer any real assurances. Lastly, for the final part, which includes Jesus's quotation of Deuteronomy 6:13, Sedulius's text agrees with Augustine and the Persian Diatessaron against the Pepysian and the text found in the Latin Chrysostom in the absence of any form of *uade (retro) satanas*, but the limited weight of an argument *e silentio* should be taken into account.

---

[58] Augustine, *De consensu evangelistarum* 2.33. Outside Augustine, *monstrare* only occurs in Latin translations of Greek texts, e.g. Rufinus, *De principiis* 4.3.1; Jerome, *Origenis in Lucam homiliae* 30, as well as once in Jerome's homilies on the Psalms, *Tractatus siue homiliae in psalmis*.

Third Temptation

Paschale Carmen II	Pepysian Harmony, ch. 8	Persian Diatessaron, ch. 19	Augustine, De uera religione 38 [Latin Chrysostom, De lapsu primi hominis]
v. 201 (Mt. 4:5a) Tunc adsumpsit eum	Mt. 4:5a þo tok þe fende hym	...	Mt. 4:5–6 Subiecta est autem extrema etiam curiositatis illecebra, non enim, ut se de fastigio templi praecipitaret, urgebat nisi causa tantum aliquid experiendi.
v. 201 (Mt. 4:5b) sanctam sceleratus in urbem,	Lk. 4:9a & brouȝth hym to Jerusalem	Lk. 4:9a Di nuovo portò Gesù in Gerusalemme,	
v. 202 (Mt. 4:5c) Et statuens alti supra fastigia templi	Mt. 4:5c & sette hym þere vpon a pyler onheiȝ in þe temple	Lk. 4:9b e lo sollevò sul pinnacolo del tempio (bis)	Mt. 4:5c [Leuauit eum similiter in pinnam templi,
v. 203 (Mt. 4:6a) Si natum genitore Deo tete adseris, inquit,	Mt. 4:6a & seide to hym ȝif he were Goddes son	Lk. 4:9c e gli disse : se tu sei il Figlio di Dio,	Mt. 4:6a et ait ei:]
v. 204 (Mt. 4:6b) Inpiger e summo dilapsus labere tecto.	Mt. 4:6b þat he aliȝth adoune,	Lk. 4:9d gettati giù di qui	Mt. 4:6b [Mitte te deorsum,
v. 205 (Mt. 4:6c) Nam scriptura docet de te mandasse Tonantem,	Mt. 4:6c for God hym hadde so bihoten by Dauid þe prophete	Lk 4:10a perchè è scritto nei Salmi :	
v. 206 (Lk. 4:10c) Angelicis subuectus eas ut tutior ulnis,	Mt. 4:6d þat his aungel schulde hym bere ouer al, ...	Mt. 4:6d agli angeli suoi comandò su di te, chè ti sollevino sulle loro avambraccia, Lk. 4:10c e ti custodiscano,	Ps. 90:11–2 quia angelis suis mandauit de te, ut custodiant te in omnibus uiis tuis: in manibus tollent te,
v. 207 (Mt. 4:6e) Ad lapidem ne forte pedem conlidere possis.	Mt. 4:6e þat he ne hyrta hym nouȝth.	Mt. 4:6e affinchè il tuo piede non sia percosso nella pietra	ne quando offendas ad lapidem pedem tuum.]
vv. 215–7 (Mt. 4:7) Dixerat et ualidi confossus cuspide uerbi / Quod temptare suum Dominumque Deumque nequiret / ... fugit (diabolus)	Lk. 4:12 And Jesus ansuered hym and seide: 'God it defende þat man schulde hym asaaye forto helpen ȝif he wolde be saued, ac helpe hym self.'	Lk. 4:12 Gesù rispose e disse : fu detto : non tentare il Signore Dio tuo.	Mt. 4:7 Et respondit ei dominus, Non tentabis dominum et [et om.] deum tuum.] ...
v. 217 (Mt. 4:11a) tunc hoste repulso	Mt. 4:11a Þo left þe fende hym þere,	Lk. 4:13 E quando il diavolo compì tutte le sue tentazioni, alla stessa ora si separò da presso lui	...
vv. 218–9 (Mt. 4:11b) Caelicolae adsistunt proceres coetusque micantes / Angelici Christo famulantur rite ministri.	Mt. 4:11b & þe aungels comen doune fram heuene & serueden hym in al þinge.	Mt. 4:11b e gli angeli servivano Gesù.	

The third and final temptation maintains the pattern seen thus far: Sedulius's text is principally Matthean with a single Lukan insertion, in this instance the detail in Psalm 90 that the angels keep Jesus safe. As we have seen above, this detail is also present in the Latin Chrysostom text, albeit in the form found in the Psalm. The origin of this reading is unclear, but it is also found in one manuscript of Peter Cantor's Harmony commentary, a witness to the *Unum ex quattuor* tradition, suggesting that the Lukan reading could quite independently find itself in the Matthean text in a variety of traditions.[59] Its presence in the Latin Chrysostom reveals the difficulty of drawing conclusions when there is a third source (in this case the Psalms) in addition to the Matthean/Lukan dichotomy. For this reason, it is difficult to see the presence of Luke 4:10 in the Persian Diatessaron as evidence of it witnessing Sedulius's source.

Textually, Augustine's *De uera religione* text is largely paraphrased for the third temptation, but we can reconstruct much of his text and supplement it with the text of Latin Chrysostom. The reading *fastigium templi* is another African reading, occurring in Codex Bobiensis (VL 1) in Matthew and Codex Palatinus (VL 2) in the equivalent Lukan passage, as well as in Augustine and Hilary.[60] This appears to be present both in *fastigio templi* as found in *De uera religione* and Sedulius's *fastigia templi*. The Latin Chrysostom text retains *pinna*, a reading that is also found in Sedulius's text in his exegesis of the Temptations.[61] It is Moretti Pieri's opinion that *pinna*, and not *fastigium*, is the word found in Sedulius's base text, on the basis that it is unlikely that both *pinna* and *fastigium* were present together in Sedulius's text and thus of the two *pinna* is the likelier candidate.[62] In turn, she explains the presence of *fastigium* at line 202 (but not the second occurrence at line 210) by referring to a suggestion by Mayr that *fastigium templi* is an allusion to *Aeneid* 8.366, describing Evander's house as seen by Aeneas (*at angusti subter fastigia tecti / ingentem Aeneam duxit*).[63] This is probably coincidental, since a deliberate allusion would require us to understand an association between the Temple, the symbol of Jewish and Christian faith,[64] and the Pantheon of

---

[59] Schmid, *Unum ex quattuor*, p. 332.

[60] Hilary of Poitiers, *Tractatus super Psalmos* 138.6.

[61] *Paschale Carmen* 2.209–11, *hunc ardua templi / culmina et erectae quamuis fastigia pinnae / credidit in praeceps horrescere.*

[62] Moretti Pieri, *Fonti*, p. 141.

[63] Moretti Pieri, *Fonti*, 140. Mayr, *Studien*, 39.

[64] Maximus of Turin, *Sermones* 70.2: *super hanc ergo pinnam templi saluator stare*

Greco-Roman gods, represented by the home of Evander, the bringer of Greek divinities to Italy. Sedulius does imitate classical passages portraying Greco-Roman gods in the *Carmen*, but to portray Jesus as the conqueror or superior of these gods, not their heir or equal.[65] On the other hand, the word *pinna* was so widespread in its use in commentaries, homilies and sermons on the Temptations at the time that it would be impossible for Sedulius not to have encountered the word in this context.[66] Therefore, we prefer to retain *fastigium* as Sedulius's base text reading and consider *pinna* as stemming from a secondary source.

The harmonies do not contain any words that offer a sure parallel to *fastigium*, with the Persian Diatessaron offering *kongereh*, a battlement or pinnacle, and the Pepysian *vpon a pyler onhei3 in þe temple*, with *pyler* apparently a rendering of *pinnaculum*, perhaps via the Old French *pinacle*. There does not appear a case either for an influence from the Syrian *Vorlage* on the Latin tradition or for the Pepysian preserving an Old Latin reading found in Sedulius. Sedulius's text departs in one other point from the traditions preserved in the harmonies, most obviously in the absence of the Lukan variant *Ierusalem* for the Matthean *ciuitatem sanctam*, but since *Ierusalem* is un-metrical, this difference is insignificant.

The final lines concern the confirmation of Jesus's victory and the descent of the Angels to minister to him. The latter, taken from Matthew 4:11, is present in Sedulius and the harmonies. It is not found in the two texts selected as witnesses to the African tradition, which break off the account after the third temptation, but as mentioned above, there are two

---

dicitur, hoc est quasi in quodam templo fidei nostrae consistere, unde ait apostolus: '*Vos estis templum dei, et spiritus dei habitat in uobis*'. Also see Hilary of Poitiers, *Commentarius in Evangelium Matthaei* 3.4: *et positum in templi summo, id est, super leges et prophetas eminentem*; Arnobius, *Expositiunculae in Matthaeum* 5: *Templum autem Christianos homines demonstrat, Paulo apostolo dicente: Vos estis templum dei.*

[65] See especially Paul W.A.Th. Van der Laan, 'Imitation créative dans le Carmen Paschale de Sédulius' in *Early Christian Poetry: A Collection of Essays* ed. J. den Boeft and A. Hilhorst (Leiden: E.J. Brill, 1993). pp. 135–66.

[66] The use of *pinna* at 210 could have been suggested by Psalm 17:11: *et ascendit super cherubin et uolauit uolauit super pinnas uentorum*. Sedulius interprets the second temptation using the previous verse, *et inclinauit caelos et descendit*, both at *Paschale Carmen* 211–12, *qui membra poli caelosque per omnes / Vectus in extremae discendit humillima terrae*, and in the equivalent position in the *Paschale Opus* (2.14.4-5; p. 218). Similarily, Psalm 103:3, *et ambulauit super pinnas uentorum*, is used by Maximus of Turin *Sermones* 70.2 to interpret Jesus's placement on the top of the Temple.

striking parallels between the third text and Augustine's *De honorandis uel contemnendis parentibus*. The first is the repetition of *repellere*, rendered here in Sedulius's *tunc hoste repulso*, and the second far more striking parallel is the presence of the words *Et hic ex eadem lege uulnerauit inimicum, prostrauit, confusum abire fecit* just before the citation of Deuteronomy 6:16, *Scriptum est: Non temptabis dominum deum tuum*.[67] This finds a precise parallel in exactly the same place in Sedulius at lines 215–6, further strengthening the case for Sedulius's dependence on the African tradition.

In conclusion, detailed analysis of Sedulius's *Paschale Carmen* text reveals both its Matthean character and the presence of African readings. This is in contrast to his text of the *Pascale Opus* that comprises Vulgate passages selected from both Luke and Matthew. On the basis of this it appears that Sedulius was using different base texts for the composition of his twin works. Subsequent analysis of Sedulius's text reveals only two unequivocal Lukan details in his passage: the mention that he was filled with the Holy Spirit and the mention that the angels were to *protect* Jesus if he fell from the Temple. Of these, the second detail has been shown to exist in Matthean texts such as that found in Latin Chrysostom. Therefore, on the basis of a single Lukan detail that is included in the Matthean text, it does not appear possible to sustain the hypothesis that Sedulius was using a harmonised text for this episode and rule out that such an addition came from Sedulius's own hand. In addition, neither of the harmonised traditions offers any reliable lexical parallels to Sedulius's text; given the long and complicated manuscript tradition for both harmonies, a tradition that remains largely unknown, this should come as no surprise. Structurally, however, there appears a moderately strong correlation between Sedulius's text and the text preserved in the Pepysian Harmony. This text is largely Matthean and little can be made of those features not found in Sedulius's text. The only two points where Sedulius's text contains features not found in the Pepysian Harmony are in the first temptation, the comment that Jesus was filled with the Holy Spirit, and the apparent allusion to the Lukan version of Psalm 90. The Persian Diatessaron on the other hand preserves a text that has little structural correlation with that found in Sedulius. It is largely Lukan in character, omitting several of the Matthean features found in Sedulius's text. It must be concluded therefore that of the two harmonised texts, the Pepysian Harmony offers a far greater agreement with Sedulius's text than the Persian Diatessaron.

---

[67] Augustine, *De honorandis uel contemnendis parentibus* (*Sermo* 159A), p. 8.

As for the Old Latin African tradition, the text used by Augustine in his *De uera religione* from the late fourth century provides the closest match to Sedulius's text, offering notable lexical similarities, in particular the use of *fastigium* and *prostratus*. Nevertheless, the other African texts have been shown to offer similarities in the wording used in connection with Jesus's successive defeats of the devil. The presence of African readings in Sedulius's text together with the mirroring of Sedulius's unusual episode order in the African texts makes it very likely that Sedulius's text depends somehow on this African tradition that is present in homiletic texts. The extent of this connection between Sedulius and the North African homiletic tradition of this time remains to be explored. If we are to accept the hypothesis that Sedulius was based in Italy, we can speculate that Sedulius either based his Temptations text on a text that he had encountered in the writings of Augustine or that a similar homiletic tradition to that witnessed by the North African texts was in circulation in Italy at the time of Sedulius. Finally, these findings beg the question as to why Sedulius decided to change his textual source from a North African Old Latin text to a Vulgate text in the course of his two works. This can only be answered through further study of Sedulius's textual sources, but at the very least, the results of this comparison reveal the need to examine his text not only in the light of the canonical Gospel texts of the time, but also the importance of considering unusual homiletic texts preserved in the lesser-known works emanating from Africa and Italy at the time.

6. A REINTRODUCTION TO THE BUDAPEST ANONYMOUS COMMENTARY ON THE PAULINE LETTERS

R. F. MACLACHLAN[1]

The earliest commentaries on the Pauline Letters in Latin offer potentially important evidence for the biblical text used by their writers since this may be reflected in the comments made upon it and they may thus preserve a text earlier than those which survive in the manuscript tradition. Several of these works are by key figures in the early formation and interpretation of the biblical text – Jerome, Augustine, Ambrosiaster, Rufinus translating Origen – and this makes them doubly interesting. This paper, however, is interested in an anonymous commentary tradition of which manuscript VL 89 in the *Vetus Latina* Register is an important early witness.[2] The commentary is also found elsewhere in several overlapping forms which present selections, extensions and rearrangements. VL 89 is known as the 'Budapest Anonymous Commentary' since it was rediscovered by Hermann Frede in the library of the Hungarian National Museum in Budapest, where it is Codex Latinus Medii Aevi 1, and published in 1974.[3] According to Frede, the manuscript dates from the ninth century and is one of a group of

[1] The research leading to these results has received funding from the European Union Seventh Framework Programme (FP7/2007-2013) under grant agreement no. 283302 (COMPAUL: 'The Earliest Commentaries on Paul in Greek and Latin as Sources for the Biblical Text').

[2] Roger Gryson, *Altlateinische Handschriften/Manuscrits Vieux Latins. Première partie: Mss 1-275.* (Vetus Latina 1/2A. Freiburg; Herder, 1999).

[3] H.J. Frede, *Ein neuer Paulustext und Kommentar.* (AGLB 7–8. Freiburg; Herder, 1974).

manuscripts produced under Arno, Archbishop of Salzburg from 785–821.[4] It is on parchment and contains a General Prologue to the Pauline Epistles followed by the fourteen Epistles and Hebrews in the standard order with commentary on each letter. Every letter is prefaced with a short introduction; Romans, the first item, has a longer introduction. The epistles also each have *capitula*, apart from Romans, Titus, Philemon and Hebrews. The commentary on Hebrews in VL 89 does not appear in other manuscripts of the same commentary tradition, but it does appear in some additional manuscripts.[5]

The recent production of good quality digital colour images of the manuscript for the COMPAUL project at the University of Birmingham offers a good opportunity to revisit this manuscript.[6] This new record of the manuscript captures different aspects from Frede's print edition, including a clearer representation of the layout. This is not so easy to figure out from Frede's edition, partly due to the presentational limitations of the print format and partly because Frede is interested in exploring the text of the commentary tradition which is represented in VL 89 rather than representing the manuscript VL 89 itself. As part of the COMPAUL project I have transcribed Romans, 1 & 2 Corinthians and Galatians for an electronic edition now available at www.epistulae.org. These transcriptions record all the text of the manuscript, including page and line breaks, rubrication, capitals, punctuation, corrections and abbreviations. Biblical verse numeration and the numbering of comment sections introduced by Frede have been added and the pagination of Frede's edition is also indicated to facilitate cross-consultation. The plain text encoding was based on the International Greek New Testament Project transcription guidelines, converted to XML and displayed with a XSLT stylesheet. [7] The comparison of this electronic edition with Frede's edition forms the basis of the present chapter.

---

[4] Frede, *Ein neuer Paulustext*, p. 15.

[5] See Frede, *Ein neuer Paulustext*, p. 14.

[6] The COMPAUL project, funded by the European Research Council and led by Dr H.A.G. Houghton, is investigating the earliest commentaries on Paul in Latin and Greek as sources for the biblical text.

[7] For more on encoding, see H.A.G. Houghton, 'The Electronic Scriptorium: Markup for New Testament Manuscripts', in Claire Clivaz, Andrew Gregory and David Hamidovic (eds), *Digital Humanities in Biblical, Early Jewish and Early Christian Studies* (Leiden: Brill, 2013), pp. 31–60.

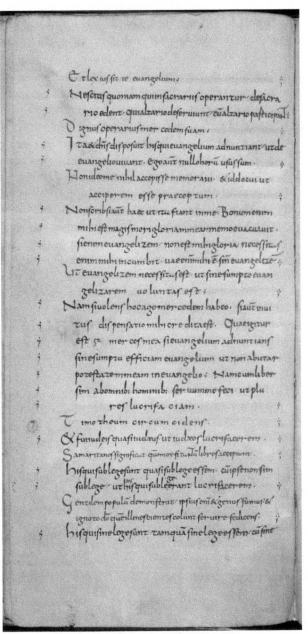

Figure 1: VL 89 fol. 33v.
(By kind permission of the Hungarian National Library)

In Frede's edition, which has a three-part apparatus, VL 89 is designated P. The printed 'biblical text' is the text of this manuscript with obvious errors, corrections and orthographic quirks tidied up; the first part of the apparatus details these corrections to VL 89, listed by verse. The text is given without layout information except for the division between sections of commentary and biblical text. The commentary text printed in Frede's edition is also based on VL 89 but supplemented with additional commentary material found in other manuscripts of the tradition; the sections added are marked with brackets with different styles for different sources. Sometimes the arrangement of sections in VL 89 has had to be adjusted to place commentary sections where they appear elsewhere in the tradition. Frede has also very usefully numbered the sections of commentary text. The second section of the apparatus is an apparatus to the commentary text indicating any editorial transpositions and giving readings from all witnesses, listed by comment section. The third section of Frede's apparatus is a guide to the commentary sections. It indicates to which biblical verse wording within the sections quotes or refers; direct quotations of biblical verses are in addition italicised in the commentary sections of the work. Also indicated is where the VL 89 commentary tradition reflects material in other early Pauline commentaries and commentary traditions possibly influenced by it, reflecting considerable effort by the editor.

Thus Frede's edition gives more information about the text of the whole tradition rather than just about VL 89 itself. This is highly useful for investigating this tradition but means that it is not easy to work out and visualise what the manuscript VL 89 itself is like and how the comment and biblical text sections relate spatially within it; these aspects of the manuscript's physicality are not an interest of the edition and are not well reproduced by it. On the other hand, aspects of the physicality of Frede's edition itself make it rather easier to navigate the work, thanks to the systematic numbering of verses and sections, and to figure out how the comments relate to the biblical text, thanks to the italicisation of wording from biblical verses in the commentary text. These features contribute to the different reading experience Frede's edition offers compared to the manuscript.

VL 89 as a whole is neatly and decently produced. The work seems to have been divided between two scribes in roughly equal stints. It has 106 folios, the first 58 by one scribe, the remaining 48 by the other. This division of the work between two scribes is shown by the quire signatures, which are used by the first scribe but not by the second. The switch between scribes is identifiable from the change in hand which occurs at Folio 59r, beginning with 2 Cor 9:10. The quires written by the first hand are detailed in the following table, in which the final quaternion of the first scribe's stint sticks out. A greater incidence of elongated *m* and reduced use of abbreviations in this short quire suggests that the scribe was trying to fill space.

Quire Signature	Folio of Quire Signature	N°. of Folios in Quire	Epistle
I	8v	8 folios	Rm
II	14v	6 folios	Rm
(III)	Expected on 22v but this coincides with incipit of 1 Cor	8 folios	Rm + 1 folio of 1 Cor
IIII	30v	8 folios	1 Cor
V	38v	8 folios	1 Cor
VI	46v	8 folios	2 Cor
VII	54v	8 folios	2 Cor
VIII	58v	4 folios	2 Cor
No further quire signatures from folio 59r			

Both scribes begin biblical text sections on a new line with a hanging capital in ordinary ink; they have diples in the outer margin of the page for each line and are generally in a slightly heavier script than the comment sections. Commentary sections also begin on a new line with a rubricated hanging capital; they have no diples in the margins and are generally in slightly closer script than the biblical text. The first scribe alone uses symbols consisting of a group of three dots with a stroke below at the end of sections, in red after commentary and black after biblical text. These are illustrated in Figures 1 and 2.

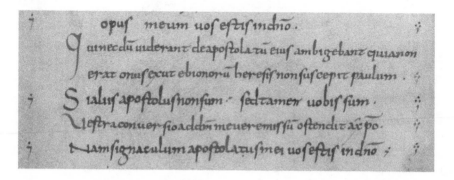

Figure 2: VL 89, fol. 32v: 1 Cor. 9:1–2 with comments 39D & 39E, Scribe 1.
(By kind permission of the Hungarian National Library)

The layout of the manuscript with defined sections of text and
comment, including the use of colour to distinguish them, gives the
manuscript a neat orderly appearance, making it look like a regular
lemmatised commentary. In this conventional type of commentary a piece
of text (lemma) is set out, followed by a comment. This fairly
straightforward relationship between lemma and comment, namely that
comment follows text, runs through the work and is undoubtedly how the
work was composed. There is, of course, some variability in this pattern.
Longer passages of comment may have a lemma or parts of a lemma
reiterated within them. There may be overlap between the comments on
neighbouring lemma, especially when they are thematically close, and there
may be cross references to other more distant verses too. The lemmata
themselves are usually 'sense units', but may vary in length from short
phrases to several verses; occasionally larger chunks may be left
uncommented. But the basic pattern, lemma followed by comment, is
regular through the whole work since it is an integral part of that work. This
remains true for commentaries that have less formally set-out sequential
citations rather than distinct lemmata; the same text-comment structure is
integral to the work. This is the format of other early Pauline commentaries.
     A closer look at the relationships between biblical text and comments,
however, reveals that VL 89 does not conform to the standard sequential
lemma-comment pattern, as shown in the following extract from the
beginning of 1 Corinthians:

04 Orat pro ipsis ut usque in finem uitae suae inrepraehensi in
aduentum d̄n̄i nostri īh̄u x̄p̄i permaneant ·

1 Cor 1:8 *Qui et [...]⁸ confirmauit uos usque ad finem sine crimine in die
aduentus d̄n̄i nostri īh̄u x̄p̄i ;* **9** *Fidelis d̄s̄ per quem uocati estis in societatem filii eius
īh̄u x̄p̄i d̄n̄i nostri*

05 Hoc contra Arrianos ualet qui ministrum praeceptorum patris filium
dicunt quoniam scriptum est · omnia per ipsum facta sunt · hic autem
ostenditur quia et per d̄m̄ patrem uocati sunt in communionem īh̄u x̄p̄i
d̄n̄i nostri

Here, Comment 05 refers as expected to the preceding biblical text with
uocati sunt in communionem corresponding to *uocati estis in societatem* in 1 Cor.
1:19, (note in passing that *communionem* appears to be an alternative for
societatem). The preceding comment, however, Comment 04, refers to the
text below it: *usque in finem uitae suae inrepraehensi in aduentum domini nostri Iesu
Christi* corresponds to *usque ad finem sine crimine in die aduentus domini nostri Iesu
Christi*. This sort of forward reference is also seen at the beginning of 1 Cor.
2, where Comments 11B and 11C both precede 1 Cor 2:3:

> **2:1b** *Aut sapientiae adnuntians uobis testimonium d̄ī*
>
> **11B** In illis talibus non semet ipsum ideo addit et ego in timore et
> tremore multos fui apud uos et cetera
>
> **2:2a** *Neque enim iudicaui me scire aliquid inter uos nisi x̄p̄m īh̄m̄*
>
> **11C** Persecutionis memorat quas passus in principio simul dum suum
> replicat timorem d̄ī gratiam per quem uicit ostendit
>
> **2:2b** *et hunc crucifixum · **2:3a** et ego in infirmitate · et timore ·*
>
> **11D** Hoc est stultum et infirmum d̄ī
>
> **2:3b** *et tremore · multo fui apud uos **2:4** et sermo meus· et praedicatio mea non in
> persuasione*

As can be seen, most of the verse is quoted in Comment 11B. The 'textual
geography' is further complicated by references to other parts of the work
and the New Testament, as identified in Frede's apparatus: Acts 18:9, 18:12,
and 1 Cor. 15:10 in Comment 11C, plus 1 Cor. 1:25 in Comment 11D. The
most notable thing, however, is how Comment 11D is positioned in the
middle of a sense unit in the biblical text and, indeed, the sense unit upon
which Comments 11B and 11C also make unrelated comments.

---

⁸ Three characters have been erased at this point.

On other occasions it is harder to tell how the text and comment relate. For example in Comment 09 *sapientia dei* could refer backwards to 1 Cor. 1:20 or forwards to 1 Cor. 1:21:

> **1:19** *Scriptum est enim· perdam sapientiam sapientium· et prudentiam prudentium perprobabo* ; **20** *Ubi sapiens· ubi scriba· ubi conquisitor huius saeculi· Nonne stultam fecit d̄s sapientiam huius mundi·*
>
> **09** Hoc loco sapientia d̄i in ordinatione creaturarum per quae creator intellegitur ostendit ex quibus d̄m auctorem uenerari et agnoscere debuerunt
>
> **1:21** *Nam quia d̄s sapientiam non cognouit hic mundus per sapientiam d̄n̄m̄ placuit d̄o per stultitiam praedicationis saluos facere credentes*
>
> **9A** Inde filium crucifixum · et mortuum credere
>
> **1:22** *Quoniam quidem iudaei signa petunt· et graeci sapientiam quaerunt·*
>
> **1:23** *Nos autem praedicamus Christum crucifixum . Iudaeis quidem scandalum gentibus autem stultitiam ·* **1:24a** *Ipsis autem uocatis iudaeis atque graecis xp̄m d̄i uirtutem*
>
> **9B** Uirtutem ad iudęos · sapientia ad graecos refert
>
> **1:24b** *et d̄i sapientiam ·* **1:25a** *quia quod stultum est*
>
> **10A** Stultum d̄i et infirmum uocationem ecclesiae significauit ex ignobilibus et rusticis denique ita sequitur · uidete enim uocationem uestram fratres quia non multi sapientes · et reliqua ·
>
> **1:25b** *d̄i · sapientius est hominibus et infirmum d̄i fortius est hominibus*

Other comments in this passage sit awkwardly with the text they comment upon. Comment 9B comes in the middle of 1 Cor. 1:24 to which it refers, while Comment 10A cuts through the sense unit *quod stultum est dei* to come before the rest of the verse upon which it comments. What is not so apparent from this transcription but immediately apparent from the digital image of the folio is that something seems to have gone amiss with the copying such that Comment 9A and Comment 9B have been written in between the lines of biblical text with insertion marks used to show where they fit into the biblical text.

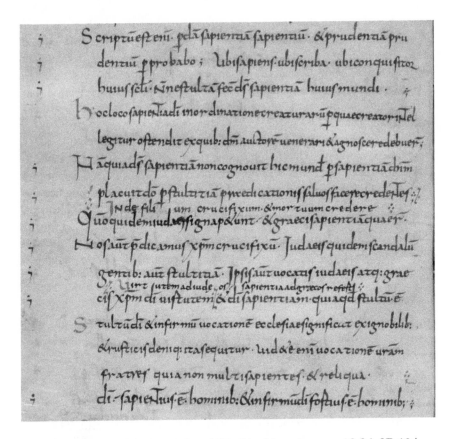

Figure 3: VL 89, fol. 23v: 1 Cor. 1:20–24 with comments 09 9A 9B 10A
(By kind permission of the Hungarian National Library)

This appears to be all the work of the same first-hand scribe. A plausible scenario is that the scribe has carried on writing the more familiar biblical text and overlooked these short comments before going back and adding them in. Note the continued use of rubricated capitals to begin the comment text sections and symbols to end them even when they have been written in between the lines. This passage suggests how the positioning of comments in relation to text might become distorted in transmission.

While the electronic edition conveys some physical features of the manuscript quite aptly and can present the general layout, its ability to represent the manuscript has its limitations when the general pattern is disrupted and especially when the disruption is not textual. Corrections to the text itself appear where they occur in the passage and hover-over notes can alert and explain that there is something further going on but the more rigid format of the transcription requires lines of text to be lines of text and cannot replicate the spatial flexibility of the manuscript itself in instances such as lines being squeezed in. In Frede's edition the manuscript's lineation is not reproduced and the only indication of this incident is that the apparatus to the commentary text records that the first hand in VL 89 omitted Comments 9A and 9B.

As well as comments which cut across each other and the biblical text, there are comments which duplicate material. On fol. 31v, *uirginem hic alicuius non filiam sed carnem uocat* appears both as Comment 35G between 1 Cor. 7:35 and 7:36 and as Comment 36D in 1 Cor. 7:40. A copying error at some point could be one explanation for the repetition of the comment. Elsewhere, however, the content rather than the wording of comments overlaps. So, for example, both Comment 52A (*angelos significat qui humanas res administrant siue qui praesunt ecclesiis*) and Comment 52B (*hoc loco uel angelos ecclesiis presedentes dicit*) make the same point in different ways about *angelos* in 1 Cor. 11:10, the verse positioned between the two comments.

The positioning of comments is not insignificant, since they may well require reading in relation to the biblical text in order to make sense. For example, the start of Comment 6a, *aut nomen mulieris aut turbis aut regionis alicuius*, needs to be read as a comment on the proper name *Cloes* in 1 Cor. 1:11 which appears at the start of the text section immediately below the comment. Other comments, such as 11D reported above, provide cross references to elsewhere in the work which need to be associated with a verse in the text to complete their sense. Similarly, Comment 23B (*haec ironicos dicit*) makes an observation on the authorial tone in the biblical text above it which is incomplete unless read in relation to that text. Comment 52C, *dixit de principio reuertitur ad consequentiam*, comments on the structure of the work and guides the reader through it. This illustrates how comments are made on different levels from individual words to the overall structure of the work. There are also, of course, longer comments with more discussion of the theological implications of the biblical text, as well as longer passages of biblical text without comments.

The overlapping and loosely-positioned comments, the sometimes awkward placing of comments in the text, the competing comments and the other tensions evident in the relationship of comment-text and biblical text suggest the commentary and biblical text were not brought together in one coordinated compositional exercise. VL 89 does not present a lemmatised commentary, even one with sequential lemmata written through the exegesis that has been visually re-styled with biblical text and exegesis more spatially separated on the page. Indeed, it seems unlikely that VL 89 presents an ordered attempt to produce a coherent and consistent commentary even by selecting and arranging pre-existing material. And it seems unlikely that the comments which make up this commentary originated in the form in which they are now presented in VL 89.

Marginal comments, or possibly interlinear comments, seem to be the likely original source for the commentary material now in VL 89. The first scribe's use of symbols which resemble the *hederae* sometimes used to indicate where comments relate to a text could be a reminiscence of this sort of origin for the material.[9] The change in page geography from comments in the margins to comments in the text presents an explanation for the sometimes clumsy positioning of the comments found in VL 89 as stemming from difficulties in synchronising comment and text in a new format. Whereas multiple items of marginal material can be accommodated on a page without interfering with each other and linked to the text quite flexibly using insertion signs, inserting this commentary text into the biblical text requires accommodating it in a more constrained and rigid structure. The comments that cut across the biblical text in VL 89 could plausibly result from mechanically inserting comments into the biblical text at points where an insertion symbol once indicated that there was a comment on the text. This compositional process would produce comments that indeed roughly aligned with their corresponding biblical text but did not always maintain precision in their placement within the biblical text and adhere to sense units; the latter is the case with the lemmatised commentaries which were composed in a different, sequential way.

It would be interesting to know more about how the VL 89 commentary tradition came together and why marginal comments may have been transformed in this manuscript into sections of commentary within the biblical text. Some material in VL 89 has been traced to sequential commentaries or other works, though taken selectively rather than reformatted wholesale. It has probably been drawn together from more than one such source and perhaps at more than one time.[10] At some point, it seems, someone systematically brought this commentary material physically into the biblical text and made the whole into a visually coherent work with biblical text and comments in the same space. It is possible, of course, that the change in page geography was more a pragmatic response

---

[9] This was suggested to me by H.A.G. Houghton in conversation.

[10] See Frede, *Ein neuer Paulustext*, volume 1.

to how to reproduce efficiently a manuscript with multiple marginal comments than intentionally significant. The decision to refashion this text and commentary material in this form may however hint at the development of an aesthetic idea of the commentary with a page geography of alternating defined sections of text and comment. It certainly suggests that at quite an early period people were prepared to refashion commentary material. This bringing of comment and biblical text into the same main region of the page must have affected the reading experience fostered by the work, since what had been in the margins was now encountered in the main text rather than alongside it. The short, unlinked comments that rely on positioning in their context for sense weigh against the commentary being read out of conjunction with the text, but the overlapping and disparate comments militate against a coherent continuous reading experience such as offered by more consciously designed and systematically composed lemmatised commentaries. VL 89 itself, however, presents frustratingly little evidence of being read. There are some not very remarkable corrections and occasional markings in the text, which are difficult to date due to their brevity; there are also some examples of obvious errors which remain uncorrected. Nothing in the condition of the manuscript suggests heavy use.

Underlying questions about how changing the page geography of VL89 may have changed the way it read are questions about what the alteration in layout may have meant for the comparative status of the biblical text and comment material in the work. Was the work still perceived as a biblical text with marginal comments once these were not marginal by position? Did it become – or was it already – something to be read for its commentary text? Again, evidence from VL 89 itself about the status of comment and biblical text is thin and ambiguous. The commentary is in slightly smaller characters than the biblical text; this is more noticeable and consistent in the work of Scribe 2. Biblical text and comment are often distinguished in commentary texts by the use of rubrication: lemmatised commentaries typically use rubrication for the running biblical lemmata, yet VL 89 uses rubricated initial capitals to pick out the start of the comments while the biblical text sections begin with plain ink capitals. It is not clear that rubrication has to have a hierarchical significance rather than more neutrally differentiating between elements in a text.[11]

---

[11] Thus the *incipit* and *explicit* to a work may be rubricated to distinguish them

It does seem likely that VL 89's immediate predecessor was a manuscript much like VL 89. It would otherwise have been difficult to divide the task of copying between two scribes for VL 89 and, if the process of assembling the commentary had been carried out while producing VL 89 itself, there would undoubtedly be more errors evident in the manuscript accompanied by less general neatness in its the layout; I must confess that I have been slightly unrepresentative by drawing attention to places where the scribes have made interesting but actually exceptional mistakes in their work. The copying scenario suggested may find some support towards the bottom of fol. 24r where the physical division of comment and biblical text has gone awry such that the biblical text runs into the text of Comment 11H rather than the comment starting in a new line. This layout error would seem more indicative of accidentally overlooking the division of text and comment material while copying the work sequentially from a similar exemplar than of the scribes of VL 89 adding the comments into the biblical text in the course of their work. The passage considered above, where comments have been initially omitted then added back between lines of biblical text, seems aberrant and could perhaps be explained as resulting from scribal inattention while copying the more familiar biblical text.

VL 89 should perhaps not be regarded as a single coherent commentary; it is more 'Budapest Anonymous Comments' than 'Budapest Anonymous Commentary'. There is a corresponding need not to think of the 'Budapest Anonymous Commentator' as a known author, though it is always worth considering at what point the selection and representation of comments might become sufficiently creative and exegetical to form something that might be considered commentary rather than comments. The composite nature of the work must raise particular problems in trying to identify and study the biblical text used in composing the comments. There may be practical problems determining to what biblical text comments relate and using methods and database technology designed for commentaries with a more regular lemma-comment compositional pattern. The difficulty of distinguishing paraphrase or loose reference to the biblical text from echoes of different textual forms attested elsewhere is increased the more fluid and diffuse the compositional scenario of the manuscript. Answers to the question 'Do the lemmata match the text reflected in

---

from the text and perhaps to make them easier to find in the manuscript for practical purposes but not with the implication that they are more important than the work itself.

comments?' may produce unconnected and contradictory results. Pre-existing commentary material could well have been brought together with a non-coordinating pre-existing text during the phase when the work existed as marginal notes. Furthermore, the comments indeed may not relate directly to the notably Old Latin biblical text which now accompanies them in VL 89, especially since the change in page geography could conceivably have involved inserting the comments into a biblical text other than the one which had originally had the comments in the margin. To be more positive however, there is also the possibility that comments to VL 89 might, by happenstance, conserve something unexpected.

7. PRELIMINARY INVESTIGATIONS OF ORIGEN'S TEXT OF GALATIANS

MATTHEW R. STEINFELD[1]

Comparative methodologies have dominated the field of textual criticism for decades.[2] There is no lack of patristic citations of the New Testament, yet this vast amount of data is often misrepresented when compared to biblical documents. Conclusions often omit an explanation of textual development and the transmission history of the citations. The typical routine of determining each Church Father's use of the New Testament is as follows. First, locate patristic citations in critical editions. Then, categorise the citations according to their intention to cite biblical text (i.e. 'quotation', 'reference', 'allusion', 'adaptation', 'locution', and even 'echo').[3]

[1] The research leading to these results has in part received funding from the European Union Seventh Framework Programme (FP7/2007-2013) under grant agreement no. 283302 (COMPAUL: 'The Earliest Commentaries on Paul in Greek and Latin as Sources for the Biblical Text').

[2] e.g. Ernest C. Colwell, 'The Significance of Grouping of New Testament Manuscripts' *NTS* 4 (1958) pp. 73–92; *id.* The Quantitative Relationships Between MS Text-Types,' in J. N. Birdsall and R. W. Thomson (eds), *Biblical and Patristic Studies in Memory of Robert Pierce Casey*; *id.,* 'Genealogical Method: Its Achievements and its Limitations.' *JBL* 66 (1947) pp. 109–33; Bart D. Ehrman, 'The Use of Group Profiles for the Classification of New Testament Documentary Evidence' *JBL* 106.3 (1987) pp. 465–86; E. J. Epp, 'The Claremont Profile-Method for Grouping New Testament Minuscule Manuscripts' in B. Daniels and M. J. Suggs (eds), *Studies in the History and Text of the New Testament.* (SD 29. Salt Lake City: University of Utah Press, 1967), pp. 27–38; The *SBL New Testament in the Greek Fathers* Series (SBLNTGF. Atlanta GA: Scholars Press, 1986–).

[3] e.g. Gordon D. Fee, 'The Text of John in Origen and Cyril of Alexandria: A

Third, consider the context to help with categorisation, because some citations have introductory formula such as 'it is written' or 'the apostle said', which may indicate an attempt to cite a document. Last, the citations are compared to New Testament readings, which determines the citation's affinity in the tradition.

The above steps appear to be a linear process that results in a better understanding of patristic citations and their relationship to the primary texts. However, this process is more circular than linear. Finding citations requires a choice of search text. This is usually a critical edition, set up as the standard by which a citation is categorised. From the start, citations are judged against what has been deemed the ideal text with only the closest forms of the Father's citation considered as a true citation. In other words, a modern form of text is forced upon the citation, which is then used as a witness for the text by which it was judged. False conclusions are then used in the editorial process that often falsely represents the patristic witnesses in critical editions or apparatuses. This circular process still holds sway over much research in the field. A better approach is to allow the citations to speak for themselves.

In reality, Church Fathers often cite different forms of text or one text inconsistently, and even quote according to their own mental text.[4] Sometimes the citations have been changed in a later time period, accommodated to a text form the Father never knew. The way in which we evaluate these variations must be descriptive, but more importantly explanatory: this is much more beneficial than the common attempt to reconstruct a 'patristic text'. The biblical citations of the Church Fathers potentially provide much needed information concerning the development of the New Testament.

Origen of Alexandria, when citing the Letter to the Galatians, for example, appears to have many citing techniques. He employed many forms of text(s?) and used them freely to create different citations. So how, for example, can one demonstrate the nature of Origen's citations in a helpful way? If Origen is inconsistent, then a methodology that is based on deviance and affinity is not helpful. Origen's citations must be described

---

Contribution to Methodology in the Recovery and Analysis of Patristic Citations.' *Biblica* 52 (1971) pp. 357–94; Carroll D. Osburn, 'Methodology in Identifying Patristic Citations in NT Textual Criticism.' *NovT* 47.4 (2005) pp. 313–43.

[4] For the term 'mental text', see H.A.G. Houghton, 'Augustines' Adoption of the Vulgate Gospels' *NTS* 54 (2008) pp. 450–64.

and explained or we will use him to tell us what we want to know instead of what we need to know about the Greek New Testament.

This paper will survey some examples of Origen's citations of Galatians and some characteristics of his presentation. He uses introductory material to 'mark' his citations, but this does not guarantee that he will not implement lexical accommodation to his context or take liberty in his stylistic variations. These examples will demonstrate the first step in assessing patristic citations. They are followed by a brief examination of the presence of Origen in Galatians in NA28.

CHARACTERISTICS OF ORIGEN'S CITATIONS

The most common way citations of Galatians are identified in Origen's works is through the use of either introductory or concluding markers. The markers typically indicate author (i.e. 'Paul', 'the apostle', 'his letter') or the audience ('To the Galatians'). Some citations have both of these elements while others only have one. While markers can introduce a single citation, they often appear before citation chains. The following examples are introductory markers.[5]

Galatians 1:3–4 [Ps.Frag 134:12:100]
ὡς καὶ γράφων τοῖς Γαλάταις ὁ Παῦλος εἰπὼν γάρ ...
'and as written to the Galatians, for Paul said ...'

Galatians 1:4 [Eph.Com 9:177]
Καὶ ἐν τῇ πρὸς Γαλάτας ...
'and in 'To the Galatians'"

Galatians 1:8 [Ps.Frag 68:14:9]
ἢ διδάξῃ ἡμᾶς παρ' ὃ ὁ Παῦλος ἐδίδαξεν ...
'the teaching according to that which Paul taught you'

Galatians 1:15–16 [Basil.Phil A 25:1:3]
καὶ ἐν τῇ πρὸς Γαλάτας ὁ ἀπόστολος ...
'and in 'To the Galatians' the apostle ...'

---

[5] The text of all Origen's works has been taken from the online *Thesaurus Linguae Graece*. The abbreviations differ slightly from those in the *Clavis Patrum Graecorum* in order to disambiguate certain groups of works.

Galatians 1:19 [Matt.Com B 10:17:29]
ὃν λέγει Παῦλος ἰδεῖν ἐν τῇ πρὸς Γαλάτας ἐπιστολῇ εἰπών ...
'which Paul said he had seen in his letter 'To the Galatians', saying ...'

Galatians 2:9 [Ps.Sel 12:1533:52]
... φησὶν ὁ Ἀπόστολος ...
'the apostle said ...'

Galatians 2:20 [1Cor.Com 30:5]
διὸ λέγει ὁ Παῦλος...
'therefore Paul said ...'

Galatians 3:1 [Ps.Frag 9:6:17]
Καὶ Γαλάταις δὲ Παῦλος ἐπετίμα ...
'But Paul also admonished the Galatians ...'

Galatians 4:16 [Ps.Sel 12:1129:53]
ὡς ὁ Ἀπόστολός φησιν ...
'as the Apostle said ...'

Galatians 4:21 [Princ 4:2:6:28]
ἀλλὰ μὴν καὶ ἐν τῇ πρὸς Γαλάτας ἐπιστολῇ ...
'but indeed also in the epistle 'To the Galatians' ...'

Galatians 4:26 [Matt.Com C 16:15:25]
ἐν δὲ τῇ πρὸς Γαλάτας ...
'but in 'To the Galatians' ...'

Galatians 5:19 [Eph.Com 25:69]
καὶ λέγειν ...
'and he said ...'

Galatians 6:14 [Matt.Com C 13:21:28]
...ἀλλὰ λεγέτω κατὰ Παῦλον...
'but say, according to Paul ...'

The next two markers occur after a citation. These are unique as they are the only two that appear in Origen's works when citing Galatians.

Galatians 1:4 [Orat 25:1:21]
... κατὰ τὰ ἐν τῇ πρὸς Γαλάτας εἰρημένα ἐπιστολῇ.
'according to what was said in the epistle 'To the Galatians'.'

Galatians 5:19 [Ps.Sel 12:1132:38]
... φησὶν ὁ θεῖος Ἀπόστολος.
'... he said, the godly Apostle.'

One would think the specificity of these markers should warrant confidence in the text to follow. However, such detail does not require any citation to be an attempt to cite an exemplar or refrain from stylistic variation. The following is a good example of how Origen's markers are not formulaic indicators of his citation presentation:

Galatians 2:12 [Cels 2:1:50]
Καὶ ἐν τῇ πρὸς Γαλάτας δὲ ἐπιστολῇ Παῦλος ἐμφαίνει ὅτι Πέτρος ἔτι φοβούμενος τοὺς Ἰουδαίους, παυσάμενος τοῦ μετὰ τῶν ἐθνῶν συνεσθίειν, ἐλθόντος Ἰακώβου πρὸς αὐτὸν ἀφώριζεν ἑαυτὸν ἀπὸ τῶν ἐθνῶν, φοβούμενος τοὺς ἐκ τῆς περιτομῆς πρὸ τοῦ γὰρ ἐλθεῖν τινας ἀπὸ Ἰακώβου μετὰ τῶν ἐθνῶν συνήσθιεν· ὅτε δὲ ἦλθον, ὑπέστελλεν καὶ ἀφώριζεν ἑαυτὸν φοβούμενος τοὺς ἐκ περιτομῆς.
[NA28 and Maj]

As this citation of Galatians 2:12 shows, an introductory marker naming author, recipient church and letter-format precedes a citation not found in any New Testament manuscript. In fact, it is unique among the citations in Origen's works where Galatians is recognisable. Specific markers cannot predict an attempt to cite a specific text and, conversely, attempts to cite specific text do not require specific formulaic markers. These examples have shown two general citation practices of Origen: introductory markers and final markers. The next examples will show another presentation style, the use of citation markers within the citation.

Internal markers typically serve as a continuation or resumption of broken chains of text. Citation chains often have specific introductory markers, but if they are interrupted by exposition or commentary, one way Origen resumes citations of Galatians is the use of these markers. These markers appear as a verbal post-positive, usually φησίν and γάρ. Once again, marker specificity does not indicate an intention to cite a specific reading or a manuscript.

Galatians 2:9 [John.Com B 32:17:208:2]
Δεξιάς, γάρ φησιν, ἔδωκαν ἐμοὶ καὶ Βαρνάβᾳ κοινωνίας, ἵνα ἡμεῖς εἰς τὰ ἔθνη, αὐτοὶ δὲ εἰς τὴν περιτομήν.

Galatians 4:21 [Princ 4:2:6:28]
λέγετέ μοι φησὶν οἱ ὑπὸ νόμον θέλοντες εἶναι, τὸν νόμον οὐκ ἀκούετε

Galatians 5:9 [Luke.Frag 107:14]
μικρὰ γάρ φησι ζύμη ὅλον τὸ φύραμα ζυμοῖ.

The text of all of these citations corresponds to readings preserved in the manuscript tradition of Galatians (without the markers). Internal markers, as well as introductory and final markers, indicate a switch from Origen's prose to a biblical citation. So far, the examples given of Origen's text have shown ways that distinguish between Galatians and Origen. The following section will present some examples of how Origen accommodates biblical text to his own context.

Sometimes a single lexical change is the only difference between Origen's citations and a manuscript. The following reading (mentioned above) is a clear example of accommodation to the context of his writing, yet has an introductory formula with ἐν τῇ πρὸς Γαλάτας. Despite the label as text, Origen uses different prepositions for the same verse in different works.

Galatians 1:4
... ἑαυτὸν ὑπὲρ τῶν ἁμαρτιῶν ἡμῶν... [Ps.Frag 134:12:10]
... ἑαυτὸν περὶ τῶν ἁμαρτιῶν ἡμῶν... [Orat 25:1:21]

In Galatians 2:9, Origen exchanges ἐμοὶ for Παύλῳ to avoid the Pauline first-person reference, yet still claims explicitly that they are the words spoken by the apostle:

Galatians 2:9
δεξιὰς ἔδωκαν Παύλῳ καὶ Βαρνάβᾳ κοινωνίας... [Cels 2:1:56]
δεξιὰς ἔδωκαν ἐμοὶ   καὶ Βαρνάβᾳ κοινωνίας... [NA28/Maj]

Though carrying the same meaning, Galatians 2:19 is a place where Origen shows freedom in using different verb/participle forms. But which one was Paul's words? Or better, which words were Origen's, if not both?

Χριστῷ συνεσταύρωμαι [Cels 2:69:8]
Χριστῷ συνεσταύρωται [John.Com A 10:35:230:3]

Galatians 5:14
πεπλήρωται, ἐν τῷ ἀγαπήσεις τὸν πλησίον σου ὡς σεαυτόν [NA28]
πληροῦται ἐν τῷ ᾿Αγαπήσεις τὸν πλησίον σου ὡς ἑαυτόν [Maj]
πεπληρωκέναι τὴν ἀγαπήσεις τὸν πλησίον σου ὡς ἑαυτόν [Matt.Com C 15:14:41]

Typically, Origen's non-commentary works, such as the apologetical *Contra Celsus*, have more idiosyncratic readings. While Origen's commentaries present a form of the text closer to our modern critical editions, Origen's other works are more likely to abandon verse structure and lexical usage to fit his polemical purposes if necessary. For obvious reasons, Origen's citations which employ stylistic variation are harder to recognize than single lexical changes. One reason is that changes to grammar, structure, and word order can change the appearance of the biblical text. However, other than Galatians 2:12, there are not many places where Origen significantly diverges from well-attested forms of text. However, these examples quite possibly could not have originated with Origen. Similar to the New Testament tradition, Origen's tradition could be accommodated to any contemporary text of his readers of over 2,000 years. The citations of the Church Fathers were quite often adjusted to fit the biblical texts they were copied in.

ORIGEN'S PRESENCE IN THE NA28 CRITICAL APPARATUS

In general, not much has been published on Origen's citations of Paul, though some publications describe his use of the biblical text.[6] This may be seen by his presence (or lack thereof) in modern critical editions. Origen is not frequently cited as a witness in places of variation where his text is extant. This section offers a review of the places where Origen appears in the critical apparatus of the NA28 in the Galatians, along with some suggestions of other passages where his testimony is worthy of mention. The first variant is found in Galatians 4:14:

τὸν πειρασμὸν ὑμῶν ἐν τῇ σαρκί μου... [NA28]
τὸν πειρασμόν μου   τὸν ἐν τῇ σαρκί μου... [Maj]
τὸν πειρασμόν ὑμῶν τὸν ἐν τῇ σαρκί μου... [Eph.Com 14:32]

---

[6] On Origen's use of Scripture, see C.P. Hammond Bammel, *Der Römerbrieftext des Rufin und seine Origenes-Übersetzung.* (AGLB 10. Freiburg im Breisgau: Herder, 1985), pp. 213–30; B. Ehrman, G. Fee & M. Holmes, *The Text of the Fourth Gospel in the Writings of Origen* (SBLNTGF 3. Atlanta GA: Scholars Press, 1992); Darrell D. Hannah, *The Text of I Corinthians in the Writings of Origen.* (SBLNTGF 4. Atlanta GA: Scholars Press, 1997); R.P.C. Hanson, *Allegory and Event: A Study of the Sources and Significance of Origen's Interpretation of Scripture* (London: SCM, 1959; repr. Louisville, KY: Westminster John Knox, 2002); Ronald E. Heine, *The Commentaries of Origen and Jerome on St. Paul's Epistle to the Ephesians* (Oxford: Oxford UP, 2002).

υμων τον Or(a) 6. 1739. 1881.] υμων NA28 א* A B C² D* F G 33 bo,
μου τον Maj C*(vid) D¹ K L P Ψ 365. 630. 1175. 1505 ar vg(ms) sy(h)
sa bo(ms)
ου P46, τον א^C 0278. 81. 104. 326. 1241. 2464.

Here, Origen's reading corresponds with manuscripts 6 1739 1881 and not
with NA28 or Majority Text. This could be an example of Origen's stylistic
variation, or an accurate citation of the textual form found in 1739 and
1881. The next two units are found in Galatians 4:23:

ἀλλ' ὁ μὲν ἐκ τῆς παιδίσκης [NA28]
ἀλλ' ὁ μὲν ἐκ τῆς παιδίσκης [Maj]
ἀλλ' ὁ μὲν ἐκ τῆς παιδίσκης [Jer.Hom A 05:15:11]
ἀλλ' ὁ μὲν ἐκ τῆς παιδίσκης [Princ 4:2:6]
ἀλλ' ὁ μὲν ἐκ τῆς παιδίσκης [Basil.Phil A 1:13:32]
ἀλλ' ὁ μὲν ἐκ τῆς παιδίσκης [Basil.Phil A 9:1:32]
ἀλλ' ὁ μὲν ἐκ τῆς παιδίσκης [Rom.Frag A 36a:22]
⠀⠀⠀ὁ⠀⠀⠀ἐκ τῆς παιδίσκης [Matt.Com C 17:34]
και⠀ὁ μὲν ἐκ τῆς παιδίσκης [Cels 4:44:27]

μεν Or(abcdeg) NA28 Maj א A B C D F G K L P Ψ 062(vid). 0278. 33.
81. 104. 365. 630. 1175. 1241. 1505. 1739. 1881. it sy(h) Amb] *omit*
Or(f) P46 B f vg; Pel

In 4:23a, six of Origen's seven citations contain μεν, matching NA28,
Majority Text and 1739 1881. There is one citation that does not contain
μεν, Matt.Com C, which appears to be an abbreviation of his other
citations. In 4:23b, Origen is a witness against the editorial text of NA28:

τῆς ἐλευθέρας δι'⠀⠀⠀ἐπαγγελίας. [NA28]
τῆς ἐλευθέρας διὰ τῆς ἐπαγγελίας. [Maj]
τῆς ἐλευθέρας διὰ τῆς ἐπαγγελίας. [Jer.Hom A 05:15:11]
τῆς ἐλευθέρας διὰ τῆς ἐπαγγελίας. [Princ 4:2:6]
τῆς ἐλευθέρας διὰ τῆς ἐπαγγελίας. [Basil.Phil A 1:13:32]
τῆς ἐλευθέρας διὰ τῆς ἐπαγγελίας. [Basil.Phil A 9:1:32]
τῆς ἐλευθέρας διὰ τῆς ἐπαγγελίας. [Rom.Frag A 36a:22]
τῆς ἐλευθέρας διὰ τῆς ἐπαγγελίας. [Matt.Com C 17:34]
τῆς ἐλευθέρας διὰ τῆς ἐπαγγελίας. [Cels 4:44:27]

δια της Or(abcdefg) Maj B Δ Φ Γ K Λ Π 062. 0278. 365. 630. 1175. 1505.
1739. 1881. it sy(h); Ambst] δι NA28 P46 א A C Ψ 33. 81. 104. 1241.
2464., κατ 323. 945.

This is a rare occurrence of Origen consistently corresponding with the Majority Text where it disagrees with NA28. This unit of variation has strong witnesses on both sides and is a place where Origen should contribute. As a witness, Origen could tip the scale in one direction where strong sources conflict. Again, he is in correspondence with 1739 and 1881 as expected. The question remains whether these citations are early examples of the presence of this reading or whether Origen's text was later adjusted to match the text of a copyist or reader.

Overall, it is surprising to see Origen cited for only three verses for Galatians in the NA28 apparatus. In the first chapter of Galatians alone there are several examples where his presence in the apparatus would have been helpful. For example, in Galatians 1:3:

ἀπὸ   θεοῦ πατρὸς ἡμῶν καὶ κυρίου   Ἰησοῦ Χριστοῦ [NA28]
ἀπὸ   θεοῦ πατρός,   καὶ κυρίου ἡμῶν Ἰησοῦ Χριστοῦ [Maj]
ἀπὸ του θεοῦ πατρός ἡμῶν καὶ κυρίου   Ἰησοῦ Χριστοῦ
[Ps.Frag 134:12:10]

του Or(a)] omit NA28 Maj

ημων και κυριου Or(a) NA28 ℵ A P Ψ 33. 81. 326. 365. 1241. 2464. ar b; Ambst] και κυριου ημων Maj P46 P51(vid) B D F G H K L 104. 630. 1175. 1505. 1739. 1881. vg sy sa bo(mss), και κυριου 0278 vg(mss)

In the latter unit of variation, NA28 and Majority Text disagree, with Origen corresponding with the NA28 text. Unusually, however, 1739 and 1881 agree with the Majority Text against Origen, which is uncommon in Galatians. Both readings have strong evidence, yet although another witness would be helpful here, Origen is not listed.

Another unit where Origen could help is the very next verse. Galatians 1:4 has been quoted above, but it deserves a second look:

ὑπὲρ Or(a) NA28 P51 ℵ² B H 0278. 6. 33. 81. 326. 365. 630. 1175. 1505. 2464] περὶ Or(b) Maj P46 X A D F G K L P Ψ 104. 1739. 1881.

αἰῶνος τοῦ ἐνεστῶτος Or(bcdef) NA28 P46. 51(vid) ℵ* A B 33 81. 326. 630. 1241. 1739. 1881] ἐνεστῶτος αἰῶνος Maj ℵ² D F G H(vid) K L P Ψ 0278. 104. 365. 1175. 1505. 2464 latt.

Here, NA28 and Majority Text disagree in two different units. Origen corresponds with NA28 in one place and with Majority Text in the other. This is the second time within the examples of this paper that the corrector of Sinaiticus changed text to correspond to the Majority Text, which could also have happened in Origen's citations.

Galatians 1:8

… ἄγγελος ἐξ οὐρανοῦ εὐαγγελίζηται ὑμῖν [NA28 & Maj]

… ἄγγελος ἐξ οὐρανοῦ εὐαγγελίσηται   [Ps.Frag 68:14:9]

εὐαγγελίσηται Or(a) ℵ* b g Mcion(T) Tert(pt) Lcf] εὐαγγελίσηται ὑμῖν ℵ² A 81. 104. 326. 1241. d Tert(pt) Ambst, εὐαγγελίζηται F G Ψ ar Cyp, ὑμῖν εὐαγγελίζηται P51(vid) B H 630. 1175. 1739. εὐαγγελίζεται ὑμῖν K P (0278). 365. 614. 1505. 1881. 2464. pm, εὐαγγελίζηται ὑμῖν Maj D*(c).2 L 6. 33. 945 pm vg.

In 1:8, Origen does not correspond to NA28 or Majority Text. The apparatus presents six variant readings, and includes five Church Fathers as witnesses. However, Origen is not present. This is another place of interest to investigate Origen's transmission history as he stands against most evidence except for a correction in Codex Sinaiticus. It is curious that this reading has stood the test of time with so much evidence against it. Regardless of its genesis, the presence of this minority reading shows the tenacity of the transmission history of Origen.

CONCLUSION

To sum up, although Origen is often very clear about marking his citations, these markers are not necessarily indicators of an intention to cite accurately. Origen shows many techniques for marking his citations of Galatians. He also cites text in a unique way by incorporating his own stylistic variation. Nonetheless, the evidence which Origen's citations supply for the history of the text of Galatians is more substantial than currently witnessed in the critical apparatus of hand editions.

The examples cited in this paper were not for the purpose of establishing some level of accuracy for Origen's citations, nor even to provide arguments against current trends in patristic textual studies. Descriptive and explanatory analyses of patristic citations are imperative before any type of comparison with the primary documents.

Knowing this, an academically sound assessment of patristic citations must never begin with the prejudgment of citations only to be evaluated later. Origen can be very inconsistent in his presentation of Galatians, but this is a reason why scholars working with patristic citations should focus all the more on the development of the citations. The previous comparative methodologies assume the initial text is the standard by which a citation's character is determined. Assessing a Father's affinity to a chosen text results in a false representation of the patristic citations, their exemplars, and a confused understanding of transmission history and development of the text. We may say that critical editions of the New Testament are incomplete unless they make proper use of patristic evidence to construct a critical apparatus from all the earliest witnesses. The role reversal, of using the text to assess the value of the citations limits the contribution of the Church Fathers. If textual studies of the Church Fathers remain the same, the results will continue along a methodological road that always leads to circular comparative models, diminishing the value both of patristic sources and the Greek New Testament.

8. FAMILY 1 IN MARK: PRELIMINARY RESULTS

AMY S. ANDERSON[1]

The ground-breaking work on Family 1 of the Gospels was undertaken by Kirsopp Lake in the early 1900s.[2] Later studies have repeatedly shown his results to be of high quality and accuracy but have discovered additional Family 1 manuscripts and proposed more complexity to the relationships between the various manuscripts.

In 1999, the author completed a doctoral dissertation on Family 1 in Matthew with a particular focus on Codex 1582.[3] All evidence from the investigation in Matthew pointed to 1 and 1582 as the best representatives of the archetype, and emphasis was placed on Codex 1582 as the somewhat better candidate for leading family member because of its age and the care taken by the scribe Ephraim in reproducing his exemplar. An expanded

---

[1] When this paper was presented at the Eighth Birmingham Colloquium in March 2013, early results had been compiled from the Family Readings Collation. By the time the publication of the colloquium proceedings went to press, the research had advanced significantly, so that more results are reported here. The author would like to thank North Central University for assisting in the progress of this research with both finances and release time.

[2] Kirsopp Lake, *Codex 1 of the Gospels and Its Allies* (T&S 1.7. Cambridge: Cambridge UP, 1902). This is discussed in Amy S. Anderson, *The Textual Tradition of the Gospels: Family 1 in Matthew* (Leiden: Brill, 2004), pp. 1ff and 103ff, and the work of Welsby, cited in note 4 below.

[3] This was subsequently published as Anderson, *Family 1 in Matthew*. All manuscript numbers in the present article refer to the Gregory–Aland classification of Greek New Testament manuscripts.

family tree and several types of collations with accompanying results were provided for Matthew.

Alison Welsby's thorough research on the Gospel of John led her to similarly confirm that 1 and 1582 are leading Family 1 manuscripts in John. She also found that

> a new subgroup exists, represented by 565, 884 and 2193, that rivals the textual witness of 1 and 1582. This subgroup descends from the Family 1 archetype through a different intermediate ancestor to that shared by 1 and 1582.[4]

Welsby's research resulted in a full collation of John, an expanded family tree, and a new edition of the Family 1 text in John. The present article will provide preliminary results for comparable research in the Gospel of Mark.

THE PROJECT

Developing Methodology

In the late 1990s, collation methodology had not advanced much beyond that used by Lake and others nearly one hundred years earlier. Microfilms were consulted and the textual complexion of each manuscript in Matthew was judged by means of a large selection of 'family readings' plus two chapters of continuous text collations, one each in the earlier and later parts of the Gospel.

The present work on Mark began in 2008, by which time textual scholars were making significantly more use of computer technology, in particular the COLLATE software developed by Peter Robinson.[5] Each manuscript of a text is transcribed into electronic form so that it becomes fully searchable and thereby comparable with every other transcribed manuscript. Such a computer collation of a group of manuscripts, though

---

⁴ Alison Sarah Welsby, 'A Textual Study of Family 1 in the Gospel of John.' (PhD thesis, University of Birmingham, 2011). This is available in electronic form at http://etheses.bham.ac.uk/3338/. This appeared in print after the submission of this article as Alison Welsby, *A Textual Study of Family 1 in the Gospel of John* (ANTF 45. Berlin & New York: De Gruyter, 2013). The quotation is taken from the dissertation abstract.

⁵ P.M.W. Robinson, *Collate: Interactive Collation of Large Textual Traditions, Version 2* (Computer Program distributed by the Oxford University Centre for Humanities Computing. Oxford, 1994).

valuable as a complete source of information, yielded its output in the form of hundreds of pages of readout that was difficult to decipher for anyone who did not work with it constantly.

Sixteen manuscripts were transcribed between 2008 and 2013, namely 1 22 118 131 205 209 565 872 1192 1210 1278 1582 2193 2372 2542 and 2886. A number of collations were run with COLLATE but as the final transcriptions were being finished in the summer of 2013, the successor to this programme (CollateX developed by the Interedition consortium) was used for collation, as implemented in the New Testament Virtual Manuscript Room.[6] The online collation of the Family 1 manuscripts in Mark was the first project in this environment to be completed using CollateX. Yet the work of recording the results of a full collation must still be done by the scholar, one variation unit at a time. The Full Collation of 16 manuscripts plus the *Textus Receptus* (TR) resulted in 170 pages of data, which are still being processed at the time of publication of this article. This rich resource will yield additional information about relationships between manuscripts, including percentage of agreement, and will be an excellent starting point for the production of a new edition of the text of Family 1 in Mark.

Choice of Manuscripts

As mentioned above, the number of manuscripts included in Family 1 has grown over the past 120 years. Lake recognized Codices 1 118 131 205 and 209 to be closely related and gave them the name 'Family 1' because Codex 1 was at that time the best representative of the archetype. The work in Matthew, while continuing to value the text of Codex 1, supported 1582 as a slightly better candidate for leading member of the family. Additional manuscripts were investigated as a result of findings of other textual scholars. These are 22 872 1192 1210 1278 2193 and 2542. Some of these were found to be family members in Matthew and others were not. Welsby's work in John added 565 884 2372 2713 and 2886.[7]

---

[6] http://ntvmr.uni-muenster.de/.

[7] Codex 884 is not extant in Mark; Codex 2713 came to the attention of this researcher too late for the present article, but will be included later. Codex 2886 was previously named 205abs because it was thought to be a copy of 205. Detailed physical descriptions and histories of all the manuscripts studied can be found in the relevant sections in Lake, Anderson, and Welsby and will not be repeated here.

The Family Readings List

Most of the variation units listed in this paper are from the Family Readings Collation.[8] They can be differentiated from other readings cited because they are identified by a bold number preceding the chapter and verse. The Family Readings list was created during the initial transcriptions of Codices 1 and 1582. Codex 1 was transcribed first, using an existing electronic copy of the TR as the base text to which changes were made, resulting in an electronic copy of Codex 1. At most points of variation between Codex 1 and the TR, NA27 and Robinson–Pierpont (RP) were consulted.[9] Variation units were compiled into an initial list if the reading of Codex 1 was different from the RP text *and* was either not mentioned at all in Nestle–Aland, or was included in the apparatus with little additional support beyond Family 1.

This list of Codex 1 readings was then constantly consulted during the transcription of Codex 1582. In almost every instance, 1582 had the same reading as 1,[10] and the reading was established as a Family Reading. This process produced a list of 262 variation units in Mark, plus several additional items of interest. The transcriptions of the other 14 manuscripts were then collated and added to this list, and, finally, each variation unit was investigated in NA28, Legg, Swanson, and Tischendorf.[11] All manuscripts in support of the Family 1 reading are cited, as well as witnesses for other readings if they represent a non-Byzantine text.

The complete Family Readings list, divided into three sections,[12] is found in the Appendix to the present article, where one additional

---

[8] I would like to express my gratitude to undergraduate research assistant Bethany Bostron for checking the results of the Family Readings List.

[9] Maurice A. Robinson and William G. Pierpont, eds, *The New Testament in the Original Greek According to the Byzantine/Majority Textform* (Atlanta GA: Original Word Publishers, 1991).

[10] In already existing results from the Full Collation of Mark, Codex 1 and 1582 have 97% agreement in chapters 1–5 and 98% agreement in chapters 6–10.

[11] S.C.E. Legg, *Nouum Testamentum Graece: Euangelium Secundum Marcum* (Oxford: Clarendon, 1935); Reuben J. Swanson, ed., *New Testament Greek Manuscripts: Mark* (Pasadena CA: Wm Carey International, 1995); Constantine Tischendorf, *Novum Testamentum Graece: Editio Octava Critica Maior: Volumen 1* (Leipzig: Giesecke & Devrient, 1869).

[12] Mark 1–5 has 51 possible Family Readings, Mark 6–10 has 116, and Mark 11–16 has 93.

designation is added: the number of outside witnesses in support of any Family 1 reading has been used as a guideline to designate that reading as rare (supported by 0 to 5 other witnesses and marked with **X**), somewhat rare (less than 10 witnesses from the 6th century or later and marked with •), or common (more broadly supported by non-RP manuscripts and marked with ■).

The resulting Family Readings list became a source of valuable information, allowing the researcher to quickly locate variation units in which a particular manuscript demonstrated affinity with the Family 1 text, as well as hinting at possible relationships between manuscripts. This information will be used in the discussions below.

The Full Collation of Family 1 in Mark

A Full Collation of all 16 manuscripts plus the TR has recently been completed for Mark and results are still being compiled as work in progress. Percentage agreement between the various family members will be one of the most useful results, as well as unique agreements that can provide further evidence of potential relationships. Mark has been divided into the same three sections as in the Family Readings list,[13] and many results already compiled will be reported in this paper.[14]

PRELIMINARY CONCLUSIONS FROM THE FAMILY READINGS COLLATION

Codex 2193 is an Outstanding Representative of the Archetype[15]

During preparatory research in the Gospel of Matthew, full chapter collations were completed for both 1 and 1582 in Mark, Luke, and John as well. These collations demonstrated that both the quality and the close

---

[13] Mark 1–5 (in which there are 320 possible variation units), 6–10 (510 units), and 11–16 (543 units).

[14] Many thanks to postgraduate research assistants Timothy Mitchell and Jessica Shao, who have provided immense amounts of data as a result of their careful compiling of the Full Collation, and will continue to do so in the coming months.

[15] Two postgraduate dissertations have added to awareness of Codex 2193 in recent years, Welsby, 'A Textual Study' and Timothy A. Koch, 'Manuscript 2193 and its Text of the Gospel according to John' (Unpublished STM thesis at Concordia Seminary, St Louis MO, 2013). In addition, the present writer is working on an article about Codex 2193 which will be published in 2015.

relationship between the two core codices was consistent throughout the four Gospels. Because Codex 2193 was not available except on microfilm at the *Institut für neutestamentliche Textforschung* in Münster, chapter collations for this relatively unknown manuscript were made in all four Gospels during a visit there to collect data for the research on Matthew. It was noted that 2193 appeared to change its textual complexion in moving from Matthew to Mark, or perhaps even earlier. I speculated that

> the exemplar of 2193 was rigorously corrected to the Byzantine standard text in the first part of Matthew, with the enthusiasm of the corrector decreasing somewhat in the later chapters, and possibly ceasing altogether before Mark, which appears from preliminary investigation to provide a core Family 1 text.[16]

The expectation that 2193 would have a core Family 1 text in the other Gospels is confirmed by both Welsby's work on John and the present work on Mark.[17]

Among the 262 agreements between 1 and 1582 that make up the Family Readings list, Codex 2193 had a different reading only 10 times, nine of which were in agreement with RP.[18] There were two additional variation units where 2193 had the Family 1 reading, but with minor variation. In Full Collation results already calculated, Codex 1's agreement with 2193 is 92% in chapters 1–5 and 91% in chapters 6–10. (Agreement between 1 and 1582 is 97% and 98%, respectively.) Several variation units that point out the close relationship of these three MSS are as follows:

50   5:39 *om.* **1 565 1582 2193**] εισελθων 22 118 131 205 209 872 1192 1210 1278 2372 2542 (2886) NA RP

56   6:16 ουτος εστιν ιωαννης αυτος **1 565 1582 2193** Θ 700] ιωαννην ουτος ℵ² B L W Δ 28 69 543 892 | ιωαννην ουτος εστιν αυτος 22 118 131 205 209 872 1192 1210 1278 2372 2542 2886 RP

---

[16] Anderson, *Family 1 in Matthew*, pp. 142ff. See also pp. 96 (fn. 25) and 105.

[17] Welsby, 'A Textual Study', p. 42ff.. Welsby finds that in John 2193, together with 565 and 884, represents an intermediate exemplar, which she designates as Codex B. In John, B is an independent witness to the archetype of Family 1. The Full Collation results will show whether a relationship between 565 and 2193 can be posited in Mark. However, the Family Readings list and initial compilations from the Full Collation do not appear to support such a close relationship.

[18] The one non-RP variation from 1 1582 is a spelling variant. See Variant 226.

85   6:55 και εκπεριδραμοντες **1 1582 2193**] και περιδραμοντες 118 205 209 565 700 2886 | περιεδραμον ΝΑ | περιδραμοντες 22 131 872 1192 1210 1278 2372 2542 RP

117   9:9 διεστελλετο **1 209 1582 2193**vid C] διεστελετο **205 2886** | διεστειλατο 22 118 131 565 872 1192 1210 1278 2372 2542 ΝΑ RP

204   13:8 *om.* **1 1582 2193 2542** (W)] ταυτα 22 118 131 205 209 (565) 872 1192 1210 1278 2372 2886 ΝΑ RP

224   14:31 πετρος μαλλον εκπερισσου οτι **1 1582 2193**] εκπερισσως ελαλει ΝΑ | εκπερισσου ελεγεν μαλλον 131 1278 RP | πετρος μαλλον περισσως ελεγεν W 13 69 124 346 2542 | πετρος εκπερισσου ελεγε μαλλον 22 118 1192 1210 2372 | πετρος μαλλον εκπερισσου ελεγεν οτι 205 209 2886 | πετρος περισσως ελεγεν 565 | εκπερισσου ελεγεν οτι 872

244   14:70 περιεστωτες **1 1582 2193** G] παρεστωτες 22 118 131 205 209 565vid 872 1192 1210 1278 2372 2542 2886 ΝΑ RP

The colophon after 16:8 provides a remarkable agreement:

εν τισι μεν των αντιγραφων εως ωδε πληρουται ο ευαγγελιστης εως ου και ευσεβιος ο παμφιλου εκανονισεν εν πολλοις δε και ταυτα φερεται **1 209 1582 2193 2886**] *om.* 118 131 205 565 872 1278 2372 2542 ΝΑ RP[19]

Finally, this agreement shows up in the longer ending of Mark:

262   16:12 *om.* **1 1582 2193** Arm] περιπατουσιν 22 118 131 205 209 565 872 1192 1210 1278 2372 2542 2886 ΝΑ RP

Because it is a 10th century manuscript that appears to have been copied with care, 2193 must be seen as a representative of the Family 1 archetype equal or nearly equal to Codices 1 and 1582. Evidence yet to be mined from the Full Collation will assist in a final evaluation.

Codex 565 and Possible Relationship to 2193

Codex 565 is discussed next because Welsby has already identified its connection with Codex 2193. For John, she groups Codex 565 with 2193

---

[19] 22 1192 1210 have εν τισι των αντιγραφων εως ωδε πληρουται ο ευαγγελιστησ εν πολλοισ δε και ταυτα φερεται.

and 884 (which is not extant in Mark), then reconstructs their common exemplar as a witness comparable to 1 and 1582. 565 was not collated for Matthew, but the results in John caused it to receive attention in Mark.

The fact that Codex 565 contains 69 Family 1 readings, many of which are rare, means that it is certainly descended from the Family 1 archetype in Mark. Significant Family 1 agreements include:[20]

50   5:39 *om.* **1 565 1582 2193**] εισελθων 22 118 131 205 209 872 1192 1210 1278 2372 2542 (2886) NA RP

56   6:16 ουτος εστιν ιωαννης αυτος **1 565 1582 2193** Θ 700] ιωαννην ουτος ℵ² B L W Δ 28 69 543 892 | ιωαννην ουτος εστιν αυτος 22 118 131 205 209 872 1192 1210 1278 2372 2542 2886 RP

80   6:48 *om.* **1 205 209 565 1582 2193 2886**] αυτοις 22 118 131 872 1192 1210 1278 2372 2542 NA RP

129   9:26 κραξαν πολλα και **1 118 205 209 565 1582 2193 2886** Φ] κραξας και πολλα NA | κραξαν και πολλα 22 131 872 1192 1210 1278 2372 RP | και κραξαν πολλα 2542

163   10:35 σε ερωτησωμεν **1 565 1582 2193** D Θ] αιτησωμεν 22 131 1192 1210 2542 RP | αιτησωμεν σε B C L Δ Ψ | σε αιτησωμεν Υ Κ Ν Π 28 69 118 205 209 579 872 1278* 2372 2886

189   12:4 *om.* **1 205 209 565 1582 2193 2886**] προς αυτους αλλον 22 118 131 872 1192 1210 1278 2372 2542 NA RP

It will be noted that in each of these readings that are unique or nearly unique to Family 1, Codex 2193 is also a supporting witness. However, 2193 nearly always agrees with 1 and 1582, so it is important to look for evidence of 565 and 2193 agreeing against 1 and 1582. This occurs only at 14:32, where they join a larger tradition in a spelling variant.

226   14:32 γηθσεμανει **1 1582**] γεθσημανει ℵ A C L M N S 131 565 2193 | γεθσημανι 209 2542 NA | γεθσημανη 22 118 205 209 872 1192 1210 1278 2372 2886 RP

In the Family Readings list, Codex 565 also has 123 RP readings, 43 readings which are non-RP and non-Family 1, and another 29 'singular'

---

[20] See also variants 31, 32, 55, 59, 63, 90, 95, 99, 115, 126, 134, 136, 154, 156, 160, 190, 239, 241, 257, and 260.

readings (not shared with any manuscript used in this study, including those cited by Swanson, NA27, Legg, and Tischendorf). It was noticed during the compilation of the Full Collation of Family 1 manuscripts in Mark that 565 exceeds any other manuscript in number of 'singular' readings (that is, it differs from the TR and all the Family 1 manuscripts included in the collation). A quick comparison with Swanson demonstrates that many of these apparent singulars are in agreement with a great number of other witnesses, including frequent alignment with the leading Alexandrian manuscripts. Even with this observation, however, 565 persists in often reading apart from all known witnesses. Indeed, this codex is listed in *Text und Textwert* as having the sixth-highest percentage (nearly 32%) of *Sonderlesarten* in the passages chosen by that study for collation.[21]

A comparison has been run between 565 and 2193 in the Full Collation. In Mark 1–5 their total agreement is 51%, of which 81 readings are non-TR. In Mark 6–10, the total agreement is 57%. This is not enough to demonstrate relationship between 565 and 2193 at this stage in the research. However, the results in John require further serious investigation of this possibility.

Codex 872 and Possible Relationship to 2193(C)

A relationship has also been suggested between Codex 872 and the corrected form of Codex 2193. Both of these manuscripts were basically Byzantine in Matthew, but an alignment was perceived: 872 appeared to follow the readings of 2193 unless 2193 was corrected, in which case it agreed with 2193C. However, the amount of evidence was not sufficient to draw a final conclusion.

Welsby noted this observation in Matthew along with the report in *Text und Textwert* that 872 had Family 1 affinity in Mark.[22] Her investigation of John showed that the situation in that Gospel is significantly different, with 2193 turning out to be a core family member while 872 remains strongly aligned to the majority text. In addition, Welsby pointed to two variation units in which 872 agreed with 565 in rare readings not carried by 2193 (which in those two readings agreed with Family 1 and the majority

---

[21] Kurt Aland and Barbara Aland, *Text und Textwert der griechischen Handschriften des neuen Testaments: IV. Die synoptischen Evangelien: 1. Das Markusevangelium: Band 1,2* (Berlin: de Gruyter, 1998), p. 37. Other Family 1 manuscripts are not far behind, with 1 2542 205 and 1582 making the top 15, in that order.

[22] Welsby, 'A Textual Study', p. 195 n. 307.

text). For this reason Welsby found that 872 is not related to 2193C and would not be classified as a Family 1 member at all if it were not for the *Text und Textwert* results that appear to show a relationship to the core members in Mark.

The Family Readings list in Mark does indeed show Codex 872 to be a member of Family 1 in this Gospel. 872 agrees with 94 Family Readings and 140 RP readings.[23] Some of the more impressive agreements with the core Family 1 MSS are listed below.[24]

19   4:16 δεχονται **1 118 131 205 209 872 1582 2193 2886**] λαμβανουσιν αυτον 22 1192 1210 1278 2372 2542 NA RP | λαμβανουσιν 565

40   5:11 *om.* **1 872 1582 2193** 33[vid]] προς τω ορει 22 118 131 205 209 565 1192 1210 1278 2372 2542 2886 NA RP

41   5:16 εσωθη ο δαιμονισθεις **1 22 118 131 205 209 872 1192 1210 1278* 1582 2193 2372 2886** 251] εγενετο τω δαιμονιζομενω 565 1278[C] 2542 NA RP

83   6:51 εξεπλησσοντο **1 118 205 209 872 1582 2193 2886**] εξισταντο א B L Δ 28 892 | εξισταντο και εθαυμαζον 22 131 565 1192 1210 1278 2372 2542 RP

91   7:13 την εντολην **1 118 205 209 872 1582 2193 2886** (W)] τον λογον 22 131 565 1192 1210 1278 2372 2542 NA RP

128   9:25 (οχλοσ) πολυς **1 118 205 209 872 1582 2193 2886**] *om.* 22 131 565 1192 1210 1278 2372 2542 NA RP

154   10:20 εποιησα **1 118 205 209 565 872* 1582 2193 2542 2886** Arm] εφυλαξαμην 22 131 872[c] 1192 1210 1278 2372 NA RP

219   14:11 συνεθεντο **1 118 205 209 872 1582 2193 2886**] επηγγειλαντο 22 (131) 565 1192 1210 1278 2372 2542 NA RP

---

[23] In the Full Collation, 872 agrees with Codex 1 60% in chapters 1–5 and 52% in chapters 6–10. There are also 9 readings in which 872 agrees with other MSS in a non-Family 1, non-RP reading, as well as 17 'singular' readings.

[24] See also 4, 6, 13, 27, 30, 39, 46, 55, 57, 67, 68, 71, 72, 76, 81, 82, 99, 101, 106, 115, 125, 126, 133, 137, 141, 147, 151, 156, 158, 159, 168, 171, 177, 179, 183, 186, 203, 206, 218, 221, 236, 241, 242, 252, 253, and 260.

227   14:33 λυπεισθαι **1 205 209 872 1582 2193 2886**] λυπυσθαι **118** | εκθαμβεισθαι 22 131 565 1192 1210 1278 2372 2542 NA RP

254   15:23 και γευσαμενος **1 205 209 872 1582 2193 2886** G] γευσαμεν **118** | ο δε 22 131 565 1192 1210 1278 2372 2542 RP | ος δε ℵ B Γ 33 579 892 1424 2542

It will be noted that, as in the case of 565, in all of these readings that are unique or nearly unique to Family 1 Codex 2193 is also a supporting witness. Again, however, 2193 nearly always agrees with 1 1582, so it is important to look for evidence of 2193 and 872 agreeing against 1 1582. This does not occur in this selection of variation units.[25]

The Venice Group

Welsby calls Codices 118 205 209 2886 (formerly identified as 205[abs]) the 'Venice Group' because the latter three were owned by Cardinal Bessarion and are now preserved at the *Biblioteca Nazionale Marciana* in Venice.[26] These manuscripts are strong members of Family 1, and can be shown to derive from a common intermediate exemplar.

Of the 262 Family Readings, 118 has 163, 205 has 224, 209 has 232, and 2886 has 227. There are a number of non-Family 1, non-RP readings shared by the group. One example is the following:[27]

85   6:55 και εκπεριδραμοντες **1 1582 2193**] και περιδραμοντες 118 205 209 565 700 2886 | περιεδραμον NA | περιδραμοντες 22 131 872 1192 1210 1278 2372 2542 RP

Lake and Welsby both point out that the manuscripts of the Venice group share swings in textual affinity in sections of Matthew, Luke, and John, clear evidence that they descend from a common exemplar. This switching back and forth between the majority text and the Family 1 text does not occur in the same way in Mark, perhaps because their common exemplar was not

---

[25] Complete results of the Full Collation are not yet available. However, 872 was collated against 2193C ahead of schedule and the following was found: 85% agreement with 2193C in Mark 1–5 and 84% in Mark 11–16.

[26] Welsby's inclusion of 2713 in this group did not come to the attention of this researcher in time to include it in the present article. Because it clearly represents the Family 1 text in John, ongoing research in Mark will need to add 2713 into the investigation.

[27] See also Family Reading units 61, 69, 85, 163, 224, 234, 248.

damaged in Mark. However, the agreement among the four manuscripts is strong throughout, and certain relationships among them can be posited on the basis of smaller shared omissions.

In the Full Collation results of Mark 1–5, 205 209 2886 all have agreement with Codex 1 in the 86–87% range. In Mark 6–10 the agreement drops only by 1% and the results available in Mark 11–16 stay above 80%.[28] This makes them the group of manuscripts most closely related to the core group in Mark 1–10, and probably in 11–16 as well.

Similarly, relationship among the manuscripts of the Venice Group can be demonstrated by the presently available Full Collation results in Mark 1–5. Codex 118 agrees with the other three 86–87%. Codex 205 agrees with 209 95% and with 2886 an impressive 98%. In addition, 205 and 2886 are alone in omitting a section of text from Mark 1:32 through the first part of 1:34.

This close agreement between 205 and 2886 corresponds to other discussions about the relationship between the two. In earlier research, Wisse and others assumed 2886 to be a direct copy of 205, hence its original designation as 205[abs].[29] Welsby, in her recent study of John, however, finds reason to turn this assumption on its head.[30] She demonstrates that 205 has more majority text readings and more singular readings than 2886. As a result she concludes that 205 is not an independent witness to the common exemplar of the Venice Group, and she did not use 205 for the determination of the text of the exemplar. Further exploration of the relationship between 205 and 2886 will be pursued in the ongoing work in Mark.

Codex 118 is the weakest member of the Venice Group. Lake speculated that the scribe of 118 had two exemplars in front of him and occasionally hesitated when their readings differed, often leaving a space or not finishing a word.[31] The following examples of this hesitation are from the Full Collation of Mark:

---

[28] Codices 205 and 209 agree with Codex 1 in 82% of the variation units in chapters 11–16.

[29] Frederik Wisse, *The Profile Method for Classifying and Evaluating Manuscripts.* (SD 44. Grand Rapids MI: Eerdmans, 1982), p. 106.

[30] Welsby, 'A Textual Study', p. 120ff..

[31] Lake, 'Codex 1 of the Gospels', p. xiv. His list of these hesitations is on pp. xxxvii-xxxix.

1:44 αυτοις 1 22 131 205 565 872 1192 1210 1278 1582 2193 2372 2542 2886 TR] αυτ 118 | αυτης 209

6:4 συγγενευσιν 1 205 209 1582* 2193 2542 2886] συγγενεσι 22 131 565 872 1192 1210 1278 2372 TR | συγγενοι 118

9:35 *om.* 1 205 209 1582 2193* 2886] παντων εσχατος και 22 131 565 872 1192 1210 1278 2193c 2372 2542 TR | παντων 118

Codex 118 also has more singular readings and more agreements with RP than do the other members of the Venice Group.[32] The majority text readings in particular may have derived from the second exemplar that was consulted.

Manuscripts Related to Codex 22

In the Gospel of Matthew, Codex 22 was found to be statistically a representative of the majority text. However, it retained 27 family readings, some of which were nearly unique to Family 1, and thereby demonstrated that it is a descendent of the Family 1 archetype. In Mark, the picture is much the same. The tendency to carry the Byzantine text continues,[33] but Family Readings appear throughout.[34] The following are noteworthy.[35]

30 4:37 βυθιζεσθαι **1 22 118 131 205 209 872 1210 1278* 1582 2193 2372 2886** G 33] γεμιζεσθαι 565 1192 1278ᶜ 2542 NA RP

113 8:38 *om.* **1 22 205 209 1582 2193 2542 2886**] των αγιων 118 131 565 872 1192 1210 1278 2372 NA RP

---

[32] There are 84 RP readings spaced throughout the Family Readings list, yet agreement with 1 and 1582 is significant, with a total of 163 family readings. Agreement with Codex 1 in the Full Collation is 78% for chapters 1–5, 60% for chapters 6–10, and 69% for chapters 11–16.

[33] In the Family Readings list, Codex 22 agrees with RP in 222 of 262 variation units. In the Full Collation, agreement with Codex 1 and 1582 was only 48% each in Mark 1–5, and 36% and 33%, respectively, in Mark 6–10. *Text und Textwert* lists all of the manuscript in the 22 Group as Koinehandschriften for Mark.

[34] There were 8 of 51 in Mark 1–5, 5 of 116 in Mark 6–10, and 14 of 95 in Mark 11–16.

[35] Similar agreements of 22 with Family 1 can be seen in Family Reading Variants 31, 41, 43, 177, 218, 253, 258, and 261.

217   14:5 (αυτη) πολλα **1 22 118 205 209 1210 1278* 1582 2193 2372 2886** 59 697 Arm] *om.* 131 565 872 1192 1278ᶜ 2542 NA RP

240   14:65 νυν **1 22 118 205 209 1210 1582 2193 2886** G W 1071] *om.* 131 565 872 1192 1278 2372 2542 NA RP

In addition, there is strong evidence of relationship between 22 and several other manuscripts. The calculations for Codex 22 are complete in the Full Collation of Mark 1–5 and 6–10. In the Full Collation results available for Mark 1–5, the only manuscripts with which 22 has more than 59% agreement are 1192 (92%), 1210 (89%), 1278 (83%), and 2372 (83%). In Mark 6–10, the agreement is 1192 (91%), 1210 (94%), 1278 (83%), and 2372 (83%).[36]

These Family Readings variation units provide a number of non-Family 1, non-RP readings for 22 et al.[37]

120   9:13 ηλιας ηδη ηλθεν **1 118**ᵐᵍ **205 209 1582 2193 2886** 700] και ηλιας ηδη εληλυθεν 22 1192 1210 1278 2372 | και ηλιας εληλυθεν 131 NA RP | ηλιας εληλυθε 118 565 872 | ηλιας ηλθε 2542

211   13:27 ακρων ουνων **1 118 205 209 1582 2193 2886** W] ακρων ουνου 22 1192 1210 2372 | ακρου ουρανου 131 1278 NA RP | ακρου του ουρανου 565 872 2542

245   14:72 αναμνησθεις **1 118 205 209 872 1582 2193 2886** G W 13 69 495 543] ανεμνησθεις 131 | αναμνησθη 565 NA RP | ανεμνησθη 22 565 1192 1210 1278 2372 | εμνησθης 2542

Most interestingly, 22 1192 and 1210 share a variation on the typical Family 1 colophon after 16:8:

εν τισι των αντιγραφων εως ωδε πληρουται ο ευαγγελιστης εν πολλοις δε και ταυτα φερεται

The relationship to 1192 and 1210 seems obvious. These two manuscripts follow the tendency of 22 to provide a mostly Byzantine text, but when they have Family 1 readings, they are almost always in agreement with 22. Codex 1192 has only 18 Family Readings, [38] while 1210 has 31.[39]

---

[36] Similarly, the Münster test passages in Mark show Codex 22 to be the closest relative to 1192 (97.4%) and 1210 (96.8%).

[37] See also Variants 61, 65, 76, 224, and 239.

[38] Codex 1192 carries the Family 1 text without 22 1210 in Family Reading

In the study of Matthew, Codex 1278 did not demonstrate sufficient Family 1 agreement, nor enough agreement with the 22 Group to draw any conclusions about relationships. [40] It appears that the exemplar of Matthew copied by the scribe of 1278 was highly corrected to the Byzantine text. Codex 2372, for its part, was not investigated in Matthew. In Mark, the story is different. Though somewhat weaker in affiliation, both codices are clearly part of the 22 Group as is already demonstrated in the Full Collation results listed above.

In addition, speculation can be raised about a possible relationship between 1278 and 2372. Welsby places them within the 22 Group in John, and demonstrates that they are closely related to each other, arguing that they have a common exemplar.[41] In Mark they both tend to agree with the RP text, especially at the beginning of the Gospel, but when they vary, they frequently vary together. The following readings deserve attention:[42]

23 4:22 ει μη ινα **1 118 131 205 209 1582 2193 2886** 13] αλλ ινα 22 565 872 1192 1210 2542 NA RP (1278 and 2372 omit this part of the verse.)

39 5:10 εξω της χωρας αυτους αποστειλη **1 118 (131) 205 209 872 1582 2193 2542 2886**] αυτους αποστειλη εξω της χωρας 2 22 28 69 124 157 565 700 788 1071 1192 1210 1346 1424 RP | αποστειλη αυτους εξω της χωρας 1278 2372

96 7:25 αυτω **1 205 209 872 1582 2193 2542 2886** f13 28 543 Arm] προς τους ποδας αυτου 22 118 131 565 1192 1210 NA RP | εις τους ποδας αυτου 1278 2372

Variants 27, 215, and 239.

[39] Codex 1210 carries the Family 1 text without 22 1192 in Family Reading Variants 14, 121, 157, 181, 216, 217, 225, and 240. While the evidence in John leads Welsby ('A Textual Study', pp. 161ff) to find that Codex 1210 is a copy of Codex 22, the investigation of Mark has not thus far provided a compelling case.

[40] Anderson, *Family 1 in Matthew*, pp. 139ff.

[41] Welsby, 'A Textual Study', pp. 167ff..

[42] See also Variants 42, 65, 71, 76, 101, 103, 162, 239, and 245. In addition, attention is drawn to Family 1 readings shared by both 1278 and 2372 (often in agreement with the other group members): 30, 31, 35, 41, 43, 107, 108, 177, 217, 218, 253, 258, 259, and 261. The Full Collation agreements between 1278 and 2372 have not yet been compiled.

Codex 131

Kirsopp Lake found that Codex 131 is a Family 1 member only in Mark 1–5.[43] He found Family 1 affiliation for 131 otherwise only in Luke 1–24. Lake's opinion was that, in these two sections, 131 is an independent witness to the archetype, not descended from Codex 1 nor from the intermediate exemplar behind 118 205 209 2886. Welsby agrees that 131 is 'not a clear Family 1 manuscript' in John, but did find evidence that 131 'may descend from either a very distant Family 1 ancestor or an ancestor that was heavily corrected to the Majority Text.'[44]

The findings of Lake for Mark are supported by the results of the current study, with some nuance. The division of the Family Readings list into three sections demonstrates this nicely:

Mark 1–5: Of 51 readings in Codex 131, 34 are Family 1 and 15 are RP.[45]

Mark 6–10: Of 116 readings, 11 are Family 1 and 96 are RP.[46]

Mark 11–16: Of 95 readings, only 1 is Family 1 and 85 are RP.[47]

Examples of Family 1 agreement in Mark 1–5:[48]

1 1:15 omit **1 131 205 209 1582 2193 2886**] οτι 22 118 565 872 1192 1210 1278 2372 2542 NA RP

8 3:13 ανεβη **1 118 131 205 209 1582 2193** P] αναβαινει 22 565 872 1192 1210 1278 2372 2542 NA RP | αναβας W (2886 does not have verse 13.)

---

[43] Lake, *Codex 1 of the Gospels*, pp. xxxiv–xxxv.

[44] Welsby, 'A Textual Study', pp. 182–3.

[45] Similarly in the Full Collation results compiled thus far Codex 131 agrees with the core family members, including the Venice Group, between 71 and 77% in chapters 1–5.

[46] In the Full Collation of chapters 6–10, Codex 131 agrees with Codex 1 only 36%.

[47] In the Full Collation of chapters 11–16, Codex 131 agrees with Codex 1 only 39%.

[48] See also 4, 6, 9, 10, 14, 21, 25, 29, 31, 32, 34, and 35.

19   4:16 δεχονται **1 118 131 205 209 872 1582 2193 2886**] λαμβανουσιν αυτον 22 1192 1210 1278 2372 2542 NA RP | λαμβανουσιν 565

23   4:22 ει μη ινα **1 118 131 205 209 1582 2193 2886** 13] αλλ ινα 22 565 872 1192 1210 2542 NA RP (1278 and 2372 omit this part of the verse.)

26   4:29 τοτε **1 118 131 205 209 1582 2193 2886**] ευθυς NA | ευθεως 22 565 1192 1210 1278 2372 2542 RP | ευθεως τοτε 872

30   4:37 βυθιζεσθαι **1 22 118 131 205 209 872 1210 1278* 1582 2193 2372 2886** G 33] γεμιζεσθαι 565 1192 1278^C 2542 NA RP

41   5:16 εσωθη ο δαιμονισθεις **1 22 118 131 205 209 872 1192 1210 1278* 1582 2193 2372 2886** 251] εγενετο τω δαιμονιζομενω 565 1278^C 2542 NA RP

After a more broadly attested agreement with Family 1 in 5:23, Codex 131 does not have another Family Reading in Mark 5.

In Mark 6–10, there are a few verses that testify to a possible Family 1 ancestry:[49]

79   6:46 ανηλθεν **1 118* 131 205 209 1582 2193 2886**] απηλθεν 22 118^c 565 872 1192 1210 1278 2372 2542 NA RP

101   8:2 ημερας ηδη τρεις **1 118 131 205 209 872 1582 2193 2886**] ηδη ημεραις τρισιν B | ηδη ημερας τρεις Δ f13 157 565 1192 1278 1424 2372 2542 | ηδη ημεραι τρεις 22 1210 RP

151   10:13 τοις φερουσιν **1 118 131 205 209 872 1582 2193 2886** Θ 1424] τοις προσφερουσιν 22 565 1192 1210 1278 2372 2542 RP | αυτοις ℵ B C L

The only Family 1 reading in the entire third section is shared by a broader tradition:

205   13:9 αχθησεσθε **1 118 131 205 209 872 1278 1582 2193 2886** G U 2 13 33 479 480 517 579 1424] σταθησεσθε 22 1192 1210 1582^{mg} 2372 2542 NA RP | στησεσθε 565

---

[49] See also 87, 90, 125, and 156.

Thus one might surmise, that rather than a switch of exemplar at the end of Mark 5, Codex 131 may descend from an exemplar that was corrected somewhat sporadically at first and then with ever increasing vigour until the corrector was determined to replaced all non-majority readings.

In addition to the somewhat gradual switch from Family 1 to majority text affiliation, Codex 131 varies in the amount of other affiliation. In Mark 1–5, 131 is not in a group with any non-Family 1/non-RP manuscript, but in the other sections this occurs several times. The agreements with other manuscripts in non-Family 1/non-RP readings do not otherwise appear to follow a pattern.

Codex 2542

Until this study of Mark, Codex 2542 had been recognized as a Family 1 member only in Luke 10 and 20.[50] In the investigation of Matthew, 2542 had the distinction of being the most Byzantine of the MSS studied.[51] It is not extant in John. Therefore, this study of Mark is the first to demonstrate that Codex 2542 deserves status as a member of Family 1 in this Gospel. The following variation units from the Family Readings collation are of interest:[52]

63 6:25 ειπεν **1 205 209 565 1582 2193 2542 2886** D Δ Θ 28] ητησατο λεγουσα 22 131 872 1192 1210 1278 2372 NA RP | ειπε θελεγουσα 118 (originally wrote θελω and changed it into θελεγουσα θελω

82 6:49 φαντασμα εδοξαν ειναι **1 205 209 872 1582 2193 2542 2886** W 28] εδοξαν οτι φαντασμα εστιν NA | εδοξαν φαντασμα ειναι 22 118 131 565 1192 1210 1278 2372 RP

97 7:27 *om.* **1 205 209 1582 2193 2542 2886** 28 90] αυτη 22 118 131 565[vid] 872 1192 1210 1278 2372 NA RP

99 7:29 υπαγε δια τουτον τον λογον **1 118 205 209 565 872 1582 2193 2542 2886** (D) 700 Arm] δια τουτον τον λογον υπαγε 22 131 1192 1210 1278 2372 NA RP

---

[50] See the brief discussion in Anderson, *Family 1 in Mark*, pp. 144–5.

[51] Although two variation units hinted at a possible relationship with the 22 Group.

[52] See also variants 10, 36, 38, 66, 96, 103, 110, 119, 138, 149, 172, 180, 197, 198, 199, 239, 241, 252, and 257.

113   8:38 *om.* **1 22 205 209 1582 2193 2542 2886**] των αγιων 118 131 565 872 1192 1210 1278 2372 NA RP

121   9:14 *om.* **1 205 209 1210 1582 2193 2542 2886** W 28 Arm] πολυν 22 118 131 565 872 1192 1278 (2372) NA RP

154   10:20 εποιησα **1 118 205 209 565 872* 1582 2193 2542 2886** Arm] εφυλαξαμην 22 131 872ᶜ 1192 1210 1278 2372 NA RP

171   11:2 λεγων **1 205 209 872 1582 2193 2542 2886** 28] και λεγει αυτοις 22 118 131 565 1192 1210 1278 2372 NA RP | λεγων αυτοις W Θ 13 69 91 346 543 700

183   11:23 αρθηναι και βληθηναι **1 205 209 872* 1582 2193 2542 2886** W 28 124] αρθητι και βληθητι 22 118 131 565 872ᶜ 1192 1210 1278 2372 NA RP

204⁵³ 13:8 *om.* **1 1582 2193 2542** (W)] ταυτα 22 118 131 205 209 (565) 872 1192 1210 1278 2372 2886 NA RP

235   14:54 της αυλης **1 118 205 209 1582 2193 2542 2886** 237] την αυλην 22 131 565 872 1192 1210 1278 2372 NA RP

In the Family Readings list, Codex 2542 had 82 Family Readings, with the frequency appearing to increase in the last third of Mark. In addition, there were 133 RP agreements, 25 readings in which 2542 agreed with other manuscripts in a non-Family 1, non-RP variation, and 19 'singular' readings. The pattern was similar to that of Codex 565 and indeed the two often agreed against all the other family manuscripts.⁵⁴ However, it also frequently occurred that they each had a different 'singular' reading. This will require further investigation.

REMAINING RESEARCH ON FAMILY 1 IN MARK

A number of witnesses not transcribed for this study, but associated with the so-called Caesarean text-type, were listed if they were cited in the

---

⁵³ 1582 has a space after ωδινων with ταυτα written above the space in the first hand. This is connected with the omission of βλεπετε δε υμεισ εαυτουσ in the following verse. 1582mg has that reading. Though 2542 omits after ωδινων, it has ταυτα after λοιμοι, which appears to be an otherwise unknown reading.

⁵⁴ In the Full Collation, 565 and 2452 agreed 65% in chapters 1–5, 62% in chapters 6–10, and 69% in chapters 11–16.

resources used. These include W Θ 28 157 579 700 1424 and Family 13, which was listed as individual manuscripts whenever possible. These manuscripts certainly do show up in agreement with Family 1 frequently, raising the question of a textual tradition that may have affected the readings of manuscripts in a local area. Lake speculated about a

> lost recension which was based on a knowledge of all the early types of text and has been preserved in several late forms, all of which have been mixed with the Antiochian text.[55]

He found that the Family 1 text of Mark differed from the other Gospels in its great number of readings that did not fit into any generally recognized family. It is not clear if by 'family' he means text-type, but he goes on to discuss manuscripts that belong to the loosely grouped Caesarean text. He puzzles over how to explain this situation:

> This connection admits theoretically of two explanations: - (1) some one of the group may represent the original archetype of a lost family, and the variations of the other manuscripts may be due to mixture with different types of text: (2) no one of the group may be a faithful representative of the original text, but all may have suffered mixture with the more ordinary types.

Lake favours the second option, and ongoing research in the so-called Caesarean manuscripts in the years since his results were published would seem to support that idea. Recent work in Family 1 makes clear that there is a group of manuscripts that can be called a family in the Gospels. The core members are being identified with little question, and a number of additional manuscripts are clearly also descendants of the archetype that the core members represent. The question that is more difficult to answer is what to think of manuscripts that contain some readings that are nearly unique to Family 1 but are otherwise statistically not in close agreement. One could add ever more manuscripts to the collation, but in most cases they would not provide more information about the archetype than can be gained from the current choices.

The attainable goal of the current research in Mark is to work on establishing the archetype represented by 1 1582 and now 2193, as well as other close relatives that can be shown to have an independent descent. The marginal readings in 1582 helped to connect the Matthean text of

---

[55] Lake, *Codex 1 of the Gospels*, p. 1.

Family 1 to the text of Origen and thereby to third century Caesarea. This does not prove the existence of a Caesarean text type but it does raise the possibility that the wider, loosely related group of manuscripts has that locale as a source of variant readings.

A few additional manuscripts will need to be tested for Family 1 membership in Mark. Codex 2713, which is a member of the Venice Group in John, will need to be transcribed and collated into both the Family Readings list and the Full Collation. Lake[56] pointed out that Family 1 in Mark has significant support from 22 28 565 700. In the mean time 22 and 565 have been included in Family 1, and a glance at the Family Readings list indicates that perhaps 28 and 700 should be transcribed and collated as well.[57]

The Full Collation results, which are about one-third compiled at the time of writing will be completed relatively quickly, thanks to several research assistants mentioned earlier in this paper. Finally, it is hoped that the current research will result in a family tree of Family 1 in Mark, as has been produced for Matthew and John. The resulting understanding of lineage will allow for the reproduction of the text of the archetype behind Family 1.

APPENDIX: FAMILY 1 READINGS IN MARK

The creation of this list is described in the article above. Family 1 readings are listed first and the members of the family that contain the reading are marked in bold. If the Family 1 reading is not in the text of NA27 and also not in the majority text edition by Robinson-Pierpont (RP), all known witnesses are cited, using NA, Legg, Swanson, and Tischendorf as sources. The variation units are numbered in bold if they were used for compilations. The designation in front of the variant number describes how common the Family 1 reading is, using the following symbols:

X   = Fewer than 5 known witnesses outside of Family 1 have this reading.

●   = Fewer than 10 witnesses of the sixth century or later have this reading.

■   = This reading has broad support in non-RP manuscripts.

---

[56] Lake, *Codex 1 of the Gospels*, pp. 1ff.

[57] In the Münster test passage results, Codex 28 has as its closest relatives Codex 2542 (66.7%) and Codex 209 (65.6%). 1582 and 2193 are 6th and 7th. In the Family Readings lists, variants 10, 29, 32, 46, 55, 56, 63, 82, 93, 95, 97, 100, 103, 110, 115, 120, 121, 134, 136, 138, 141, 171, 186, 190, 196, 197, 198 and 241 demonstrate that 28 and 700 need to be given further attention.

X 1   1:15 omit **1 131 205 209 1582 2193 2886**] οτι 22 118 565 872 1192 1210 1278 2372 2542 NA RP

● 2   1:17 omit **1 118 131 205 209 1582 2193 2886** 13 28 579 700 1071 1424] γενεσθαι 22 565 872 1192 1210 1278 2372 2542 NA RP

■ 3   2:24 οι μαθηται σου **1 118 209 565 1582 2193 2542** D M Θ Σ Φ 13 28 61 69 124 346 472 543 700 1071] οι μαθηται 205 2886 | *om.* 22 131 872 1192 1210 1278 2372 NA RP

X 4   2:27 εκτισθη **1 131 205 209 872* 1582 2193 2886** W 700] εγενετο 22 118 565 872ᶜ 1192 1210 1278 2372 2542 NA RP

■ 5   3:2 παρετηρουντο **1 118 131 205 209 565 1582 2193 2542 2886** A C* D W Δ Θ Σ 074 10 67 238 579 700] παρετηρουν 22 872 1192 1210 1278 2372 NA RP

X 6   3:3 ο ις **1 118 131 205 209 872 1582 2193 2886** 472] *om.* 22 565 1192 1210 1278 2372 2542 NA RP

● 7   3:4 τι (εξεστι) **1 22 118 131 205 209 1192 1210 1582 2193 2372 (2542) 2886** E 16 115 251 271 569 700] *om.* 565 872 1278 NA RP
3:7–8[58]

X 8   3:13 ανεβη **1 118 131 205 209 1582 2193** P] αναβαινει 22 565 872 1192 1210 1278 2372 2542 NA RP | αναβας W (2886 does not have verse 13.)

X 9   3:20 οχλος πολυς **1 118 131 205 209 1582 2193 2886** 61] ο οχλος ℵᶜ A B D Δ Θᶜ 2 67 157 209 252 300 472 476 565 892 2542 | οχλος ℵ* C E F G H K L M W S U V W Γ Θ Π 22 28 157 543 579 700 872 1071 1192 1210 1278 1241 1424 2372 RP (NA includes f1 in this group.)

X 10 3:33[59] απεκριθη αυτοις και λεγει **1 131 205 209 1582 2193 2542 2886** 700] και απεκριθη αυτοις και λεγει 28 69 788 1346 | και αποκριθεις αυτοις λεγει ℵ B C L Δ 61 238 892 1071 | και απεκριθη αυτοις λεγων A D 2 22 118 124 157 1210 1278 1241 1424 2372 RP | απεκριθη αυτοις λεγων 565 872 1192

---

[58] See numerous Family 1 readings in verses 7 and 8. It was difficult to untangle them for use in this list.

[59] Secondary sources were in frequent disagreement on presence or absence of first και.

● **11** 3:34 τους κυκλω περι αυτον **1 118 205 209 872 1582 2193 2542 2886** 13
28 69 124 346 543 700] τους περι αυτον κυκλω NA | κυκλω τους περι
αυτον 22 33 157 565 1192 1210 1278 2372 RP | κυκλω περι αυτον 131

■ **12** 3:34 ιδου **1 118 131 205 209 565 872 1582 2193 2542 2886** A D G K M Y
Δ Π Σ 28 33 543 700] ιδε 22 157 892 1192 1210 1278 2372 NA RP

X **13** 4:1 συνερχεται **1 205 209 872 1582 2193 2886**] συνερχονται 131 |
συναγεται 28 543 700 892 2542 NA | συνηχθη D W 2 22 33 118 157
1192 1210 1278 1424 1071 2372 RP | συνηχθησαν A 565

X **14** 4:1 παρα την θαλασσαν² **1 118 131 205 209 1210 1582 2193 2886**] προς
την θαλασσαν B 22 565 872 1071 1192 1278 1424 2372 2542 RP | περαν
τη θαλασσης D

● **15** 4:5 τα πετρωδη **1 118 131 205 209 565 1582 2193 2886** ℵ* D W Θ 33 517
569 1424] το πετρωδες f13 2 22 28 124 157 543 700 872 892 1071 1192
1210 1278 2372 2542 NA RP

● **16** 4:8 επι την γην **1 118 131 205 209 565 1582 2193 2542 2886** C 28 36 40
106 124 237 259 1424 | εις την γην W Θ f13 2 22 157 872 1071 1192
1210 1278 2372 NA RP

■ **17** 4:11⁶⁰ τα μυστηρια **1 118 131 205 209 872 1582 2193 2886** G Σ Φ 67 106
115 201 235 258 517 569 1424] το μυστηριον W Θ 2 22 28 33 157 579
700 892 1071 1192 1210 1278 2372 2542 NA RP | τον μυστηριον 565

● **18** 4:12 συνωσι **1 118 131 205 209 565 1582 2193 2886** D L W 127 225 569
892 1071 1424] συνιωσιν f13 22 28 33 131 157 543 579 700 872 1192
1210 1278 1582ᶜ 2372 2542 NA RP

X **19** 4:16 δεχονται **1 118 131 205 209 872 1582 2193 2886**] λαμβανουσιν
αυτον 22 1192 1210 1278 2372 2542 NA RP | λαμβανουσιν 565

X **20** 4:20 *om.* **1 118 205 209 1582 2193 2886**] σπαρεντες 22 131 565 872 1192
1210 1278 2372 2542 NA RP

X **21** 4:21 λεγει **1 118 131 205 209 1582 2193 2886** W Arm] ελεγεν 22 565 872
1192 1210 1278 2372 2542 NA RP

---

⁶⁰ The Family 1 reading is within a larger variation unit, where the word order
and wording differ from NA27. RP has the same word order and wording as
Family 1, except for this variation.

● 22   4:22 ει μη ινα **1 131 205 209 565 1582 2193 2886** Θ 13 28 69 543 579 700]
       εαν μη ινα NA | ο εαν μη 2 22 33 118 124 157 1071 1210 1278 1424
       2372 RP | ο ου μη 872 | εαν μη 1192 2542

X 23   4:22 ει μη ινα **1 118 131 205 209 1582 2193 2886** 13] αλλ ινα 22 565 872
       1192 1210 2542 NA RP (1278 and 2372 omit this part of the verse.)

X 24   4:24 λεγει **1 118 205 209 1582 2886** 7 244] ελεγεν 22 131 565 872 1192
       1210 1278 2193 2372 2542 NA RP

X 25   4:26 την γην **1 118 131 205 209 1582 2193 2886** W 579] της γης 22 565
       872 1192 1210 1278 2372 2542 NA RP

X 26   4:29 τοτε **1 118 131 205 209 1582 2193 2886**] ευθυς NA | ευθεως 22 565
       1192 1210 1278 2372 2542 RP | ευθεως τοτε 872

X 27   4:30 ομοιωσομεν **1 205 209 872 1192 1582 2193 2372 2542 2886** 2^C 1278^C
       ] ομοιωσωμεν 22 131 565 1210 1278* NA RP | ομοιωματι 118^61

■ 28   4:33 *om.* **1 118 131 205 209 1582 2193 2542 2886** C* L S W Θ Σ 28 33 579
       700 788 892 1424 Arm] πολλαις 22 157 565 872 1071 1192 1210 1278
       2372 NA RP

X 29   4:36^62 τα αλλα τα οντα μετ αυτου πλοια **1 118 131 205 209 1582 2193**
       2886 28] αλλα πλοια ην μετ αυτου B C* 157 579 788 892 | αλλα δε
       πλοια ην μετ αυτου 2542 | αλλα δε πλοιαρια ην μετ αυτου 2 22 124
       1192 1210 1278 2372 RP | τα αλλα τα οντα πλοια μετ αυτου 565 |
       αλλα δε πλοιαρια ην τα μετ αυτου 872

X 30   4:37 βυθιζεσθαι **1 22 118 131 205 209 872 1210 1278*** 1582 2193 2372
       2886 G 33] γεμιζεσθαι 565 1192 1278^C 2542 NA RP

X 31   4:38 προσκεφαλαιου **1 22 118 131 205 209 565 1192 1210 1278 1582 2193**
       2372 2886 D W Θ 1424] προσκεφαλαιον 872 2542 NA RP

X 32   4:39 και τη θαλασση και ειπεν **1 118 131 205 209 565 1582 2193 2886** D
       W 700] και ειπεν τη θαλασση 22 1192 1210 1278 2372 2542 NA RP |
       και τη θαλασση ειπεν 872

---

⁶¹ The variation in 118 appears to be due to haplography. 118 has skipped ahead to the Family 1 reading in the second half of the verse. Because the formatting of 209 could be the source for the situation in 118, it would remain to explore the possibility that 209 could be the exemplar for 118.

⁶² There are half a dozen other variants in wording and order.

■ 33   4:41[63] οι ανεμοι **1 118 131 205 209 565 1582 2193 2542 2886** ℵ* D W E Θ
Φ 31 33 38 157 179 229 235 238 271 435 472 517 700 1071 1424] ο
ανεμος 22 872 1192 1210 1278 2372 NA RP

X 34   5:3 ετι **1 118 131 205 209 1582 2193 2886** 517 1424] *om.* 22 565 872 1192
1210 1278 2372 2542 NA RP (This could be described as ουδεις ετι vs
ουκετι ουδεις.)

X 35   5:4[64] πολλας πεδας και αλυσεις αις εδησαν αυτον διεσπακεναι και
συντετριφεναι **1 22 118 131 205 (209)** 1192 1210 **(1278) 1582 2193 2372
2886** (128) 251 697] πολλακις πεδαις και αλυσεσιν δεδεσθαι και
διεσπασθαι υπ αυτου τας αλυσεις και τας πεδας συντετριφθαι NA RP |
πολλακις αυτον πεδες και αλυσεσιν αις εδησαν διεσπακεναι και τας
πεδας συντετριφεναι 565 | αυτον πολλας πεδες και αλυσεις αις εδησαν
διεσπακεναι και τας συντετριφεναι 2542 | πολλας πεδας και αλυσεσι
δεδεσθαι και διεσπασθαι υπ αυτου τας αλυσεις και τας πεδας
συντετριφθαι 872

● 36   5:5 μνημειοις **1 118 131 205 209 565 1582 2193 2542 2886** D W 28 69 124
225 346 543] μνημασιν 22 872 1192 1210 1278 2372 NA RP

● 37   5:7 *om.* **1 118 205 209 872 1582 2193 2886** 33 84 86 238 349 446 700] ιυ 22
131 1192 1210 1278 2372 2542 NA RP (565 not readable)

● 38   5:10 παρεκαλουν (**1 118 209 2886** have παρακαλουν) **1 22 118 131 205
565**[vid] **1192 1210 1582 2193 2542** A Δ Θ 074 28 37 75 225 245] παρεκαλει
872 1278 2372 NA RP

X 39   5:10 εξω της χωρας αυτους αποστειλη **1 118 (131) 205 209 872 1582 2193
2542 2886**] αυτους αποστειλη εξω της χωρας 2 22 28 69 124 157 565 700
788 1071 1192 1210 1346 1424 RP | αποστειλη αυτους εξω της χωρας
1278 2372

X 40   5:11 *om.* **1 872 1582 2193** 33[vid]] προς τω ορει 22 118 131 205 209 565 1192
1210 1278 2372 2542 2886 NA RP

X 41   5:16 εσωθη ο δαιμονισθεις **1 22 118 131 205 209 872 1192 1210 1278*** 1582
2193 2372 2886** 251] εγενετο τω δαιμονιζομενω 565 1278[C] 2542 NA RP

● 42   5:23 (επιθης τας χειρασ) αυτω **1** (The ligature in Codex 1 is uncertain.)
(22) 118 (131) 205 209 (1192 1210) 1582 2193 2886 p45 A D S 2 31 121 244

---

[63] This is part of a larger word order variation unit.
[64] There are a variety of other readings.

435] αυτη 131 209 872 (1278 2372) 2542 NA RP | επ αυτη 565 (check this one for relationship between 22 and 1192 and between 1278 and 2372)

X   43   5:27 *om.* **1 22 118 205 209 1210 1278 1582 2193 2372 2886** 238 251 697] εν τω οχλω 131 872 1192 NA RP (565 not readable) | εις τον οχλον 2542

●   44   5:27 του κρασπεδου **1 118 205 209 565**[vid] **1582 2193 2886** M 33 579 1071 1588] *om.* 22 131 872 1192 1210 1278 2372 2542 NA RP

●   45   5:28 εν εαυτη **1 118 205 209 565 872 1582 2193 2886** D K Θ Π 33 700 1424] *om.* 22 131 1192 1210 1278 2372 2542 NA RP

X   46   5:32 πεποιηκυιαν **1 205 209 872 1582 2193 2886** W Θ 28] ποιησασαν 22 118 131 565 1192 1210 1278 2372 2542 NA RP

X   47   5:33 αιτιαν **1 1582** 28] αιτιαν αυτης W 13 69 346 543 1346 2542 | αληθειαν 22 118 131 205 209 565 872 1192 1210 1278 2193 2372 2886 RP

X   48   5:34 ο δε ις ειπεν **1 205 209 1582 2193 2886**] ο δε ειπεν αυτη 22 131 1192 1210 1278 2372 NA RP | ο δε ις ειπεν αυτη C D Θ Φ 13 28 69 118 124 234 235 238 271 543 565 700 872 2542

■   49   5:37 (τον αδελφον) αυτου **1 118 205 209 565 1582 2193 2886** D G Δ Φ 36 61 106 348 489] ιακωβου 22 131 872 1192 1210 1278 2372 2542 NA RP

X   50   5:39 *om.* **1 565 1582 2193**] εισελθων 22 118 131 205 209 872 1192 1210 1278 2372 2542 (2886) NA RP

X   51   5:42 ως ετων δεκαδυο **1 118 205 209 1582 2193 2886**] ετων δωδεκα 22 131 1192 1210 1278 2372 2542 NA RP | ωσ(ει) ετων δωδεκα ℵ C Δ Θ 33 124 238 565 579 700 788 | ετων δεκαδυο 872

●   52   6:4 ελεγεν δε ο ις **1 1582 2193** W f13 28 543] και ελεγεν αυτοις ο ιησους 565 NA | ελεγεν δε αυτοις ο ιησους 22 118 131 205 209 1192 1278 2372 2886 RP | ελεγεν δε ο ις αυτοις 872 | ελε δε αυτοις ο ις 1210 | ελεγε δε αυτοις 2542

X   53   6:11 ακουση τους λογους **1 205 209 1582 2193 2886** | ακουσωσιν 22 118 131 1192 1210 1278 2372 NA RP (565 not readable)] ακουσησωσιν 872 | ακουσας 2542

X   54   6:11 τον κονιορτον εκτιναξατε **1 118 205 209 872 1582 2193 2886** (33) 188] εκτιναξατε τον χουν 22 131 1192 1210 1278 (2372) 2542 NA RP (565 not readable)

X   55   6:15 *om.* **1 118 (131) 205 209 565 1582 2193 2886** ℵ Θ 28 700 1424 Arm] ελεγον[2] 22 872 1192 1210 1278 2372 2542 NA RP

X 56 6:16 ουτος εστιν ιωαννης αυτος **1 565 1582 2193** Θ 700] ιωαννην ουτος
ℵ² B L W Δ 28 69 543 892 | ιωαννην ουτος εστιν αυτος 22 118 131 205
209 872 1192 1210 1278 2372 2542 2886 RP

X 57 6:18 την γυναικα εχειν **1 118 205 209 872 1582 2193 (2886)**] εχειν την
γυναικα 22 565 1192 1210 1278 2372 2542 NA RP | εχειν γυναικα 131

X 58 6:20 *om.* **1 205 209 1582 2193 2886** 111 119 485] και αγιον 22 118 131 872
1192 1210 1278 2372 2542 NA RP (565 not readable)

X 59 6:22 *om.* **1 205 209 565 1582 2193 2886** C D Δ 238] εαν 22 118 131 872
1192 1210 1278 2372 2542 NA RP

● 60 6:22 θελεις **1 118 131 205 209 565 1582 2193 2886** D H L N 188 238 244
253 1424] θελης 22 872 1192 1210 1278 2372 2542 NA RP

X 61 6:23[65] εως ημισους της βασιλειας μου και ωμοσεν αυτη **1 1582 1278***
2193] εως ημισους της βασιλειας μου 22 118 131 872 1210 | και ωμοσεν
αυτη οτι εαν με αιτησης δωσω σοι εως ημισους της βασιλειας μου RP |
και ωμοσεν αυτη 205 209 2886 | και ωμοσεν αυτη πολλα οτι ο αν μοι
αιτησης δωσω σοι και το ημισους της βασιλειας 565 | και ωμοσεν αυτη
οτι ο εαν αιτησης με δωσω σοι εως ημισους της βασιλειας μου 1192 |
και ωμοσεν αυτη οτι ο εαν με αιτησης δωσω σοι 2372 | και ωμοσεν
αυτη οτι ο εαν με αιτησης δωσω σοι εως ημισους της βασιλειας μου
2542

X 62 6:25 *om.* **1 205 209 1582 2193 2886** D L 489 892 1424] ευθυς ℵ B C N W Δ
Θ Σ p45 28 33 565 700 2542 NA | ευθεως A 22 118 131 157 543 579 872
1071 1192 1210 1278 2372 RP

X 63 6:25 ειπεν **1 205 209 565 1582 2193 2542 2886** D Δ Θ 28] ητησατο
λεγουσα 22 131 872 1192 1210 1278 2372 NA RP | ειπε θελεγουσα 118
(originally wrote θελω and changed it into θελεγουσα θελω

● 64 6:26 ηθελεν **1 22 209 1192 1278*** **1582 2193 2372 2886** Π 17 258 271 435
697 (1071)] ηθελησεν 118 131 565 872 1210 2542 NA RP | εθελεν 205

X 65 6:27 απολυσας **1 205 209 1582 2886**] αποστειλας D W 22 28 118 251 470
565 697 700 872 1192 1210 1278 2372 2542 | αποστειλας ο βασιλευς 131
2193 NA RP

---

[65] Most manuscripts read a slight variation on the RP wording and word order,
as does NA27.

● **66**   6:28 *om.* **1 118 205 209 1582 2193 2542 2886** L W Δ 487 892] αυτην[1] 22
131 565 872 1192 1210 1278 2372 NA RP

X **67**   6:33[66] ιδοντες **1 118 205 209 872 1582 2193 2886**] ειδον 22 131 1192 1210
1278 2372 2542 NA RP | ιδων 565

X **68**   6:33 εγνωσαν **1 118 205 209 872 1582 2193 2886**] και επεγνωσαν αυτον
22 565 1192 1210 (1278) 2372 RP | και επεγνωσαν αυτους ℵ A K L M N
U Δ Π 33 579 1424 | και επεγνωσαν 131 2542 | και εγνωσαν B* D W Θ

X **69**   6:33[67] και ηλθον εκει **1 1582 2193**vid 240 244] εκει και προηλθον 22 118
872 (1192) 1210 1278 2372 RP | εκει και προσηλθον 131 | *om.* W 205 209
2886 | και ηλθον 565 | και ηλθον προς αυτον 2542

● **70**   6:35 *om.* **1 205 209 872 1582 2193 2542 2886** W 13 28 69 261 282 346 543
1071 Arm] αυτου 22 118 131 565 1192 1210 1278 2372 NA RP

X **71**   6:35 η ωρα ηδη **1 118 205 209 872 1582 2193 2886** 569] ηδη ωρα 131 565
1192 1210 (1278) 2372 2542 | ηδη ωρας 22 NA RP

X **72**   6:36 τας κυκλω κωμας και αγρους καταλυσωσι **1 209 872 1582 2193**]
τους κυκλω αγρους και κωμας καταλυσωσιν 22 | τους κυκλω αγρους
και κωμας αγορασωσιν 118 131 205 209 1192 1210 1278 2372 NA RP |
τους κυκλω αγρους και κωμας αρτους αγορασωσιν 565 | τας κυκλω
κωμας και αγρους αγορασωσιν 2886 | τας κυκλω αγρους και κωμας
αγορασωσιν 2542

X **73**   6:37 *om.* **1 205 209 1582 2193 2886**] αυτω 22 118 131 565 872 1192 1210
1278 2372 2542 NA RP

X **74**   6:38 *om.* **1 205 209 1582 2193 2886** 59 Arm] και (γνοντεσ) 22 118 131 565
872 1192 1210 1278 2372 2542 NA RP

X **75**   6:42 και εχορτασθησαν παντες **1 205 209 1582 2193 2886** 579] παντες
και εχορτασθησαν 22 118 131 565 1192 1210 1278 2372 NA RP | και
εχορτασθησαν 872 2542

X **76**   6:43 δωδεκα κοφινων πληρωματα **1 205 209 872* 1582 2193 2886**]
κλασματα δωδεκα κοφινων πληρωματα 2542 NA | κλασματων
δωδεκα κοφινων πληρεις 118 RP | κλασματων δωδεκα κοφινους
πληρεις 22 118 131 565 872c (1192 appears to have πληροισ) 1210 1278
2372

---

[66] There are several other variants.
[67] There are several other variants.

● 77 6:45 (προαγειν) αυτον **1 118 205 209 565 1582 2193 2542 2886** D N Θ Σ Φ
13 28 32 40 69 220 435 472 543 700 1346 Arm] *om.* 22 131 872 1192 1210
1278 2372 NA RP

● 78 6:45 τους οχλους **1 565 1582 2193 2886** 20 40 69 247 700 1071] τον
οχλον 22 118 131 205 209 872 1192 1210 1278 2372 2542 NA RP

X 79 6:46 ανηλθεν **1 118* 131 205 209 1582 2193 2886**] απηλθεν 22 118ᶜ 565
872 1192 1210 1278 2372 2542 NA RP

X 80 6:48 *om.* **1 205 209 565 1582 2193 2886**] αυτοις 22 118 131 872 1192 1210
1278 2372 2542 NA RP

X 81 6:48 επι της θαλασσης περιπατων **1 205 209 872 1582 2193 2886**]
περιπατων επι της θαλασσης 22 118 131 565 1192 1210 1278 2372 2542
NA RP

X 82 6:49 φαντασμα εδοξαν ειναι **1 205 209 872 1582 2193 2542 2886** W 28]
εδοξαν οτι φαντασμα εστιν NA | εδοξαν φαντασμα ειναι 22 118 131
565 1192 1210 1278 2372 RP

X 83 6:51 εξεπλησσοντο **1 118 205 209 872 1582 2193 2886**] εξισταντο ℵ B L Δ
28 892 | εξισταντο και εθαυμαζον 22 131 565 1192 1210 1278 2372 2542
RP

● 84 6:54 οι ανδρες του τοπου εκεινου **1 118 205 209 872 1582 2193 2886** A G
Δ 13 33 472 1071 Arm] οι ανδρες του τοπου W Θ Φ 28 32 38 40 61 69
121 238 282 435 543 565 700 1346 | *om.* 22 131 1192 1210 1278 2372 2542
NA RP

X 85 6:55 και εκπεριδραμοντες **1 1582 2193**] και περιδραμοντες 118 205 209
565 700 2886 | περιεδραμον NA | περιδραμοντες 22 131 872 1192 1210
1278 2372 2542 RP

● 86 6:55 φερειν **1 118 205 209 565 1582 2193 2886** M Θ 32 38 435 472]
περιφερειν 22 131 872 1192 1210 1278 2372 2542 RP

X 87 6:56 οποτ αν **1 118 131 205 209 1582 2193 2886** W] οπου αν 22 118ᶜ 872
1192 1210 1278 2372 2542 NA RP | οταν 565

X 88 6:56 ασθενεις **1 205 209 1582 2193 2886**] ασθενουντας 22 118 131 565
872 1192 1210 1278 2372 2542 NA RP

● 89 6:56 διεσωζοντο **1 205 209 1582 2193 2886** N Σ 69 271 543 700]
εσωζοντο 22 118 131 872 1192 1210 1278 2372 2542 NA RP
(565 not readable)

X 90 7:6 ειπεν[2] **1 118 131 205 209 565 1582 2193 2886** D Θ Arm] γεγραπται
(οτι) 22 872 1192 1210 1278 2372 2542 NA RP

X 91   7:13 την εντολην **1 118 205 209 872 1582 2193 2886** (W)] τον λογον 22
        131 565 1192 1210 1278 2372 2542 NA RP

● 92   7:17 επηρωτησαν **1 205 209 1582 2193 2886** Θ 33 56 60 579 Arm]
        επηρωτων 22 (118) 131 565 872 1192 1210 1278 2372 2542 NA RP

X 93   7:18 ελεγεν **1 118 205 209 1582 2193 2886** 28] λεγει 22 131 565 872 1192
        1210 1278 2372 2542 NA RP

X 94   7:21 *om.* **1 118 205 209 1582 2193 2886**] των ανθρωπων 22 131 565 872
        1192 1210 1278 2372 2542 NA RP

X 95   7:23 *om.* **1 205 209 565 1582 2193 2886** 700] τα πονηρα 22 (118) 131 872
        1192 1210 1278 2372 2542 NA RP

● 96   7:25 αυτω **1 205 209 872 1582 2193 2542 2886** f13 28 543 Arm] προς τους
        ποδας αυτου 22 118 131 565 1192 1210 NA RP | εις τους ποδας αυτου
        1278 2372

X 97   7:27 *om.* **1 205 209 1582 2193 2542 2886** 28 90] αυτη 22 118 131 565[vid] 872
        1192 1210 1278 2372 NA RP

● 98   7:28 λεγουσα **1 118 205 209 565 1582 2193 2542 2886** p45 D W Θ 28 69
        700] λεγει αυτω 22 131 872 1192 1210 1278 2372 NA RP

X 99   7:29 υπαγε δια τουτον τον λογον **1 118 205 209 565 872 1582 2193 2542
        2886** (D) 700 Arm] δια τουτον τον λογον υπαγε 22 131 1192 1210 1278
        2372 NA RP

X 100 7:37 υπερεκπερισσως **1 118 205 209 1582 2193 2886** D U 435 700]
        υπερπερισσως 22 131 565 872 1192 1210 1278 2372 2542 NA RP

X 101 8:2 ημερας ηδη τρεις **1 118 131 205 209 872 1582 2193 2886**] ηδη ημεραις
        τρισιν B | ηδη ημερας τρεις Δ f13 157 565 1192 1278 1424 2372 2542 |
        ηδη ημεραι τρεις 22 1210 RP

X 102 8:6 την γην **1 118 205 209 1582 2193 2886** 33 579 1424] της γης 22 118
        131 565 872 1192 1210 1278 2372 2542 NA RP

X 103 8:10 εμβας ευθυς **1 118 205 209 1582 2193 2542 2886** W f13 28] εμβας
        ευθεως A K M N U Π 124 872 1071 1278 1424 2372 | ευθυς εμβας NA |
        ευθεως εμβας 22 131 1192 1210 RP | ευθεως ανεβη 565

● 104 8:15 απο[2] **1 118 205 209 1582 2193 2886** G W Δ 28 124 482 Arm] *om.* 22
        131 565 872 1192 1210 1278 2372 2542 NA RP

X 105 8:17 *om.* **1 205 209 1582 2193 2886**] ουδε συνιετε ετι 22 118 131 872 1192
        1210 1278 2372 RP | ουδε συνιετε ℵ C D L W 28 33 124 579 788 2542 |
        ουδε μνημονευετε Θ 565

X   106   8:21 ειπεν **1 118 205 209 872 1582 2193 2886**] ελεγεν 22 131 1192 1210
1278 NA RP | λεγει 565 2372 2542

■   107   8:22 βηθσαιδα **1 118 205 209 1278 1582 2193 2372 2542 2886** C N Δ Σ 28
33 46 69 90 157 349 478 482 517 579 697] βηθσαιδαν 131 565 1192 1210
NA RP | βηθσαιδαμ 22 | βεθσαιδα 872

●   108   8:24 *om.* **1 22 118 205 209 565 1192 1210 1278 1582 2193 2372 2542 2886** D
W Θ 28 700 788 1071 1424] οτι 131 872 NA RP

■   109   8:24 *om.* **1 22 118 205 209 1192 1210 1278 1582 2193 2372 2542 2886** D W Θ
28 225 248 349 472 517 565 700 788 892 1071 1424] ορω 131 565 872 NA
RP

X   110   8:29 λεγει αυτοις **1 118 205 209 1582 2193 2542 2886** W Θ 28 788] και
αυτος λεγει αυτοις 22 131 872 1192 1210 1278 2372 RP | και αυτος
επηρωτα αυτους NA | αυτος δε επηρωτα αυτους 565

●   111   8:31 τη τριτη ημερα **1 118 205 209 565 872 1582 2193 2542 2886** W 13 28
33 69 124 543 579 1342 Arm] μετα τρεις ημερας 22 131 1192 1210 1278
2372 NA RP

X   112   8:34 μου **1 1582**] μοι 22 118 131 205 209 565 872 1192 1210 1278 2193
2372 2542 2886 NA RP

X   113   8:38 *om.* **1 22 205 209 1582 2193 2542 2886**] των αγιων 118 131 565 872
1192 1210 1278 2372 NA RP

X   114   9:3 *om.* **1 205 209 1582 2193 2886** 346 1346] στιλβοντα 22 118 131 565
872 1192 1210 1278 2372 2542 NA RP

X   115   9:4 συνελαλουν **1 205 209 565 872 1582 2193 2886** D Θ 700 Arm]
συλλαλουντες 22 118 131 1192 1210 1278 2372 2542 NA RP

●   116   9:5 ελεγεν **1 205 209 872 1582 2193 2542 2886** 13 28 69 124 346 543 788]
λεγει 22 118 131 1192 1210 1278 2372 NA RP | ειπεν D Θ 565 700 892

X   117   9:9 διεστελλετο **1 209 1582 2193**[vid] C] διεστελετο **205 2886** | διεστειλατο
22 118 131 565 872 1192 1210 1278 2372 2542 NA RP

■   118   9:11 επηρωτησαν **1 118**[mg] **205 209 1582 2193 2542 2886** A 13 28 33 69 90
124 483 484 506 543 579 788 Arm | επηρωτων 22 118 131 565 872 1192
1210 1278 2372 NA RP

X   119   9:11 *om.* **1 118 205 209 872 1582 2193 2542 2886** D 46 52 60 108] οτι[2] 22
131 1192 1210 1278 2372 NA RP
(565 has an entirely unrelated variation.)

X 120   9:13[68] ηλιας ηδη ηλθεν **1 118^mg 205 209 1582 2193 2886** 700] και ηλιας
ηδη εληλυθεν 22 1192 1210 1278 2372 | και ηλιας εληλυθεν 131 NA RP
| ηλιας εληλυθε 118 565 872 | ηλιας ηλθε 2542

X 121   9:14 *om.* **1 205 209 1210 1582 2193 2542 2886** W 28 Arm] πολυν 22 118
131 565 872 1192 1278 (2372) NA RP

● 122   9:19 και (αποκριθεισ) **1 118 205 209 565 1582 2193 2542 2886** p45^vid D W
Θ 13 28 69 472 543 569 Arm] ο δε (αποκριθεισ) 22 131 872 1192 1210
1278 2372 NA RP

● 123   9:21 (επηρωτησεν) ο ις **1 118 205 209 (565) 872 1582 2193 (2542) 2886** Φ
28 59 124 517 569 1424] *om.* 22 131 1192 1210 1278 2372 NA RP

■ 124   9:21 παιδοθεν **1 118 205 209 1582 2193 2542 2886** E N W Σ 069 2 33 238
474 517 892 1424] παιδιοθεν 22 131 872 1192 1210 1278 2372 NA RP |
παιδος D Θ 565

X 125   9:22 εβαλλεν **1 118 131 205 209 872 1582 2886** 157 330 474] εβαλεν 22
2193 565 1192 1210 1278 2372 2542 NA RP

X 126   9:22 αυτον απολεση **1 118 205 209 565 872 1582 2193 2886** D 067 517
1424] απολεση αυτον 22 131 565 1192 1210 1278 2372 2542 NA RP

X 127   9:24 του παιδος **1 118 205 209 1582 2193 2886**] του παιδιου 22 131 565
872 1192 1210 1278 2372 2542 NA RP

X 128   9:25 (οχλοσ) πολυς **1 118 205 209 872 1582 2193 2886**] *om.* 22 131 565
1192 1210 1278 2372 2542 NA RP

X 129   9:26 κραξαν πολλα και **1 118 205 209 565 1582 2193 2886** Φ] κραξας και
πολλα NA | κραξαν και πολλα 22 131 872 1192 1210 1278 2372 RP |
και κραξαν πολλα 2542

X 130   9:28 ηρωτων **1 205 209 1582 2193 2886** D] επηρωτων 22 118 131 565
872 1192 1210 1278 2372 NA RP | ηρωτησαν 2542

● 131   9:31 εγερθησεται **1 872 1582 2193** 13 69 346 474 543] αναστησεται 22
118 205 209 565 1192 1210 1278 2372 2886 NA RP | αναστησετε 131 |
εγειρεται 2542

● 132   9:32 ερωτησαι **1 205 209 565 1582 2193 2886** W 13 69 346 424 788 1346]
επερωτησαι 22 118 131 872 1192 1210 1278 2372 2542 NA RP

---

[68] There are a variety of other combinations.

X 133 9:33 διελεχθητε **1 205 209 872 1582 2886** W 28 788 (**2193** has διηλεχθητε)
] διελογιζεσθε 22 118 131 565 1192 1210 1278 2372 NA RP |
διελλεγχθητε 2542

X 134 9:34 διηνεχθησαν **1 565 1582 2193** Θ 700] διελεχθησαν 22 118 131 205
209 872 1210 1278 2372 2886 NA RP | διηλεχθησαν 1192 |
διελλεγχθησαν 2542

X 135 9:35 *om.* **1 205 209 1582 2193 2886** (D) 63 253 349] εσχατος και παντων
22 118ᶜ 131ᵛⁱᵈ 872 1192 1210 1278 2372 2542 NA RP | παντων 118 |
εσχατος και 565

X 136 9:36 *om.* **1 118 205 209 565 1582 2193 2886** W Θ 28 Arm] αυτο (after
εστησεν) 22 131 872 1192 1210 1278 2372 2542 NA RP

X 137 9:36 λεγει **1 118 205 209 872 1582 2193 2886**] ειπεν 22 565 1192 1210
1278 2372 2542 NA RP (131 not readable)

X 138 9:38 και λεγει **1 205 209 1582 2193 2542 2886** 28] *om.* NA | λεγων 22 118
131 872 1192 1210 1278 2372 RP | λεγει 565

X 139 9:38 *om.* **1 205 209 1582 2193 2886**] διδασκαλε 22 118 131 565 872 1192
1210 1278 2372 2542 NA RP

   140 9:39 δυνησεται με κακολογησαι | omit ταχυ and με after κακολογησαι **1
205 209 565 2193 2542 2886**] δυνησεται ταχυ κακολογησαι με 22 118
131 1192 1210 1278 2372 | δυνησεται με ταχυ κακολογησαι με 872*
1582 has a space not quite big enough for ταχυ, and the word written
above the line – I think in the first hand. The presence of the word would
therefore be a first hand correction.

X 141 9:43 *om.* **1 118 205 209 872 1582 2193 2886** W 28 435 788] εις την γεενναν
22 131 565 1192 1210 1278 2372 2542 NA RP

X 142 9:48 τελευτησει **1 205 209 1582 2193 2886**] τελευτα 22 118 131 565 872
1192 1210 1278 2372 2542 NA RP

● 143 9:50 *om.* **1 118 205 209 1582 2193 2886** M 206 232 255 299 474 517 1424]
αυτο 22 131 565 872 1192 1210 1278 2372 2542 NA RP

● 144 9:50 αρτυθησεται **1 118 209 1582 2193 2886** K 14 91 206 255 299 474]
αρτυσετε 22 131 565 872 1192 1210 1278 2372 2542 NA RP | *om.* 205

● 145 10:1 συμπορευεται **1 118 205 209 1582 2193 2542 2886** W 13 28 69 91 299
433 543] συμπορευονται 22 131 872 1192 1210 1278 2372 NA RP |
συνερχονται 565

X 146 10:1 οχλος πολυς **1 118 205 209 1582 2193 2886** 91 299] οχλοι 22 131
1192 1210 1278 2372 NA RP | ο οχλος 565 | οχλος 872 2542

X 147   10:4 μωυσης ενετειλατο **1 118 (205 2886** spell it μωσησ**) 209 872 1582 2193** 299 472] επετρεψεν μωυσης ℵ B D Δ Ψ 579 | μωυσης επετρεψεν (22 1192 1210 1278 2372 spell it μωσης) 2542 RP | *om.* 131 (565 not readable)

● **148**   10:7 τη γυναικι **1 118 131 205 209 1582 2193 2886** A L N Δ Σ 67 91 579 1342] *om.* ℵ B Ψ | προς την γυναικα 22 565 872 1192 1210 1278 2372 2542 RP

X 149   10:11 γυνη τον ανδρα αυτης και γαμηση αλλον **1 205 209 1582 2193 (2542** has εαυτησ**) 2886** W] την γυναικα αυτου και γαμηση αλλην 22 118 (131) 565 1192 1210 1278 2372 NA RP | γυνη τον ανδρα αυτης και γαμηθη αλλω 872

    150   10:12[69] ανηρ απολυση την γυναικα αυτου και γαμηση αλλην 872 2193 (2542 has εαυτης) (205 209 2886 omit the verse.)

X 151   10:13 τοις φερουσιν **1 118 131 205 209 872 1582 2193 2886** Θ 1424] τοις προσφερουσιν 22 565 1192 1210 1278 2372 2542 RP | αυτοις ℵ B C L

X 152   10:19 *om.* **1 118 205 209 1582 2193 2886** (D) Γ 300 330] μη φονευσης 22 (131) 565 872 1192 1210 1278 2372 2542 NA RP

● **153**   10:20 *om.* **1 118 205 209 872 1582 2193 2542 2886** Κ Π 11 68 114 229 253 1342] διδασκαλε 22 131 565 1192 1210 1278 2372 NA RP

X 154   10:20 εποιησα **1 118 205 209 565 872* 1582 2193 2542 2886** Arm] εφυλαξαμην 22 131 872ᶜ 1192 1210 1278 2372 NA RP

■ **155**   10:21 αρας τον στρον **1 22 118 131 205 209 872 1192 1210 1278 1582 (2193** W 13 69 124 238 346 543 1346 add σου**) 2372 2542 2886** G N 28 299 Arm] *om.* 565 NA RP

X 156   10:24 (μαθηται) αυτου **1 118 131 205 209 565 872 1582 2193 2886** D Δ Θ 91 474 | *om.* 22 1192 1210 1278 2372 2542 NA RP

● **157**   10:24 τεκνια **1 118 205 209 1210 1582 2193 2886** A N Ψ 50 91 299 300 405 700] τεκνα 22 131 565 1192 1278 2372 2542 NA RP | *om.* 872

X 158   10:25 εις την βασιλειαν του θυ πλουσιον **1 872 1582 2193** W 299] πλουσιον εις την βασιλειαν του θυ 22 118 131 205 209 565 1192 1210 1278 2372 2542 2886 NA RP

---

[69] This variation unit was too complex to use as a Family Reading variation unit. However, the groupings listed above provide hints of relationship between manuscripts.

X 159 10:28 αυτω λεγειν ο πετρος **1 872 1582 2193** W 124] λεγειν ο πετρος αυτω NA | ο πετρος λεγειν αυτω 22 118 131 205 209 1192 1210 1278 2372 2886 RP | λεγειν αυτω ο πετρος 565 2542

X 160 10:29 (εμου) η **1 118 205 209 565 1582 2193 2886** D Θ Arm] και 22 131 872 1192 1210 1278 2372 2542 NA RP

X 161 10:30 απολαβη **1 205 209 1582 2193 2886** ℵ] λαβη 22 118 131 565 872 1192 1210 1278 2372 2542 NA RP

■ 162 10:30 και πρα και μρα **1 118 205 209 872 1582 2193 2542 2886** ℵ² K M N X Π 92 220 234 237 517 575 579 892 1278ᶜ] και μητερας B (A C D W Θ) 22 131 1192 RP | και μρα 565 1210 1278* 2372

X 163 10:35 σε ερωτησωμεν **1 565 1582 2193** D Θ] αιτησωμεν 22 131 1192 1210 2542 RP | αιτησωμεν σε B C L Δ Ψ | σε αιτησωμεν Y K N Π 28 69 118 205 209 579 872 1278* 2372 2886

X 164 10:37 *om.* **1 205 209 1582 2193 2886** (579 omits second occurrence)] retain both occurrences of εις 22 118 131 565 872 1192 1210 1278 2372 2542 NA RP

■ 165 10:38 αποκριθεις **1 205 209 565 872 1582 2193 2542 2886** D W Θ 13 28 69 91 124 346 543 788] *om.* 22 118 131 1192 1210 1278 2372 NA RP

X 166 10:41 *om.* **1 118 205 209 1582 2193 2886** 579] ηρξαντο 22 131 565 872 1192 1210 1278 2372 2542 NA RP

X 167 10:41 ηγανακτησαν **1 118 205 209 1582 2193 2886** A 579] αγανακτειν 22 131 (565) 872 1192 1210 1278 2372 2542 NA RP

X 168 10:48 ο υιος **1 118 205 209 872 1582 2193 2886** (D F 28 124)] υιε 22 131 565 1192 1210 1278 2372 NA RP (2542 omits this verse.)

X 169 10:49 θαρσων εγειρου **1 118 205 209 1582 2193 2886** 13 69 346 1346] θαρσει εγειρε 1278* NA | θαρσει εγειραι 22 131 872* 1192 1210 1278ᶜ 2372 2542 RP | θαρσει και εγειρε 565 872ᶜ

● 170 11:1 απεστειλε **1 205 209 1582 2193 2886** F H 20 46 91 125] αποστελλει 22 118 (131) 565 872 1192 1210 1278 2372 2542 NA RP

X 171 11:2 λεγων **1 205 209 872 1582 2193 2542 2886** 28] και λεγει αυτοις 22 118 131 565 1192 1210 1278 2372 NA RP | λεγων αυτοις W Θ 13 69 91 346 543 700

X 172 11:3 *om.* **1 118 205 209 1582 2193 2542 2886** W 91 299 1542] ποιειτε τουτο 22 (131) 872 1192 1210 1278 (2372) NA RP | λυετε τον πωλον D Θ 28 69 124 565 700 788 1071 1346 Arm

● **173** 11:4 (απηλθον) ουν **1 118 205 209 1582 2193 2542 2886** 13 28 69 91 124
299 346 433 543] και (απηλθον) (565) NA | (απηλθον) δε (22?) 131 872
1192 1210 1278 2372 RP

● **174** 11:5 (τινεσ) δε **1 205 209 1582 2193 2542 2886** W 13 28 69 346 543 788]
και (τινεσ) 22 118 131 565 872 1192 1210 1278 2372 NA RP

● **175** 11:8 εστρωννυον[1] **1 118**[vid] **205 209 565 872 1582 2193 2542 2886** D W Θ
28 63 91 241 299 700 Arm] εστρωσαν 22 118[c] 131 1192 1210 1278 2372
NA RP

● **176** 11:10[70] *om.* **1 205 209 872 1582 2193 2886** Δ 53 71 299 579] ερχομενη 22
118[c] 131 565 1192 1210 1278 2372 2542 NA RP

X **177** 11:10 ειρηνη εν ουνω και δοξα **1 22 118** (205 adds τω) **209 872 1192 1210
1278 1582 2193 2372 2886** Θ 91 299] *om.* 131 565 2542 NA RP

X **178** 11:12 *om.* **1 205 209 1582 2193 2886** 299] απο βηθανιας 22 118 131 565
872 1192 1210 1278 2372 2542 NA RP

X **179** 11:14 καρπον μηδεις **1 118 205 209 872 1582 2193 2886** W 299 1071]
μηδεις καρπον 22 131 565 1192 1210 1278 2372 2542 NA RP

X **180** 11:19 εξω της πολεως εξεπορευετο **1 118 205 209 1582 2193 2542 2886**]
εξω της πολεως εξεπορευοντο W 28 872 | εξεπορευετο εξω της πολεως
א C (D) Θ 22 1192 1210 1278 2372 RP | εξεπορευοντο εξω της πολεως A
B Δ M 124 565 700 1071 (131 not readable)

■ **181** 11:21 εξηρανθη **1 118 205 209 565 1210 1278* 1582 2193 2372 2886** D L N
Δ Θ Σ Ψ 22[c] 33 245 349 433 517 579 700 1342 1424] εξηρανται (22) 872
1192 1278[c] NA RP | εξηραντε 131 | εξηραται 2542

■ **182** 11:23 εαν[1] **1 118 205 209 872 1278 1582 2193 2372 2542 2886** A Φ f13 33
543 481 788] αν[1] 22 131 565 1192 1210 NA RP

X **183** 11:23 αρθηναι και βληθηναι **1 205 209 872* 1582 2193 2542 2886** W 28
124] αρθητι και βληθητι 22 118 131 565 872[c] 1192 1210 1278 2372 NA
RP

X **184** 11:25 ανη **1 205 209 1582 2886** W] αφη 22 118 131 872 1192 1210 1278
2193 2372 2542 NA RP | αφισει 565

X **185** 11:27 *om.* **1 205 209 1582 2193 2372 2886** 91] και οι πρεσβυτεροι 22 118
131 565 872 1192 1210 1278 2542 NA RP

---

[70] Codex 118 has been corrected to ερχομενη. However, the first hand appears
to have read ερχομενη as well.)

X 186   11:29 λογον ενα **1 205 209 872 1582 2193 2886** Θ 28 124 299] ενα λογον
        22 118 131 565 1192 1210 1278 2372 NA RP | λογον 2542

X 187   11:30 απ (ουνου) **1 205 209 1582 2193 2886**] εξ (ουνου) 22 118 131 565
        872 1192 1210 1278 2372 2542 NA RP

■ 188   11:31 ημιν **1 118 205 209 565 872 1582 2193 2542 2886** M W Θ 13 69 124
        225 299 543 700 788 Arm] *om.* 22 131 1192 1210 1278 2372 NA RP

X 189   12:4 *om.* **1 205 209 565 1582 2193 2886**] προς αυτους αλλον 22 118 131
        872 1192 1210 1278 2372 2542 NA RP

X 190   12:4 κεφαλαιωσαντες **1 118 205 209 565 1582 2193 2886** (W) 28 700]
        εκεφαλιωσαν NA | εκεφαλαιωσαν 22 131 872 1192 1210 1278 2372
        2542 RP

■ 191   12:9 (γεωργουσ) εκεινους **1 118 205 209 1582 2193 2886** G N Σ 10 11 15
        68 80 91 218 299 472 517] *om.* 22 131 565 872 1192 1210 1278 2372 2542
        NA RP

■ 192   12:14 ανου **1 118 205 209 1582 2193 2542 2886** G K 28 91 116 242 253 299
        349 435 517 1424] ανθρωπων 22 131 565 872 1192 1210 1278 2372 NA
        RP

X 193   12:16 *om.* **1 1582**] και λεγει αυτοις 22 118 131 205 209 872 1192 1210
        1278 2193 2372 2542 2886 NA RP | και ειπεν αυτοις 565

● 194   12:18 αναστασις ουκ εστι **1 205 209 1582 2886** 13 (28) 69 124 346 543]
        αναστασιν μη ειναι 22 118 131 565 872 1192 1210 1582^mg 2193 2372 NA
        RP | μη ειναι αναστασιν 1278 2542

● 195   12:20 απεθανεν **1 118 205 209 565 872 1582 2193 2542 2886** D W Θ 28 91
        92 299 700 1071 Arm] αποθνησκων 22 131 1192 1210 1278 2372 NA RP

● 196   12:28 ακουων **1 118 205 209 1582 2193 2542 2886** W Θ 28 299 700]
        ακουσας 22 131 872 1192 1210 1278 2372 NA RP | ακουοντων 565

X 197   12:28 πρωτη εντολη **1 205 209 1582 2193 2542 2886** W 28 69 543]
        εντολη πρωτη παντων 131 NA | πρωτη παντων εντολη 22 118 872
        1192 1210 2372 RP | πρωτη πασων εντολη 1278 | εντολη πρωτη 565

X 198   12:29 πρωτον παντων **1 205 209 1582 2193 2542 2886** (28 700)] οτι
        πρωτη παντων των εντολων 22 118 1192 1210 1278 2372 RP | οτι
        πρωτη παντων εντολη 131 872 | οτι πρωτη εστιν ℵ B L Δ Ψ 579 892 |
        παντων πρωτη D W Θ 91 565

X 199   12:33 καρδιας, ισχυος, συνεσεως, **1 118 205 209 1582 2193 2542 2886** 299
        Arm] καρδιας, συνεσεως, ισχυος B L W Δ Θ Ψ 28 565 892 1241 |

καρδιας, συνεσεως, ψυχης, ισχυος 22 131 1192 1210 1278 2372 RP |
καρδιασ, δυναμεως, ισχυος 565 | καρδιας, ισχυος, συνεσεως, ψυχης 872

■ **200**   12:37 πως **1 118 205 209 565 872 1582 2193 2542 2886** ℵ* M W Θ Σ Ψ 13
27 28 33 69 91 108 435 543 579 1071 Arm] ποθεν 22 131 1192 1210 1278
2372 NA RP

● **201**   12:43 *om.* **1 118 205 209 1582 2193 2886** W 13 28 248 788] των
βαλλοντων 22 (131) 565 872 1192 1210 1278 2372 (2542) NA RP

● **202**   12:44 ουτοι **1 118 205 209 872 1582 2193 2886** D 33 67 91 299 433 579
1424] *om.* 22 565 1192 1210 1278 2372 2542 NA RP (131 not readable)

X **203**   13:2 λεγω υμιν **1 118 205 209 872 1582 2193 2886** (D) 299] αμην λεγω
σοι G Θ Σ 13 28 61 69 91 115 124 543 565 700 788 1346 Arm | *om.* 22 131
1192 1210 1278 2372 2542 NA RP

X **204**   13:8 *om.* **1 1582 2193 2542** (W)] ταυτα 22 118 131 205 209 (565) 872 1192
1210 1278 2372 2886 NA RP

1582 has a space after ωδινων with ταυτα written above the space in the
first hand. This is connected with the omission of βλεπετε δε υμεις
εαυτους in the following verse. 1582mg has that reading. Though 2542
omits after ωδινων, it has ταυτα after λοιμοι, which appears to be an
otherwise unknown reading.

■ **205**   13:9 αχθησεσθε **1 118 131 205 209 872 1278 1582 2193 2886** G U 2 13 33
479 480 517 579 1424] σταθησεσθε 22 1192 1210 1582ᵐᵍ 2372 2542 NA
RP | στησεσθε 565

X **206**   13:11 λαλησετε² **1 118 205 209 872 1582 2193 2886** 90 484] λαλειτε 22
131 565 1192 1210 1278 2372 2542 NA RP

● **207**   13:19 ουδ ου **1 118 205 209 565 872 1278 1582 2193 2542 2886** F G Θ 13
69 157 253 346] και ου 22 131 1192 1210 2372 NA RP

■ **208**   13:20 (ημερασ¹) εκεινας **1 118 205 209 1582 2193 2542 2886** E F G M Δ Θ
Σ Ψ 2 13 69 127 349 517 579 1071 1424] *om.* 22 131 565 872 1192 1210
1278 2372 NA RP

● **209**   13:20 δια δε **1 118 205 209 1582 2193 2542 2886** 9 13 28 69 91 299 543
1542] αλλα δια 22 131 565 872 1192 1210 1278 2372 NA RP

● **210**   13:26 νεφελη **1 118 205 209 565 1582 2193 2542 2886** W Θ 13 28 69 543
788] νεφελαις 22 131 565 872 1192 1210 1278 2372 NA RP

X **211**   13:27 ακρων ουνων **1 118 205 209 1582 2193 2886** W] ακρων ουνου 22
1192 1210 2372 | ακρου ουρανου 131 1278 NA RP | ακρου του
ουρανου 565 872 2542

■ **212** 13:28 τα φυλλα εκφυη **1 872 1582 2193** U Ψ 78 108 127 517 700 1071 1342 1424] εκφυη τα φυλλα 22 118 (131) 205 209 565 1192 1210 1278 2372 (2542) 2886 NA RP

● **213** 13:30 εως αν **1 118 205 209 872 1582 2193 2542 2886** 13 28 69 124 299 346 543] μεχρις ου 22 131 1192 1210 1278 2372 NA RP | εως W Θ 565

X **214** 13:34 ωσπερ **1 118 205 209 1582 2193 2886** 299 474] ωσπερ γαρ W Θ Σ 13 28 69 91 124 472 543 565 788 2542 | ως 22 131 872 1192 1210 1278 2372 NA RP

■ **215** 13:34 αποδημων **1 118 205 209 565 1192 1582 2193 2542 2886** D X Θ 28 245 299 349 472 517 1342 1424] αποδημος 22 131 872 1210 1278 2372 NA RP

■ **216** 14:3 πολυτιμου **1 22ᶜ 118 205 209 565 872 1210 1278* 1582 2193 2542 2372 2886** A G Mᵐᵍ W Θ 13 22ᶜ 28 69 59 91 108 299 435 697 1071 1342] πολυτελους 22* 131 1192 1278ᶜ NA RP

X **217** 14:5 (αυτη) πολλα **1 22 118 205 209 1210 1278* 1582 2193 2372 2886** 59 697 Arm] *om.* 131 565 872 1192 1278ᶜ 2542 NA RP

X **218** 14:8 προς **1 22 118 205 209 872 1192 1210 1278* 1582 2193 2372 2886** 59 238 251] εις 131 565 1278ᶜ 2542 NA RP

X **219** 14:11 συνεθεντο **1 118 205 209 872 1582 2193 2886**] επηγγειλαντο 22 (131) 565 1192 1210 1278 2372 2542 NA RP

● **220** 14:14 φαγομαι **1 205 209 1582 2542 2886** D W Θ 13 69 124 346 543] φαγωμαι G 22 28 118 346 | φαγω 131 565 872 1192 1210 1278 2193 2372 NA RP

X **221** 14:15 κακεινος **1 118 205 209 872 1582 2193 2886**] και αυτος 22 131 565 1192 1210 1278 2372 2542 NA RP

● **222** 14:29 αποκριθεις λεγει **1 118 205 209 565 872 1582 2193 2542 2886** W Θ 13 69 124 346 543 700 1346] εφη 22 131 1192 1210 1278 2372 NA RP

● **223** 14:29 εν σοι **1 118 205 209 1582 2193 2886** E G U 60 108 127 472 517 1424] *om.* 22 131 565 872 1192 1210 1278 2372 2542 NA RP

X **224** 14:31 πετρος μαλλον εκπερισσου οτι **1 1582 2193**] εκπερισσως ελαλει NA | εκπερισσου ελεγεν μαλλον 131 1278 RP | πετρος μαλλον περισσως ελεγεν W 13 69 124 346 2542 | πετρος εκπερισσου ελεγε μαλλον 22 118 1192 1210 2372 | πετρος μαλλον εκπερισσου ελεγεν οτι 205 209 2886 | πετρος περισσως ελεγεν 565 | εκπερισσου ελεγεν οτι 872

■ 225   14:31 συν σοι αποθανειν **1 118 205 209 565 872 1210 1582 2193 2542 2886**
L 0112 115 218 349 472 477 517 1071 1342 1424] συναποθανειν σοι 22
131 1192 1278 2372 NA RP

X 226   14:32 γηθσεμανει **1 1582**] γεθσημανει ℵ A C L M N S 131 565 2193 |
γεθσημανι 209 2542 NA | γεθσημανη 22 118 205 209 872 1192 1210
1278 2372 2886 RP

X 227   14:33 λυπεισθαι **1 205 209 872 1582 2193 2886**] λυπυσθαι **118** |
εκθαμβεισθαι 22 131 565 1192 1210 1278 2372 2542 NA RP

● 228   14:34 μετ εμου **1 118 205 209 1582 2193 2886** G 0112 28 61 245 300] *om.*
22 131 565 872 1192 1210 1278 2372 2542 NA RP

■ 229   14:35 επι προσωπον **1 22 118 205 209 565**[vid] **1192 1210 1278 1582 2193
2372 2886** D G Θ Σ 2 7 13 28 59 69 248 472 517 543 692 700 1424 Arm]
om. 131 872 2542 NA RP

X 230   14:35 προσηυξατο **1 118 205 209 1582 2193 2886**] προσηυχετο 22 131 565
872 1192 1210 1278 2372 2542 NA RP

● 231   14:37 ισχυσατε **1 22 118 205 209 565 1210 1278 1582 2193 2372 2886** D (Θ)
7 59 69 124 346 543] ισχυσας 131 872 1192 2542 NA RP

● 232   14:43 *om.* **1 118 205 209 565 1582 2193 2886** D W Θ Σ 13 69 346 543 700
1346 Arm] ευθεως 22 118[c] 131 872 1192 1210 1278 2372 2542 RP |
ευθυς NA

● 233   14:43 απεσταλμενοι **1 22 118 205 209 1210 1278* 1582 2193 2372 2886** 7
56 59 251 697] *om.* 131 565 872 1192 1278[c] 2542 NA RP

■ 234   14:54 ηκολουθει **1 118 205 209 565 1582 2193 2542 2886** G W (Θ) Ψ 13 69
124 543 700 788 1346 Arm] ηκολουθησεν 22 131 872 1192 1210 1278
2372 NA RP

X 235   14:54 της αυλης **1 118 205 209 1582 2193 2542 2886** 237] την αυλην 22
131 565 872 1192 1210 1278 2372 NA RP

X 236   14:58 δι ημερων τριων **1 118 205 209 872 1582 2193 2886**] δια τριων
ημερων 22 131 565 1192 1210 1278 2372 2542 NA RP

● 237   14:62 αποκριθεις ειπεν αυτω **1 118 205 209 1582 2193 2542 2886** G W 13
69 124 346 543 1071] ειπεν 22 131 1192 1210 1278 2372 NA RP |
αποκριθεις λεγει αυτω 565] αποκριθεις ειπεν 872

■ 238   14:62 επι **1 22 118 205 209 872 1192 1210 1582 2193 2886** G 11 28 33 127
238 349 472 482 517 579 1424] μετα 131 565 1278 2372 2542 NA RP

X 239   14:64 παντες την βλασφημιαν αυτου **1 565 1192 1582 2193 2542** (D) G]
της βλασφημιας ℵ B (131) 872 1278[c] RP | παντες την βλασφημιαν του

στοματος W (Θ 124 565) | παντες της βλασφημιας αυτου 22 118 205 209 1192 2886 | παντες της βλασφημιας 1210 1278* 2372

X 240 14:65 νυν **1 22 118 205 209 1210 1582 2193 2886** G W 1071] *om.* 131 565 872 1192 1278 2372 2542 NA RP

X 241 14:67 αυτον **1 118 205 209 565 872 1278 1582 2193 2542 2886** 69 346 543 700 Arm] τον πετρον 22 131 1192 1210 2372 NA RP

X 242 14:68 εις την εξω αυλην **1 118 205 209 872 1582 2193 2886** W] εις την εξω προαυλιον Θ f13 543 700 1346 | εξω εις το προαυλιον 22 131 1192 1210 1278 2372 NA RP | εις το εξω προαυλιον 565 | εξω εις την προαυλειον 2542

● 243 14:70 ηρνησατο **1 118 209 565 872 1582 2193** G M N W Δ (579) 700 2372ᶜ] ηρνησατε 205 2886 | ηρνειτο 22ᵛⁱᵈ 131 1192 1210 1278 2542 NA RP | ηρνητω 2372*

X 244 14:70 περιεστωτες **1 1582 2193** G] παρεστωτες 22 118 131 205 209 565ᵛⁱᵈ 872 1192 1210 1278 2372 2542 2886 NA RP

● 245 14:72 αναμνησθεις **1 118 205 209 872 1582 2193 2886** G W 13 69 495 543] ανεμνησθεις 131 | αναμνησθη 565 NA RP | ανεμνησθη 22 565 1192 1210 1278 2372 | εμνησθης 2542

X 246 15:5 απεκρινατο **1 118 205 209 1582 2193 2886** G 13 69 543] απεκριθη 22 131 565 872 1192 1210 1278 2372 2542 NA RP

● 247 15:10 ηιδει **1 565 872 1582 2193 2542** D W Θ 13 69 346 700] εγινωσκεν 22 118 131 205 209 1192 1210 1278 2372 2886 NA RP

■ 248 15:10 παρεδωκαν **1 565 872 1582 2193 2542** D H S W Θ 13 69 124 435 472 517 543 700 1424] παραδεδωκεισαν 22 131 (205 209 1210 2886 have παρεδεδωκεισαν) 1192 1278 2372 NA RP | παρεδωκεισαν 118

● 249 15:13 εκραζον **1 1582 2193** G 13 69 73 543 1424 Arm] εκραξαν 22 118 205 209 131 872 1192 1210 1278 2372 2886 NA RP | εκραυγαζον 565 2542

■ 250 15:14 εκραζον **1 118 205 209 872 1582 2193 2542 2886** A D G K M N P Y Π 11 69 108 248 300 346 472 482 543 1342 Arm] εκραξαν 22 131 1192 1278 2372 NA RP | εκραυγαζον 565
(1210 is missing verse 14)

● 251 15:16 εις την αυλην **1 22 118 205 209 565 1192 1210 1278 1582 2193 2372 2542 2886** Cᶜ D M P Θ 700] της αυλης 131 872 NA RP

X 252   15:17 στεφανον εξ ακανθων **1 872 1582 2193 2542** Θ 872 1342 1542]
ακανθινον στεφανον 22 118 131 205 209 565 1192 1210 1278 2372 2886
NA RP

X 253   15:20 την χλαμυδα **1 22 872 1210 1278* 1582 2193 2372** 59 61 251 697]
την πορφυραν 118 131 205 209 1192 1278ᶜ 2886 NA RP | την χλαμυδα
και την πορφυραν Θ 1213 69 124 346 330 543 565 700 1071 2542 Arm

X 254   15:23 και γευσαμενος **1 205 209 872 1582 2193 2886** G] γευσαμεν 118 | ο
δε 22 131 565 1192 1210 1278 2372 2542 RP] ος δε ℵ B Γ 33 579 892 1424
2542

▪ **255**   15:30 καταβηθι **1 118 205 209 1582 2193 2886** P 90 240 483 484 517 569
579 1071 1424] καταβας NA | καταβα 22 131 565 872 1192 1210 1278
2372 2542 RP

▪ **256**   15:36 αφες **1 22 565 872 1192 1210 1278* 1582 2193 2372 2542** ℵ D V Θ Ω
13 28 59 61 69 258 543 579 697 700 2542] αφετε B (118) 131 205 209
1278ᶜ 2886 RP

256a   15:41 both 1 and 1582 leave an unusual amount of space after this verse.
For 1 it is at the bottom of the page. This is not the case in 2193. 565
leaves almost a whole line after the end of the verse. 2886 has an unusually
large space after the verse, similar to another space after the end of chapter
15.

X 257   15:45 παρα **1 565 1582 2193 2542** D W Θ 72 124] απο 22 118 131 205 209
872 1192 1210 1278 2372 2886 NA RP

X 258   15:46 προσκυλισας **1 22 205 209 1210 1278* 1582 2193 2372 2886** D 59
697] προσκυλησας **1 118**] προσκυλισεν 872 NA RP] προσεκυλισε 131
565 1192 1278ᶜ 2542

X 259   15:46 μνημειου απηλθεν **1 22 118 205 209 1210 1278 1582 2193 2372 2886**
G 59 697] μνημειου και απηλθεν D 157] μνημειου 131 565 872 1192
NA RP] μνημειω 2542

X 260   16:5 ιδον **1 565 872* 1582 2193**] ειδον 22 118 131 205 209 872ᶜ 1192 1210
1278 2372 2542 2886 NA RP

X 261   16:7 ηγερθη απο των νεκρων και ιδου **1 22 118 205 209 1210 1278 1582
2193 2372 2886** 59 697] ηγερθη απο των νεκρων ιδου D W Θ 565] *om.*
131 565 872 1192 2542 NA RP
After 16:8:[71]

---

[71] See also Tischendorf, *Novum Testamentum Graece*, p. 404 (Comment 3).

εν τισι μεν των αντιγραφων εως ωδε πληρουται ο ευαγγελιστης εως ου
και ευσεβιος ο παμφιλου εκανονισεν εν πολλοις δε και ταυτα φερεται **1
209 1582 2193 2886**] *om.* 118 131 205 565 872 1278 2372 2542 NA RP
22 1192 1210 have εν τισι των αντιγραφων εως ωδε πληρουται ο
ευαγγελιστης εν πολλοις δε και ταυτα φερεται

X 262 16:12 *om.* **1 1582 2193** Arm] περιπατουσιν 22 118 131 205 209 565 872
1192 1210 1278 2372 2542 2886 NA RP

9. TEXTUAL CRITICISM AND THE INTERPRETATION OF TEXTS: THE EXAMPLE OF THE GOSPEL OF JOHN

HANS FÖRSTER[1]

INTRODUCTION

The full textual evidence of the Gospel of John including the early versions will be accessible in a few years' time in the *Editio Critica Maior*. It is, however, already clear – and will become even clearer – that its text seems to show a high level of stability when compared with the Hebrew Bible and its versions as well as with other texts from the early time of Christianity. This raises the question of whether the stability of the text is of importance for the evaluation of possible levels of redaction which have been detected by literary criticism.

Since the Sahidic version of the Gospel of John is currently the main focus of the author's research, examples of this translation will dominate the paper. The research is still in progress, thus far encompassing major parts of the manuscript evidence. At this stage it seems comparatively certain that, while there might be some minor disagreements between different Sahidic manuscripts (and also between the Sahidic and Bohairic versions) the overall impression is of a rather stable text. There are only a few examples of missing verses, such John 5:4 which is only attested in parts of the Bohairic version but not in the Sahidic or the other Coptic dialects which attest this passage. This, however, holds also true for

---

[1] The paper grew out of the author's following research projects: Austrian Science Fund / FWF Project P22017, P24649 and P25082. Two of these projects are concerned with the Sahidic version of John's Gospel; for project P24649, see Chapter Two in the present volume.

numerous Greek witnesses, hence its omission from the editorial text of the Nestle–Aland Greek New Testament. Another example is the pericope of the woman taken in adultery (John 7:53–8:11).[2] This passage is attested only by parts of the Bohairic version and omitted from the Sahidic, Lycopolitan and Proto-Bohairic versions. Again this is an area where the textual variation can also be found in other languages, including important Greek witnesses. This explains why many commentaries of John's Gospel do not include this pericope. It is, however, extremely rare to find manuscripts which have textual variants comparable to these examples at the level of an entire verse. One example is the identification of Mary Magdalene at the open tomb as Mary, mother of Jesus. One Sahidic manuscript attests this variation of the story in John 20:15 and reports further that Mary tried to bribe the person whom she encountered in order to receive information concerning the presumptively stolen body of Jesus. It is possible to trace this variant to homilies given in the same monastic community which obviously influenced the scribe who copied the lectionary.[3] This, however, is one of the outstanding variations of the Coptic translations of this text which otherwise show a high level of stability. Furthermore, this variant will not be included in the *Editio Critica Maior* since this must be seen as an intra-versional change of the text and not as a variant which might have its origin in the Greek tradition.

With the decision of not noting this variant in the *Editio Critica Maior* an important difference between textual criticism and literary criticism becomes obvious. Textual criticism tends to be fairly conservative regarding the inclusion of variants. One example would be the recent publication by Christian Askeland who convincingly argues for a minimalist concept of inclusion concerning the Coptic witnesses of John's Gospel, based on the methodological premise of the priority of the Greek and the value of

---

[2] Cf. also Felix Just, 'Combining Key Methodologies in Johannine Studies' in Tom Thatcher (ed.), *What We Have Heard from the Beginning*, (Waco TX: Baylor, 2007), pp. 355–8, there p. 356.

[3] Cf. Hans Förster, "... damit ich dir deinen Lohn gebe' – Eine etwas andere Begegnung am leeren Grab (Joh 20,15) in einer koptischen liturgischen Handschrift.' *Mitteilungen zur Christlichen Archäologie* 18 (2012) pp. 91–100. One could argue that this might hint at a copying process which involved dictation rather than visual copying since such a significant change of the text is unlikely to have been made when copying from an exemplar.

variants in versional evidence only with regard to the Greek text.[4] Only those variants are worth to be included which give evidence of the textual history of the Greek, whose evidence should be beyond reasonable doubt.

If one were to compare textual criticism with literary criticism it would become obvious that textual criticism seems to be a comparatively rigid approach which does not leave much leeway for interpretation while literary criticism of the same text leads to different 'original' versions of John's Gospel. This plurality of results seems to imply that a certain degree of subjectivity is involved in this approach. Most textual critics will be hesitant, at the least, to include passages which might be of intra-versional origin. Some literary critics, however, seem to be optimistic about the ability of their approach to identify the different sources which were used by the author and to unearth the layers of the text which show, what was produced first and what was added during a later revision.[5] Nonetheless, an excessively optimistic use of literary criticism as methodology has also been criticised.[6]

Thus, while the textual critic includes those versional variants into the Greek tradition which are beyond reasonable doubt, the literary critic tends to see those passages which are not 'easily understood' and therefore seem – perhaps only to the modern mind and not to the ancient author – to be

---

[4] Christian Askeland, *John's Gospel. The Coptic Translations of its Greek Text* (ANTF 44. Berlin/Boston: De Gruyter, 2012).

[5] E.g. Robert T. Fortna, *The Fourth Gospel and its Predecessor. From Narrative Source to Present Gospel* (Edinburgh: T. & T. Clark, 1989) and Folker Siegert, *Das Evangelium des Johannes in seiner ursprünglichen Gestalt: Wiederherstellung und Kommentar* (Schriften des Institutum Judaicum Delitzschianum 7. Göttingen: Vandenhoeck & Ruprecht, 2008). The word 'author' is used in this paper to designate the writer or writers of the Gospel without prejudice regarding the possible redactional layers of the text. Since, however, there is no textual evidence for these layers it is easier to designate the final redactor (of many? or the only one?) as 'author'.

[6] Udo Schnelle, 'Aus der Literatur zum Johannesevangelium 1994 – 2010. Erster Teil: Die Kommentare als Seismographen der Forschung.' *Theologische Rundschau* 75 (2010) pp. 265–303, there p. 287: 'Dabei wird rein systemimmanent argumentiert, d.h. die Stimmigkeit des Ansatzes ist vorausgesetzt und der Weg der einmal akzeptierten Logik wird konsequent beschritten. Neuere Kommentare werden dabei natürlich nicht berücksichtigt, denn S. scheint ernsthaft zu glauben, dass er die johanneische Frage gelöst hat, was die Lektüre und Diskussion anderer (falscher) Meinungen überflüssig macht.'

'disjunctures' (also termed 'aporias'), as products of a discernible literary history.[7] The attempt to see the text as unity and to let the 'aporias' stand as they are without either explaining them away or 'correcting' the text can lead to criticism.[8] One of the major theories of source criticism of John's Gospel, the hypothesis of a so called 'signs-source', has for a long time dominated the research into the 'signs' reported in this Gospel. This hypothesis has been called into question by Gilbert van Belle and seems now to have lost some of its attraction.[9] This can be interpreted as an indicator of elements of subjectivity which – by necessity – are part of every literary critical approach.

One of the goals of textual criticism is to determine what might have been the text of the Gospel when it started to circulate. The lack of discernible traces of a presumptive 'narrative predecessor' in the surviving evidence for the Gospel appears to indicate that such a document never circulated, although this does not mean that the textual critic is able to decide whether it ever existed. Literary criticism, however, has a goal of uncovering the 'narrative predecessor' regardless of the material evidence

---

[7] Tom Thatcher, 'The Fourth Gospel in First-Century Media Culture' (in Thatcher, *What We Have Heard from the Beginning*, pp. 159–162), observes on p. 162 that '[o]ne can scarcely deny that John's style and presentation are frequently puzzling, but it is also quite clear that the label "aporia" has often been applied to any aspect of the text that a particular interpreter, or school of interpreters, cannot readily understand', while Urban von Wahlde ('The Road Ahead: Three Aspects of Johannine Scholarship' in Thatcher, *What We Have Heard from the Beginning*, pp. 343–353) notes on p. 347 that '[o]ne might argue that an "alert" reader would notice the so-called 'aporias,' the various kinds of literary disjunctures and inconsistencies, that pervade the Gospel of John.'

[8] 'Historical critics […] neither seek out aporias nor invent them; but having found them in the text they prefer to explain them rather than paper them over or pretend they are not there.' John Ashton, 'Second Thoughts on the Fourth Gospel.' In Thatcher, *What We Have Heard from the Beginning*, pp. 1–18, there p. 3.

[9] Source criticism is for methodological reasons subsumed here as part of a literary critical approach to the Gospel of John. Cf. Gilbert van Belle, *The Signs Source in the Fourth Gospel. Historical Survey and Critical Evaluation of the Semeia Hypothesis.* (BETL 116. Leuven: University Press, 1994), p. 376, and Udo Schnelle, 'Literatur', p. 289: 'Innerhalb der letzten 30 Jahre hat sich auch hier die Forschungslage grundlegend geändert, denn auf internationaler Ebene bezweifelt heute eine deutliche Mehrheit der Exegeten die Existenz dieser "Semeia-Quelle".'

for its existence.[10] It is possible to argue that such a document could have been suppressed after the publication of the 'authorial text'. The destruction by an author of his or her notes is a comparatively widely known phenomenon: notes may have been used and drafts made which were never known to anybody else but the author. Right away, however, the caveat must be made that no evidence of such a text has been found *up to now*. If such a text were to be detected, either in one of the libraries holding texts from early Christianity or during an archaeological excavation, this would strengthen the argument of literary criticism with textual evidence and call into question one of the basic presuppositions of this article, namely that such a text never circulated.

Nonetheless, the possible impact and therefore the necessity of literary criticism is obvious:

> If we are able to provide a history of the development of the Johannine tradition [...], we will get a much more precise understanding of the Gospel text itself [...]. And, if we are able to understand more clearly the literary development of the Gospel, we will also understand better the various issues that the Johannine community faced in its relationship to the synagogue and in relationships within the community itself.[11]

Thus, even if it might be the case that the literary evolution of the text took place during a comparatively short time which, in consequence, would argue against too many layers of the text, the potential literary history is still of the utmost importance for the interpretation of the text. Decisions based upon a supposedly certain literary history might, on the other hand, influence – if not to say shape – the interpretation of the text. As John

---

[10] Hartwig Thyen, *Das Johannesevangelium*. (HNT 6. Tübingen: Mohr Siebeck, 2005), p. 1: 'Da die handschriftlichen Zeugen weder für die vielfach vorgeschlagenen Umstellungen von Teiltexten noch für eine nachträgliche Bearbeitung eines vorliegenden Evangeliums durch einen *kirchlichen Redaktor* irgendwelche ernstzunehmenden Indizien bieten, dürfte unser Evangelium *öffentlich* nie anders als in seiner überlieferten kanonischen Gestalt existiert haben. Darum haben wir hier auf die Erörterung aller Fragen nach der vermeintlichen *Genese* unseres Evangeliums, nach seinen mutmaßlichen *Quellen* oder gar nach einem bereits literarisch verfaßten Vorläufer (*Predecessor*, Fortna), sowie nach seiner vermeintlich sekundären Bearbeitung durch eine „kirchliche Redaktion" (Bultmann, Becker u.a.) verzichtet.'

[11] Wahlde, 'Road', p. 346.

Ashton phrases it: 'We have to allow for the possibility that a scholar's reading of the evidence may be distorted by previously formed opinions or unconscious prejudices.'[12]

These introductory remarks raise a double question. First, is textual criticism overly concerned with the 'original' text?[13] Such a preoccupation with the 'original' text and not with the text as it appears at different locations and in different languages can lead to the exclusion of textual variations which might be attested especially in the versional evidence and therefore deemed to be 'later' or 'only of versional interest'. One of the contentions of this paper is that some of these later 'versional evolutions' which are of no value concerning the 'original' text of John's Gospel may give insight into the question of how a certain passage was understood by those who produced these translations.[14] Such possible interpretations might, in consequence, be of importance as to how the passage may be understood in a different context. Second, is literary criticism overly confident of its ability to identify the sources used in the text and the layers of the text produced by the different 'redactors'? This, however, might lead to the problem that passages of the text could be identified as indicators of 'redactional layers' which – hypothetically at least – could in fact be literary devices used by the implied author which readers were intended to identify correctly and to use for the interpretation of the text.

With these introductory remarks the table is set to discuss the value of textual criticism (with particular reference to the Coptic versional evidence) for the interpretation of the Gospel of John. The first part will explore the

---

[12] Ashton, 'Second Thoughts', p. 3.

[13] The word 'original' is, on purpose, in quotation marks; it is impossible to identify 'one original' text; for the goals of textual criticism cf. David C. Parker, 'Textual Criticism and Theology' in David C. Parker, *Manuscripts, Texts, Theology. Collected Papers 1977-2007.* (ANTF 40. Berlin/New York: De Gruyter, 2009), pp. 323–333: 'The abandonment of the quest for an original text does not de-historicise textual criticism. We still find textual forms that are older than other ones, and seek to describe sequences of development. [...] If the quest for an original form is set aside, the oldest recoverable form has of course great significance.' (p. 329).

[14] This includes also any work done to the text as translated after the initial translation. Thus, all emendations made to an ancient translation are – in principle – of interest in this context if they reveal a decision as to how a passage might best be understood.

statement made above that the text of the Gospel of John 'seems to show a high level of stability' by comparing it with the Greek text of Daniel and the 'apocryphon of John' from the Nag Hammadi-Library. The former is chosen because of the explicit reference to it in the Gospel of John, while the latter represents an early Christian tradition similar to that connected with the Gospel.[15] The second part of the paper will deal with examples where minor changes in the text seem to hint at problems in its reception. It seems that translational tendencies as well as some variants of the Greek text show where users had difficulties understanding or interpreting the text, although modern scholars should be wary of the pitfalls of over-precise attribution of the reasons for individual changes.

1. THE LITERARY UNITY OF ANCIENT RELIGIOUS TEXTS IN THE JUDAEO-CHRISTIAN TRADITION

The Literary Unity of the Book of Daniel

As Sharon Pace notes, the Book of Daniel provides evidence of a somewhat convoluted textual transmission. 'The very placement of the book of Daniel in two canonical locations – in the prophetic corpus of the Septuagint, but in the Writings of the Masoretic text – attests to its complicated history.'[16] This is also apparent in the way in which the textual evidence makes it possible to trace parts, at least, of the literary history. First, there are two Greek translations: the Septuagint is less literal than the translation connected with Theodotion, a Jewish proselyte from the end of the second century AD, which scholars agree came into existence at least a

---

[15] For the use of the Septuagint in the Gospel, see Martin Hengel, 'Die Schriftauslegung des 4. Evangeliums auf dem Hintergrund der urchristlichen Exegese' *Jahrbuch für biblische Theologie* 4 (1989) pp. 249–88 (reprinted in Claus-Jürgen Thornton (ed.), *Martin Hengel. Die Evangelien. Kleine Schriften 5.* (WUNT 211. Tübingen: Mohr Siebeck, 2007) pp. 601–43); Bruce G. Schuchard, *Scripture within Scripture. The Interrelationship of Form and Function in the Explicit Old Testament Citations in the Gospel of John.* (SBLDS 133. Atlanta: Scholars Press, 1992); Maarten J.J. Menken, *Old Testament Quotations in the Fourth Gospel. Studies in Textual Form* (Contributions to Biblical Exegesis and Theology 15. Kampen: Pharos, 1996), p. 205.

[16] Sharon Pace, *Daniel.* (Smyth & Helwys Bible Commentary. Macon: Smyth & Helwys, 2008), p. 12.

century earlier.[17] There are also deutero-canonical additions which exist only in the Greek version of Daniel: The prayer of Azariah (Dan. 3:24–50), the hymn of the three young men in the oven (Dan. 3:51–90) and the stories of Susanna (Dan. 13), Daniel and the priests of Bel (Dan. 14:1–22) and Daniel and the dragon (Dan. 14:23–42).[18] Even using this means of identification already implies a decision about the transmission of the book. While Dan^LXX has this structure, Dan^Th places Susanna before the beginning of Chapter 1, making 'Chapter 14' in the LXX 'Chapter 13' of this version. The Göttingen edition of the Septuagint by Rahlfs follows Theodotion in the structure of the text, but the Stuttgart Vulgate has Susanna as part of the book, thereby following the LXX: interestingly, Jerome adopts the structure of the LXX but follows the version of Theodotion in his translation.[19] There is no full agreement as to the relationship of those two Greek versions.[20]

A second indicator of a rather convoluted literary history is that parts of the book are written in different languages: Hebrew (1:1–2:4; 8:1–12:13), Aramaic (2:4b–7:28) and Greek (3:23–50.51–90; 13:1–14:42).[21] Inconsistencies in the story further indicate that the text was not originally written as a single book. Most striking among these is the fact that Chapter 7 deals with the reign of King Belshazzar despite the fact that, according to 6:29,

---

[17] Ernst Haag, *Daniel.* (Neue Echter Bibel Lfg. 30. Würzburg: Echter, 1993), p. 9.

[18] Cf. Dieter Bauer, *Das Buch Daniel.* (Neuer Stuttgarter Kommentar. Altes Testament 22. Stuttgart: Katholisches Bibelwerk, 1996), p. 16.

[19] Haag, *Daniel,* p. 9.

[20] Cf. Klaus Koch, *Daniel. 1. Teilband: Dan 1–4.* (Biblischer Kommentar. Altes Testament 32/1. Neukirchen: Neukirchener, 2005), p. 315: 'Während die meisten Ausleger Θ für eine jüngere Revision von G halten [...], plädieren einige [...] für je selbständige Übersetzung. [...] Die Untersuchungen der Problematik leiden darunter, daß die syrische Übersetzung, die meist mit Θ, gelegentlich aber auch mit G geht oder ganz eigene Wege einschlägt, kaum je berücksichtigt wird.'

[21] Haag, *Daniel,* p. 9: 'Die Doppelsprachigkeit des protokanonischen Db – Anfang (Dan 1,1–2,4a) und Ende (Dan 8–12) sind in Hebräisch, der mittlere Teil (Dan 2,4b–7,28) dagegen in Aramäisch abgefaßt – und die Tatsache, dass die deuterokanonischen Zusätze (Dan 3,24–50.51-90; 13–14) nicht mehr im semitischen Original (hebräisch oder aramäisch?), sondern nur noch in Griechisch vorliegen, haben offenbar ihren Grund in der ungewöhnlichen Entstehungsgeschichte des Buches.'

Cyrus is ruling. Also a change of the perspective of the narrator from third person (1:1–7:1; 13–14) to first person (7:2–12:13) is seen as an indication that more than one author worked on this text.[22]

It is not necessary to present here the entire wealth of indicators for the literary history of the text: these examples already mentioned are sufficient to show how the convoluted history can lead to different hypotheses for the evolution of the text. A majority of scholars, however, are of the opinion that the oldest parts of this book were written after 539 BC; some put this phase in the fifth or fourth century BC. It seems plausible that different parts existed first as separate texts and were formed into chapters of the book. Whether this is seen as an addition to the kernel of the book or as a reworking of it is not really important. This work, however, was probably undertaken by a redactor in the third century BC. A final phase of work on the book may convincingly be shown to have occurred between 168 and 163 BC.[23] That the text has a literary history of around three centuries may be deduced from such obvious indicators as the different languages of the original and the different length and order of the text of the original and of ancient translations. Furthermore, the literary history of Daniel is much better documented by textual witnesses than that of the Gospel of John (as presupposed by literary criticism). In addition, it is also obvious that the time available for the literary evolution of Daniel is much longer than that available for the Gospel of John.

The Literary Unity of the 'Apocryphon of John'

The second example takes a text from early Christian literature which shares its name with the attributed author of the Gospel: all four witnesses describe the text as 'Apocryphon of John' in the *subscription*, further identified within the narrative frame as 'John Son of Zebedee'.[24] Such an attribution, along with the declaration of the text as a 'teaching of the

---

[22] Herbert Niehr, 'Das Buch Daniel' in Christian Frevel (ed.), *Einleitung in das Alte Testament*. 7th edn, (Kohlhammer Studienbücher. Theologie 1,1. Stuttgart: Kohlhammer, 2008), pp. 507–516.

[23] For an overview of the different hypotheses cf. Niehr, *Daniel*, pp. 509-10; note that Norman W. Porteous, *Das Buch Daniel*. (Alte Testament Deutsch 23. Göttingen: Vandenhoeck & Ruprecht, 1985), p. 7, locates the work over a considerably shorter period.

[24] Cf. NHC II/1, p. 1,6–7 and par.

saviour'[25] which 'had been hidden in a silence'[26] is characteristic of an apocryphal text and its claim to authority.[27]

Three of the manuscripts form part of the Nag Hammadi Library (NHC II,1; III,1; IV,1), while the fourth is in the collection in Berlin (BG 8502,2). The texts preserved in NHC II,1 and IV,1 are closely related and longer; NHC III,1 and BG 8502,2 are independent translations of a shorter Greek version. Irenaeus of Lyons summarizes parts of the Apocryphon of John (Irenaeus, *haer.* 1,29), which gives 180 AD as a *terminus ad quem* for the existence of the work. Despite the fact that only four witnesses survive, they demonstrate a comparatively high textual variability, witnessing to a literary history which most probably features two different Greek *Vorlagen* behind the translation of the Coptic texts.[28] In this case, then, the literary history would indeed be seen in the manuscripts. Furthermore, NHC II,1 and NHC IV,1 show that more or less identical copies of a single text can exist: variability was therefore a possibility but not a necessity.

Comparison with the Gospel of John

If the literary history of the book of Daniel is compared to that suggested for John's Gospel, two aspects immediately emerge of the question of literary unity in opposition to a convoluted literary history. The book of Daniel has a history which might have taken around 350 years to arrive at its final literary form (disregarding the question of whether or not the story of Susanna is part of the book), approximately ten times longer than the Gospel of John, based on the usually accepted hypothesis that the author

---

[25] NHC II/1, p. 1,1: ⲧⲉⲥⲃⲱ [ⲛⲧⲉ ⲡⲥⲱⲧⲏⲣ]. Cited according to Michael Waldstein and Frederik Wisse, *The Apocryphon of John. Synopsis of Nag Hammadi Codices II,1; III,1; and IV,1 with BG 8502,2.* (NHMS 33. Leiden: Brill, 1995), p. 13.

[26] NHC II, p. 1,2-3: [ⲛⲉ]ⲧⲉⲏⲡ ⲉⲛ ⲟⲩⲙⲛⲧⲕⲁⲣⲱϥ.

[27] Christoph Markschies, 'Haupteinleitung.' in Christoph Markschies and Jens Schröter (eds), *Antike christliche Apokryphen in deutscher Übersetzung. 1. Band. Evangelien und Verwandtes. Teilband 1.* (Tübingen: Mohr Siebeck, 2012), pp. 1–180, there p. 114; cf. Hans Förster, 'Geheime Schriften und geheime Lehren? Zur Selbstbezeichnung von Texten aus dem Umfeld der frühchristlichen Gnosis unter Verwendung des Begriffs ἀπόκρυφος (bzw. ⲉⲏⲡ).' *ZNW* 103 (2013) pp. 118–45.

[28] For the introduction to the text and a translation of the text cf. Michael Waldstein, 'Das Apokryphon des Johannes (NHC II,1; III,1; IV,1 und BG 2)' in Hans-Martin Schenke † et al. (eds), *Nag Hammadi Deutsch. Studienausgabe.* 2nd edn (Berlin/New York: De Gruyter, 2010), pp. 74–122.

knew the Synoptics and composed his Gospel sometime around the end of the first century AD.[29]

If, however, the Synoptics came into existence sometime between 70 and 85 AD, this does not leave much time for the author of John's Gospel to examine these other Gospels – if he ever used them[30] – and then to create his own text while leaving traces of the literary history of the revisions of his text as detected by modern scholarship. And, if one actually gives credibility to those traces as have been found by modern scholarship, these can be found only within the text and not among the textual witnesses. So in comparison with the apocryphon of John, which has four textual witnesses and gives testimony to a somewhat unstable text, the Gospel of John has a huge number of witnesses which differ only in minor matters.[31] Thus the stability of the textual tradition can point in two directions. One is the hypothesis of a later purgation of the text, which has already been set out with regard to certain tendencies in the textual tradition.[32] The other is that the text became an 'authoritative text' comparatively early and did not suffer major alterations. In the latter case one would have either to draw on the hypothesis that the comparatively short time available for the creation of the text is sufficient to cover the

---

[29] Cf. Ulrich Heckel and Peter Pokorný, *Einleitung in das Neue Testament. Seine Literatur und Theologie im Überblick.* (Tübingen: Mohr Siebeck, 2007), p. 584: 'Ende des ersten Jh.s ist […] die wahrscheinlichste Entstehungszeit.' For a somewhat later date cf. Udo Schnelle, *Einleitung in das Neue Testament.* 6th edn (Göttingen: Vandenhoeck & Ruprecht, 2007), p. 511: '[…] sowohl die Rezeptionsgeschichte als auch die textliche Überlieferung des Johannesevangeliums legen eine Entstehung zwischen 100 und 110 n.Chr. nahe.'

[30] Cf. Gilbert van Belle, 'Tradition, Exegetical Formation, and the Leuven Hypothesis' and Robert T. Fortna, 'The Gospel of John and the Signs Gospel', both in Thatcher, *What We Have Heard from the Beginning*, pp. 325–37 and 149–58 respectively.

[31] This holds also true for the two somewhat different witnesses of the Middle Egyptian version of the Gospel of Matthew. While Codex Scheide and Codex Schøyen might be quite different in the phrasing of the Coptic text, on principle they give witness to the same text; cf. Hans Förster, 'Review of Schenke, Matthäus-Evangelium im mittelägyptischen Dialekt des Koptischen (Codex Schøyen).' *Tyche* 18 (2003) p. 280.

[32] Bart D. Ehrman, *The Orthodox Corruption of Scripture. The Effect of Early Christological Controversies on the Text of the New Testament* (Oxford: Oxford UP, 1993).

textual history as deduced by scholars or conclude that the text might have a less convoluted textual history than often presupposed and changed comparatively little over time. If the comment in John 20:31 can be taken seriously, this work might have been written as a whole with a certain goal in mind. The process of canonization might explain the fact that later on the text changed comparatively little, but it does not fully explain why there are no traces of different versions comparable to those in the books mentioned above which could have come into existence after the text started to circulate and before the process of canonization was finished.[33] As David Parker puts it, 'the wealth of textual variation in our manuscripts of the Gospels is proof enough that the early Christian users of the Gospels treated them as *living texts*, which were re-worded, expanded or reduced, to bring out what these users believed to be the true meaning of the text.'[34] But, it seems, the Gospel of John did not have enough time in order to produce major textual variations comparable to those of the Book of Daniel or the apocryphon of John – and this might be connected with the fact that the text gained canonical status comparatively early.

2. EXAMPLES OF THE IMPORTANCE OF TEXTUAL VARIANTS AND TRANSLATIONAL TENDENCIES WITHIN THE GOSPEL OF JOHN

The following passages offer examples from the author's current research which suggest that it is important to pay close attention to the actual wording or phrasing of the text of John's Gospel.[35] In such cases, nuances can be detected which can lead to a deeper understanding of the text.

P[75] and John 11:12

Within the pericope of the Raising of Lazarus (John 11) there is a dialogue between Jesus and his apostles in which Jesus announces that he will raise

---

[33] Cf. however Markschies, 'Haupteinleitung', p. 9: 'Als 'living literature', deren Textgestalt nicht durch den Prozeß einer kirchlichen Kanonisierung stabilisiert und normiert wird, haben die hier gesammelten 'apokryphen' Schriften etwas sehr fließendes.'

[34] Parker, 'Textual Criticism', p. 327.

[35] For a thorough discussion of the first example, cf. Hans Förster, 'Johannes 11:11–14 – ein typisches johanneisches Missverständnis?' *NovT* 53 (2011) pp. 338–357.

Lazarus. The disciples understand that 'if he sleeps he will get better', even though the word σωθήσεται is used. This answer has often been commented on. Some stress the fact that it is a common knowledge that people who sleep will get better, while it is also described as Lazarus' 'natural recovery from an illness which would otherwise kill him.'[36] The absurdity of the situation seems to be obvious: 'Although sleep was a common euphemism for death, the disciples misunderstand. In context, their response is absurd: they reason that if Lazarus is allowed to sleep, he will recover!'[37] It has even been suggested that the disciples are remonstrating with Jesus for proposing to wake Lazarus and thereby jeopardising his chances of recovery.[38] Parallels are seen in healing during sleep at the temples of Asclepius.[39] Yet, while misunderstandings are a typical narrative device of the Gospel of John, the disciples here seem to be out of line. Their response is unusually coarse, more akin to the 'leaden-witted stooge' missing the mark by a long way rather than classic Johannine incomprehension.[40]

---

[36] Margaret Davies, *Rhetoric and Reference in the Fourth Gospel*. (JSNTSup 69. Sheffield: Sheffield Academic Press, 1992), p. 219; for an example of the former, see Jeffrey Lloyd Staley, *The Print's First Kiss: A Rhetorical Investigation of the Implied Reader in the Fourth Gospel*. (SBLDS 82. Atlanta GA: Scholars Press, 1988), pp. 105–107 and Thyen, *Johannesevangelium*, p. 517.

[37] Kevin Quast, *Reading the Gospel of John: An Introduction*. (New York: Paulist Press, 1991), p. 83.

[38] Thus John Coutts, 'The Messianic Secret in St. John's Gospel' in Frank Leslie Cross (ed.), *Studia Evangelica III: Papers presented to the Second International Congress on New Testament Studies Oxford 1961*. (TU 88. Berlin: Akademie, 1964), pp. 45–57, there p. 47.

[39] Gerhard Maier, *Johannes-Evangelium* (Edition C Bibelkommentar 6. Stuttgart: Hänssler, 1984), p. 486: 'Die Überzeugung, daß der Schlaf Heilung bringt (V. 12), ist in der Antike und Moderne weit verbreitet und wird immer wieder durch Erfahrung gestärkt. Außerbiblische Religionen entwickelten sogar ein System des 'Heilschlafes', bei dem Patienten in Kammern der Heilgötter-Tempel (z. B. des Asklepios/Äskulap) gelegt wurden.'

[40] Wendy E. Sproston North, *The Lazarus Story within the Johannine Tradition* (JSNTSup 212. Sheffield: Sheffield Academic Press, 2001), p. 140: 'It is now the disciples' turn to play the leaden-witted stooge (v. 12)'. On misunderstandings in John more generally, see Herbert Leroy, *Rätsel und Missverständnis: Ein Beitrag zur Formgeschichte des Johannesevangeliums*. (Bonner Biblische Beiträge 30. Bonn: Hanstein, 1968); for this particular example, Rudolf Bultmann, *Evangelium des Johannes*. (20.

The text of verse 12 does not provide many interesting variations. There is, however, a variant ἐγερθήσεται which, according to Nestle–Aland 27, is only attested by P[75]. This is even further off the mark than the answer according to the vast majority of manuscripts.[41] Nonetheless, it is also attested by the Sahidic version and other Coptic dialects. As Coptic has no passive voice, it therefore circumlocutes a passive if it occurs in the source text.[42] It is thus interesting that the Coptic tradition does not translate the future passive of σωθήσεται as 'he will get better' but rather prefers a wayward alternative. In context, however, it seems possible to understand this reading in a way which furthers the understanding of the entire passage. On principle, it is a truism that if a person sleeps, he or she will wake up again. This fact is even expressed in parts of the Coptic tradition by adding the word ⲟⲛ, meaning 'again', at the end of the verse. According to the Coptic tradition the disciples understand that Lazarus is not yet dead, that he simply sleeps and that Jesus will be able to raise him from his sleep. This seems to be in line with the narrative: death in antiquity was often sudden and unexpected and the outcome of illnesses unpredictable.

As regards the narrative of John 11 one may note that Jesus lingers after receiving the news of the illness of Lazarus before he sets off in order to 'raise him'. It seems that the disciples' answer in P[75] conveys their belief that Lazarus is not yet dead. The utterances of both sisters as well as the crowd of bystanders imply that death is a significant border beyond which there is no help.[43] It therefore seems possible to understand this as a true Johannine misunderstanding: although Jesus talks about 'eternal rest' the disciples understand this to be just 'sleep'. In consequence, if the passive voice of the majority of the manuscripts were taken at its face value, this

---

Druck=10. Aufl.; KEK 2. Göttingen: Vandenhoeck & Ruprecht, 1978), p. 304 note 6.

[41] 'This can scarcely be right': Morris, *John*, p. 482 note 25.

[42] Uwe K. Plisch, *Einführung in die koptische Sprache. Sahidischer Dialekt.* (Sprachen und Kulturen des christlichen Orients 5. Wiesbaden: Reichert, 1999), p. 36: 'Passivische Vorgänge werden häufig durch den Gebrauch der 3. Person pl. als unbestimmte Person ('man') umschrieben [...].'

[43] Cf. for Martha, John 11:21: εἶπεν οὖν ἡ Μάρθα πρὸς τὸν Ἰησοῦν· κύριε, εἰ ἦς ὧδε οὐκ ἂν ἀπέθανεν ὁ ἀδελφός μου. For Mary, cf. John 11:32: ἡ οὖν Μαριὰμ ὡς ἦλθεν ὅπου ἦν Ἰησοῦς ἰδοῦσα αὐτὸν ἔπεσεν αὐτοῦ πρὸς τοὺς πόδας λέγουσα αὐτῷ· κύριε, εἰ ἦς ὧδε οὐκ ἄν μου ἀπέθανεν ὁ ἀδελφός. For the crowd, cf. John 11:37: τινὲς δὲ ἐξ αὐτῶν εἶπαν· οὐκ ἐδύνατο οὗτος ὁ ἀνοίξας τοὺς ὀφθαλμοὺς τοῦ τυφλοῦ ποιῆσαι ἵνα καὶ οὗτος μὴ ἀποθάνη;

too may be taken as a true Johannine misunderstanding. The literal translation 'if he sleeps he will be saved' seems to imply that Lazarus is (still) alive when Jesus arrives, conveying also the idea that Jesus can raise him as in the other healing miracles. This makes the answer of the disciples not gross incomprehension but rather a typical Johannine misunderstanding, identifying the passive voice in the disciples' answer as a divine passive.

There are two consequences to be drawn from this example. First, the way a text is translated in an early version can give insight into how this passage was understood and, in consequence, might even be able to shed some light upon the way the Greek text might be better interpreted.[44] Second, it must be assumed that the reader was expected to understand the passage as a divine passive, which has been lost in the transmission of the text. This is an example of what Urban von Wahlde puts into words as follows: "'Real' readers interpret 'real' texts in *really* different ways!"[45]

The Variants of John 2:11 and the Interpretation of the Signs in John's Gospel

Since this passage deals with two different questions, the 'beginning of the signs' and the signs in their entirety, it is worth offering a short introduction. Both the interpretation of the Wedding at Cana and the signs in their entirety pose important problems for scholarship.[46] One of these questions is which sources the author used for his accounts of Jesus's 'signs' – a typical Johannine way of denoting the miraculous deeds of Jesus – and whether these were actually not different sources but rather a single 'signs source'. This latter has attracted a lot of interest and scholarly debate, retaining a number of adherents even though the fundamental criticism of

---

[44] This is, in fact, an expansion of how the 'Leuven Hypothesis' sees textual criticism cf. Belle, 'Tradition', p. 335: '[...] an attempt should be made to establish, provisionally at least, the most probable reading of the passages in question. Consideration must also be given to 'variant readings,' because these might reflect the earliest interpretations of the text.'

[45] Cf. Wahlde, 'Road', p. 345.

[46] Cf. Hans Förster, 'Die Perikope von der Hochzeit zu Kana (Joh 2:1-11) im Kontext der Spätantike' *NovT* 55 (2013) pp. 103–26; Hans Förster, 'Die Hochzeit zu Kana und die johanneische Erzähltechnik' *Standpunkt Heft* 210 (2013) pp. 25–37; Hans Förster, 'Die johanneischen Zeichen und Joh 2:11 als möglicher hermeneutischer Schlüssel' *NovT* 56.1 (2014) pp. 1–23.

this concept by Gilbert van Belle has led to a reconsideration. Within his discussion of a hypothetical 'signs source' he phrases his results rather carefully: 'On the basis of these remarks, I am inclined to refuse the semeia hypothesis as a valid working hypothesis in the study of the Fourth Gospel.'[47]

In the context of this article, source criticism is seen as a technique closely related to literary criticism. While literary criticism tends to focus on the text and problems of the flow of the narrative which are seen as indicative for possible layers of redaction, source criticism tries to identify the sources used by the author of a given text. Thus, the principal working hypothesis is for both methods that the modern scholar is able either to detect elements which show that a redaction of the text has taken place or to identify certain passages as coming from the same or different sources. The obvious possibility must be mentioned that a modern scholar might see some textual features as indicative of a redaction or supposed source which actually might be a textual feature put there on purpose by the author. To phrase it differently, the modern scholarly reader might by his very training be inclined to identify elements as belonging to a source or a redaction which a contemporary of the author might understand as elements which structure the text. This phenomenon may be observed in the discussion of the structure of the signs in John's Gospel and their potential sources.

The Wedding at Cana

The first problem of the text is that the transformation of water into wine is not traditionally found among those signs which are connected with the coming of the Messiah, such as the healing of the lame and the blind and the feeding of the needy.[48] In John 1:41 Jesus is called by Andrew 'Messiah', and with the first sign water is changed miraculously into wine. It is no surprise that this story has attracted a lot of scholarly discussion. The problem is exacerbated by the fact that the amount of wine seems to be huge. The water is contained in six jars which hold each two to three *metretes*.[49] Since the volume of such a measure is around 40 litres, each of the

---

[47] Belle, *Signs Source*, p. 376; Schnelle, 'Literatur', p. 289 (quoted above) claims that the majority of scholars are opposed to the hypothesis of a separate 'signs source'.

[48] Cf. Isaiah 35:5-6.

[49] John 2:6: ἦσαν δὲ ἐκεῖ λίθιναι ὑδρίαι ἓξ κατὰ τὸν καθαρισμὸν τῶν Ἰουδαίων κείμεναι, χωροῦσαι ἀνὰ μετρητὰς δύο ἢ τρεῖς.

containers holds between 80 and 120 litres. The result is between 480 and 720 litres of liquid, described as an 'enormous' amount[50] and interpreted as an 'eschatological' sign connected with the parable of the 'banquet of the king'.[51] Thus it is no surprise that this miraculous deed is also called a 'luxury miracle',[52] as an abundance of wine is given to the wedding celebration. Given that the exhaustion of the supplies for a wedding is hardly a situation of existential need like a dying child (John 4:46–54) or a decades-lame person (John 5:1–18), it has been noted that this 'luxury miracle' is not typical for the miracles done by Jesus.[53]

One might, however, be tempted to call this miracle a 'blessing in disguise'. The ancient technique of producing wine was different from the modern way in many aspects. One important difference pertinent to the present context is that there was no technology at hand to stop the fermentation. The yeast started to work immediately after pressing the grapes: there was always some natural yeast in the skins of the grapes or the

---

[50] See Ulrich Busse, *Das Johannesevangelium. Bildlichkeit, Diskurs und Ritual.* (BETL 162. Leuven: Leuven UP, 2002), p. 319; cf. also Wolfgang J. Bittner, *Jesu Zeichen im Johannesevangelium. Die Messias-Erkenntnis im Johannesevangelium vor ihrem jüdischen Hintergrund.* (WUNT 2/26. Tübingen: Mohr Siebeck, 1987), p. 115 note 25; Collins, 'Cana', p. 80. Cf. also Jürgen Becker, *Das Evangelium nach Johannes. Kapitel 1–10.* 3rd edn, (Ökumenischer TB-Kommentar 4/1. Gütersloh: Gütersloher Verlagshaus, 1991), p. 131; Ernst Haenchen, *Das Johannesevangelium: Ein Kommentar aus den nachgelassenen Manuskripten.* Edited by Ulrich Busse. (Tübingen: Mohr, 1980), p. 189; Bultmann, *Evangelium*, p. 82.

[51] Klaus Wengst, *Das Johannesevangelium. 1. Teilband: Kapitel 1–10.* 2nd edn (ThKNT 4/1. Stuttgart: Kohlhammer, 2004), p. 112; Tobias Nicklas, 'Biblische Texte als Texte der Bibel interpretiert: Die Hochzeit zu Kana (Joh 2,1–11) in "biblischer Auslegung".' *Zeitschrift für Katholische Theologie* 126.3 (2004) pp. 241–56, there p. 246: 'Zu erinnern wäre an die Parabel vom königlichen Hochzeitsmahl Mt 22,1–4, in der der Anbruch der Gottesherrschaft mit einem endzeitlichen Gerichtshandeln Gottes, aber auch dem Bild der Hochzeit verbunden wird.'

[52] Cf. for example Thyen, *Johannesevangelium*, p. 151; also Reinhard Nordsieck, *Das Geheimnis des Lazarus. Zur Frage nach Verfasser und Entstehung des Johannes-Evangeliums.* (Theologie 98. Münster/Berlin et al.: Lit-Verlag, 2010), p. 31.

[53] Siegfried Bergler, *Von Kana in Galiläa nach Jerusalem. Literarkritik und Historie im vierten Evangelium.* (Münsteraner Judaistische Studien 24. Münster/Berlin: Lit-Verlag, 2009), p. 1: 'Seit Beginn meines Theologiestudiums hat mich das für Jesus recht untypische Luxuswunder, im Rahmen einer Hochzeitsfeier Wasser in Wein zu verwandeln, gestört.'

cisterns which acted as 'starters' for the process. The process would only stop once all sugar had been converted into alcohol or if the concentration of alcohol were higher than the tolerance of the yeast. Wine in antiquity was therefore rather strong, between 15% and 16% alcohol, and was always mixed with water.[54] Based on a very rough calculation, the 720 litres of wine would have contained approximately 108 litres of pure alcohol. If this were consumed in one evening the liquid would probably be enough to kill 350 adult males. What, then, is the meaning of this miracle?

One hypothesis is that the source for this miracle lies in a competition between the followers of Jesus and adherents of the cult of Dionysus. There seems to have been a rather important place of cultic veneration of Dionysus in Scythopolis – the texts designated by John's Gospel as scripture would call this place Beth Shean – a city approximately 30 kilometres from Cana.[55] This hypothesis seems to underestimate three aspects of the text. First, there is no explicit mention of this competing cult, so the question must be raised whether this Dionysiac reference is imposed by the (modern) reader of the text. Second, if the text is compared with the other feeding miracles in John's Gospel,[56] while the volume of the wine is given in John 2:6, this is not noted as large, unlike the other miracles where twelve baskets of left-overs are collected in a context where sufficiency is explicitly mentioned (John 6:5–13) and 153 fish are caught yet with 'so many' the net did not break (John 21:11). Third, the sign at the wedding in Cana is called the 'beginning'. It is interesting to note how the Latin translation grapples with this wording. In the Vulgate it is given as *hoc fecit initium signorum*, but some manuscripts use the ordinal number instead: *hoc fecit primum signorum*[57] while the combination of ordinal number and

---

[54] Sandra Hodeček, "'Vinum laetificat cor hominis" — "Wein erfreut des Menschen Herz". Wein, Weinanbau und Weinkultur im antiken Ägypten' in Harald Froschauer and Cornelia Römer (eds), *Mit den Griechen zu Tisch in Ägypten*. 2nd edn (Nilus 12. Vienna: Phoibos, 2009), pp. 53–60, there p. 57.

[55] Wilfried Eisele, 'Jesus und Dionysos. Göttliche Konkurrenz bei der Hochzeit zu Kana (Joh 2,1–11).' *ZNW* 100 (2009) pp. 1–28, there p. 15.

[56] On wine as nutritional in antiquity, see Sean A. Kingsley, *A Sixth-Century AD Shipwreck off the Carmel Coast, Israel. Dor D and Holy Land Wine Trade.* (British Archaeological Reports. International Series 1065. Oxford: Archaeopress, 2002), p. 60.

[57] E.g. VL 9A; 27; 35; VL 4 has *hoc primum signum fecit*.

'beginning' is also attested: *hoc primum fecit initium signorum*.[58] The Sahidic version uses only the ordinal number, thereby interpreting the Greek word ἀρχή as a numerical element. It is noteworthy that the identical word found in John 1:1 is there translated into Sahidic by another word signifying a beginning (ϩογειτε). The Greek word can denote a less important beginning, like that of 'two ways'.[59] The translational variety seems to hint at a problem connected with the exact meaning of ἀρχή.[60] These two considerations, taken together, lead to the conviction that the amount of wine might not be as enormous as usually noted. It has been argued that the amount seems to be fitting for a 'common household' as attested by documentary sources and archaeological evidence.[61] This is a conclusion which meets Köstenberger's criterion of being 'grounded in a proper understanding of the place of John's Gospel in the first-century world'.[62]

The Signs in John's Gospel

It seems possible to advance the additional hypothesis that the word ἀρχή is used in John's Gospel in the same way as it is used in the Greek version of Genesis.[63] There, the word denotes a 'beginning' which unfolds within the different days of the creation of the world. It seems that the same meaning can be suggested for the word in John 2:11. This implies, in principle, that the signs in John's Gospel unfold step by step and that this unfolding is something which can be identified by the reader of the text.

This impression is strengthened by other elements on the textual level: It seems that the perception of the word used by Jesus in John 5 for the question as to whether or not the lame man wants to 'be healed' (ὑγιής) has (among other arguments) influenced the notion as to how difficult the healing must be. In this context the discussion focusses rather on the long

---

[58] Cf. VL 10.

[59] For ἀρχὴ τῶν ὁδῶν cf. Ezekiel 21:26.

[60] For an approach seeing this as a numbering cf. Fortna, 'Gospel', p. 150: 'In the source, these episodes were called 'signs' and were evidently numbered (vestiges remain in 2:11a, 4:54a, and 21:14a) and arranged in a geographically logical sequence.'

[61] Cf. Förster, 'Perikope'.

[62] Andreas J. Köstenberger, 'Progress and Regress in Recent Johannine Scholarship. Reflections upon the Road ahead' in Thatcher, *What We Have Heard from the Beginning*, pp. 105–7, there p. 107.

[63] Gen. 1:1: Ἐν ἀρχῇ ἐποίησεν ὁ θεὸς τὸν οὐρανὸν καὶ τὴν γῆν.

time of illness instead of the diagnosis: the healing might here be something which can be achieved by a medical treatment, as ὑγιαστήριον can mean hospital.[64] And the state of 'well being' (ὑγιής) is expressed, for example, in Sirach 17:28: 'Those who live and are well (ὑγιής) will praise the Lord'. Thus it might be more correct to render the word ὑγιής as 'to get well' instead of 'to be healed'.

It is interesting to observe that the Latin tradition translates this word, which occurs in John 5:6, 5:9, 5:11, 5:14 and 5:15, as *sanus* on all occasions. The reference to the healing of the lame man on the sabbath in John 7:23 (also using ὑγιής) is rendered either with *sanus* or (rarely) with *salvus*. In John 5, the Sahidic has ογχλϊ for the instances of ὑγιής, while in John 7:23 the word is translated by τογχε.[65] On the semantic level there is no difference between the healings which use Greek σώζω and the latter passage in the Sahidic version. In John 5:10 the passive voice (participle) of θεραπεύω (the Latin uses *sanare* or *curare*) is translated by the use of λο (constructed as a substantivated relative clause). The meaning of the Coptic in John 5:10 is obvious: to get well (as opposed to be healed).[66] The word ταλϬο is used for the participle of ἰάομαι (the Latin has *sanus*) in John 5:13. For most of these instances the other Coptic dialects use the same words as the Sahidic.[67] One is therefore tempted to conclude that the Coptic translation misses the difference between a 'healing' which presupposes supernatural power and a healing which is possible by medical treatment.

In other words, while the divine passive in John 11:12 seems to convey 'salvation'[68], medical 'therapy'[69] is to be the basic principle presupposed for

---

[64] Cf. LSJ *s.v.*

[65] This would be a causative form of the word ογχλϊ in the status nominalis.

[66] For the fundamental meaning of λο as 'to cease,' and 'to get well' cf. Walter E. Crum, *A Coptic Dictionary*. (Oxford: Oxford UP, 2000 (= 1939)), pp. 135a–136b; see also Wolfhart Westendorf, *Koptisches Handwörterbuch*. 2ⁿᵈ edn (Heidelberg: Universitätsverlag Winter, 2000 (=1965/1977)), p. 75.

[67] An exception is the Proto-Bohairic of 5:10 where the Greek word is used in transliteration, while in 5:11 the causative infinitive in combination with ογχλϊ is used.

[68] The verb in John 11:12 is σώζω; thus one is led to conclude that σωτηρία is semantically implied here.

[69] The verb θεραπεύω is used in John 5:10 and medical treatment seems to be implied in John 5:13a: ὁ δὲ ἰαθεὶς οὐκ ἤδει τίς ἐστιν. Thus, the words ἰατρικὴ θεραπία seems to be implied on a semantic level.

the healing of the lame in John 5, at least in Greek: in the Latin tradition it is lost at least partially for John 7:23, while the Coptic makes no distinction between these two words. It should also be mentioned that this is the only occurrence in John's Gospel of θεραπεύω, allowing us to suppose that this word is a deliberate choice. If one were to deduce its meaning based on its use in the Synoptics, where it occurs often for the healings caused by Jesus, it makes a different interpretation more plausible.[70] Even in John's Gospel the word ἰάομαι is used for a divine intervention, in a quote from Isaiah at John 12:40. Only the collocation of the three words used seems to offer an additional indicator as to the severity of the illness: it seems to be something that can be 'made well' again. The duration of the illness at John 5:5 as 38 years may have been overemphasised as an indicator of the severity of the illness.[71]

The signs and their structure have seen a lot of discussion in theological discourse. The hypothesis has been advanced by means of literary criticism that the order of John 5 and 6 should be reversed.[72] Certain commentaries implement this, in order to revert to the 'original order' as detected by literary criticism.[73] It has even been stated that the arguments of literary criticism for a repositioning of the two chapters cannot be overruled by theological arguments.[74] The evaluation of the Greek text and of the Latin and Coptic versions, however, make the conclusion possible that there are elements on the textual level, including the exact choice of words, which seem to imply that there could be a planned structure underlying the composition of all the signs. The examples given above are among those that lead to the hypothesis that the signs in

---

[70] Cf. for example only Matt. 4:23–24; Matt. 8:16 (paralleled by Mark 1:34 and Luke 8:20) and Matt. 9:35.

[71] Cf. Urban C. von Wahlde, *The Gospel and Letters of John*. Volume 2. (Grand Rapids MI: Eerdmans, 2010), p. 222: 'The severity of the illness is described with the detail ('thirty-eight years'; he can move only very slowly) necessary to exhibit properly the magnitude of problem overcome by Jesus' power (1E-19).'

[72] E.g. John Painter, 'The Signs of the Messiah and the Quest for Eternal Life' in Thatcher, *What We Have Heard from the Beginning*, pp. 233–56, there p. 252.

[73] Cf. Ulrich Wilckens, *Das Evangelium nach Johannes*. 18th edn (Neue Testament Deutsch 4. Göttingen: Vandenhoeck & Ruprecht, 2000) and Franz Zeilinger, *Die sieben Zeichenhandlungen Jesu im Johannesevangelium* (Stuttgart: Kohlhammer, 2011).

[74] Rudolf Schnackenburg, *Das Johannesevangelium II. Teil: Kommentar zu Kap. 5-12.* 4th edn (HThK, 4/2. Freiburg: Herder, 1990), p. 10.

John's Gospel have a climactic structure.[75] Such a structure would be destroyed by the hypothesis that it is necessary to reposition John 5 and 6.[76] In this case it is possible to state that the perceived dislocation which can seemingly be corrected by literary criticism might have been placed there on purpose. The necessity of a 'correction' might be more a problem of the perception of what the text should be which, in this case, seems to disregard the original conception.

It thus seems that the stories which have been identified as parts of the 'signs-source' could be more intricately connected on a basic level than hitherto proposed.[77] This makes it possible – or even probable – that the redactional activity of the author (or authors) of the Gospel of John was higher than hitherto expected. Even the designation 'signs' for the miracles in this Gospel might not stem from a source but from an author. This possibility could be seen as an argument against a hypothetical signs-source.

If, however, it is possible to argue that literary criticism undervalues the actual text on the basic level of semantics this, in consequence, is a further argument for the hypothesis that the first step for the interpretation of the Gospel of John is an intratextual interpretation with special attendance to the choice of words. Umberto Eco offers a summary of this:

> How to prove a conjecture about the *intentio operis*? The only way is to check it upon the text as a coherent whole. This idea, too, is an old one and comes from Augustine (*De doctrina christiana*): any interpretation given of a certain portion of a text can be accepted if it is confirmed by, and must be rejected if it is challenged by, another portion of the same

---

[75] This has been argued in Förster, 'Zeichen'. Due to the restriction of space in the journal it was not possible fully to unfold there the importance of the comparison of the Greek text with the versional evidence of the Latin and Coptic tradition for this insight.

[76] For the possibility of such an insight cf. Just, 'Combining', p. 356: 'Thus, the fundamental insight of narrative criticism – that the text must have 'made sense to someone' – might helpfully be applied not only to the final stage, but also to earlier, albeit hypothetical, stages in the composition of the Fourth Gospel.'

[77] Fortna, 'Gospel', p. 152: 'The signs pericopes have been barely edited internally, but almost entirely rearranged in their order (reflecting the Johannine Jesus' movements to and from Jerusalem) [...].' For a similar observation, see Robert Alter, *The Art of Biblical Narrative* (New York: Basic Books, 1981), p. 11.

text. In this sense the internal textual coherence controls the otherwise uncontrollable drives of the reader.[78]

CONCLUSION

An obvious caveat remains for every translator of an ancient text, as phrased by Simon R. Slings:

> One of the more obvious uses of general linguistic theory for the study of classical and other dead languages is to help us to determine whether what we *do* know (or rather what we think we know) is really knowledge, or the product of misunderstandings and errors committed and added to by one generation of scholars after another.[79]

As has been shown above, this seems also to be the case for certain passages within John's Gospel. A more literal translation of these passages might be of value for a better understanding of the text and the structure of the signs. What is more, the ancient translations might not only be of importance for the reconstruction of the 'original text' of John's Gospel but also for the identification of passages where modern understanding might be slightly improved by a more literal translation.

Furthermore, the text was written in an environment which is not yet fully understood. The missing knowledge concerning the group for which the text was written and seemingly contradictory evidence within the text concerning the intended reader has, in consequence, lead to hypotheses which are mutually exclusive.[80] One source that contributed to this problem might be the way this text has been analyzed with tools from literary criticism. It is possible that texts from antiquity might in some respects function differently from modern texts and that the Gospel of John might be counted among such – at least in some passages. To quote Robert Alter:

---

[78] Umberto Eco, 'Overinterpreting Texts' in Stefan Collini (ed.), *Umberto Eco: Interpretation and Overinterpretation.* (Cambridge: Cambridge UP, 1992), pp. 45–66, there p. 65. Cf. also Leroy A. Huizenga, *The New Isaac. Tradition and Intertextuality in the Gospel of Matthew.* (*NovT* Supplements 31. Leiden/Boston: Brill, 2009), pp. 29–34.

[79] Simon R. Slings, ''KAI adversativum' – some thoughts on the semantics of coordination' in Dick J. van Alkemade et al. (eds), *Linguistic Studies offered to Berthe Siertsema.* (Costerus 25. Amsterdam: Rodopi, 1980), pp. 101–125, there p. 101.

[80] For this problem and possible new approaches, Chapter Two in the present volume.

There is no point, to be sure, in pretending that all the contradictions among different sources in the biblical texts can be happily harmonized by the perception of some artful design. It seems reasonable enough, however, to suggest that we may still not fully understand what would have been perceived as a real contradiction by an intelligent Hebrew writer of the early Iron Age, so that apparently conflicting versions of the same event set side by side, far from troubling their original audience, may have sometimes been perfectly justified in a kind of logic we no longer apprehend.[81]

There is no such gross incongruence in the Gospel of John as contradictory or conflicting accounts, merely a number of 'aporias'. As discussed above, the 'signs' seem to be set out in a special way that might, on second sight, not so much hint at a 'source' and the need to reposition John 5 and 6 but rather at a 'design' of the author.[82]

In conclusion, the construction of an 'original text' of John's Gospel by means of literary criticism might, at least in some instances, deconstruct the original unity of the text as constructed by the author. The problem is obvious: the 'aporias' detected by literary criticism concern the communication between author and implied reader, and there is not even a common opinion as to the identity of this intended reader. It is not beyond the bounds of possibility that at least some of the 'aporias' identified by learned readers (mostly but not exclusively from Western societies of the 20th and 21st century) are possible means of communication in the Gospel of John for an intended audience in antiquity,[83] an audience which is not yet fully understood. Similarly, arguments may be found to contradict 'certainties' produced by the use of literary criticism. There is no need to pretend that all problems posed by literary criticism can be solved by textual criticism and versional evidence. The intention of this contribution was only to highlight areas where it seems that the textual evidence (including

---

[81] Alter, *Art*, p. 20.

[82] For a full analysis cf. Förster, 'Zeichen'.

[83] Cf. Tom Thatcher, 'The Fourth Gospel in First-Century Media Culture' in Thatcher, *What We Have Heard from the Beginning*, pp. 159–62: 'The notion that John read, reflected upon, quoted from, and added to earlier documents – a Signs Gospel, a discourse source, the Synoptics – carries explanatory power for us simply because this is exactly how we use written texts today. But John's first-century media culture was not like our own.' (p. 161).

the semantic level of the 'original' Greek text as preserved in the manuscripts as well as translations) sheds some insight into what the author of the text might have intended by constructing this text in this way. There are, however, many areas – for example the relationship between the concluding verses in John 20 and the 'second ending' of the Gospel in John 21 – for which literary criticism might have good and reasonable solutions.[84]

---

[84] Cf. also Just, 'Combining', p. 356: 'All but a small minority of readers today accept the proposal that the Fourth Gospel was not written all at once by only one author. The double endings at John 20:30–31 and 21:25, along with the third-person reference in John 21:24 to the Beloved Disciple as the author of the (main portion) of the Gospel, make it virtually indisputable that the text was edited and expanded at least once, if not numerous times.'

10. THE CORRESPONDENCE OF ERWIN NESTLE WITH THE BFBS AND THE 'NESTLE–KILPATRICK' GREEK NEW TESTAMENT EDITION OF 1958

SIMON CRISP[1]

In 1904 the British and Foreign Bible Society (BFBS) published its first modern edition of the Greek New Testament.[2] In essence this was a reproduction of the fourth edition of Eberhard Nestle's New Testament, published in Stuttgart by the Priviligierte Württembergische Bibelanstalt, with a slightly amended critical apparatus.[3] The BFBS reprinted its edition a number of times virtually unchanged; however it made only a modest impact in the British market where the most popular hand edition was that of Alexander Souter.[4]

---

[1] I offer my grateful thanks to Dr Onesimus Ngundu of the Bible Society's Library at Cambridge University Library for facilitating use of the BFBS archives, and to Mr Harry Müller of the Freie Theologische Hochschule in Giessen for arranging access to the Nestle family papers held at that institution.

[2] *Η Καινη Διαθηκη, Text with Critical Apparatus* (London: BFBS, 1904). Previously, the Society published the *Textus Receptus*, essentially in the 1624 edition of Elzevir.

[3] The main difference is that the BFBS 1904 edition included the readings of the text assumed 'avowedly or inferentially' to underlie the English Revised Version of 1881.

[4] *Novum Testamentum Graece, textui a retractatoribus anglis adhibitio brevem adnotationem criticam subiecit Alexander Souter.* (Oxford: Clarendon Press, 1910). A second, revised edition appeared in 1947.

As early as the 1930s voices were raised in both the UK and the USA concerning the need for a revision or new edition of the BFBS text, and once the Second World War was over the first steps began to be taken in this direction. In November 1946 the then Translations Secretary of the BFBS, Canon Noel Coleman, wrote to the General Secretary of the Bible Society (and first UBS General Secretary) Dr J. R. Temple:

> I consider that a new edition of our Bible Society Greek New Testament is urgently needed. The 1904 edition is quite out of date. The need for it is practically world-wide so that all our translating missionaries can use it. (Coleman to Temple 28 Nov 1946)[5]

The matter was reviewed at the meeting of the BFBS Translations and Library Sub-Committee on 19 February 1947, whose Minutes record that 'the Translations Secretary should bring forward proposals for a new Bible Society Greek Text of the New Testament when he has made enquiries from other experts in this field of scholarship.'[6]

As a result of these discussions a number of significant steps were taken. Overtures were made to the Württembergische Bibelanstalt in Stuttgart for help in contacting Dr Erwin Nestle (the son of Eberhard Nestle and his successor as editor of that Society's Greek New Testament) with a view to ascertaining his willingness to help the BFBS update its Greek New Testament on the basis of the latest Stuttgart edition. In response to these overtures, Nestle himself wrote on 21 July 1947 to the BFBS Translation Secretary Noel Coleman (reproduced in Figure 1):

> Dear Sir,
>
> From your letter to Mr. Diehl - Stuttgart, 29th May, I hear, that you are wishing a greater critical apparatus for your edition of the Greek New Testament. I am very enjoiced [sic] of your intention and would very much like to prepare that apparatus for you, if you would give me the charge.

---

[5] References to BFBS correspondence are to BFBS archives BSA/E3/3/181-183 (Ancient Greek correspondence, 19 files).

[6] References to BFBS committee minutes are to BFBS archives BSA/C17/2 (Translations and Library Sub-Committee Minutes, 12 binders).

Excuse, that I am writing bad English, not so well as my dear father Eberhard Nestle did; I can read it well, but not speak, since I was never in England.

Perhaps you are writing more on your intentions. Or shall I make you proposals, how I would think that apparatus?

Sincerely yours   [(signed) Erwin Nestle D.D., Dr.phil.]

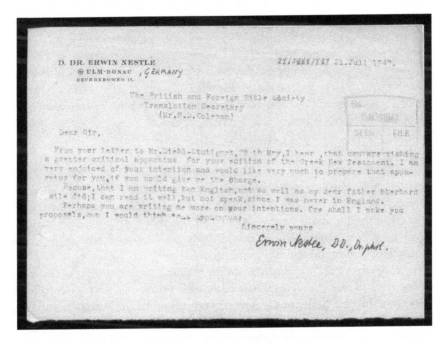

Figure 1. Nestle's letter to Coleman of 21 July 1947
(Reproduced by permission of Cambridge University Library)

So began a correspondence lasting more than a decade and spanning three BFBS Translation Secretaries. Nestle turned out to be a diligent and on occasion prolific letter-writer, and the BFBS archives, now housed in the Cambridge University Library, preserve more than one hundred of his letters and postcards. These, together with replies from his correspondents (primarily the three Translation Secretaries Coleman, Bradnock and Moulton, and also George Kilpatrick with whom – as we shall see – Nestle cooperated in preparing the BFBS Greek New Testament edition of 1958), constitute a rich resource for understanding the complex and sometimes rather fraught process by which this particular Greek New Testament edition came to birth. Unfortunately the working papers which went back and forth between Nestle and Kilpatrick as they discussed the technical details of their new critical apparatus appear not to have survived, but enough has remained to allow us to draw a picture of both the technical and the human aspects of this complex process.

Erwin Nestle was born on 22 May 1883 in Münsingen (Baden-Württemberg), the son of the well-known scholar and editor of the Greek New Testament Eberhard Nestle. Erwin was educated at the University of Tübingen, where his dissertation on Judea in the time of Josephus was published in 1911.[7] He spent most of his career as a teacher of religion in high school. In recognition of his academic achievements the title of Professor was conferred on him by the State of Baden-Württemberg in March 1963. After his father's death Erwin Nestle took over the editorship of the Novum Testamentum Graece published by the Württemberg Bible Society, which he saw through several editions. He died in Ulm-am-Donau on 21 June 1972.

Once direct contact had been made between Erwin Nestle and the BFBS matters moved ahead rather quickly. On 8 August 1947 Coleman wrote to Nestle explaining in more detail what kind and extent of critical apparatus the BFBS had in mind ('not really a larger one, but a more simplified one'), and later that month Nestle was already sending to Coleman a set of 'questions and propositions' for the proposed new edition.

The first part of Nestle's 'questions and propositions' (a two-page document dated 23 August 1947) deals with matters of **text**: essentially he asks whether the basis for the new edition should be the BFBS text of 1904 (which he mistakenly calls 1905) or the 16th/17th Stuttgart edition, and gives some account of the main differences between these editions – for example occasional changes like that of ἔχωμεν to ἔχομεν at Romans 5:1 on the one hand, and matters of orthography and layout on the other.[8] In the second part of the document, dealing with **apparatus**, he asks whether the

---

[7] Erwin Nestle, *Judaea bei Josephus. Inaugural-Dissertation zur Erlagung der Doktorwürde.* (Halle: Ehrhardt Karras, 1911; also in *Zeitschrift des Deutschen Palästina-Vereins* 34/2–3, 1911.)

[8] For a summary discussion of this variant see Bruce M. Metzger, *A Textual Commentary on the Greek New Testament*, 2nd edn (Stuttgart: Deutsche Bibelgesellschaft /United Bible Societies, 1994), p. 452.

selection of variant readings should be mechanical (as it was in the early Nestle editions of his father) or editorial; what should be done about the many variants from Westcott and Hort and from the *Textus Receptus*; and whether conjectures should be cited or not. He suggests that sigla in the text referring to variation units in the apparatus can be dispensed with 'because they could puzzle the reader', and raises the question of whether a positive or negative apparatus would be preferable. He deals with parallel passage references (suggesting that their number be reduced) and expresses doubts about the inclusion of the ancient text divisions and Eusebian canons. Finally, Nestle responds to a question from BFBS about how much time he would need for his work by saying that he cannot tell before he gets started, and asking in return when the Society would like to print the book.

Coleman had Nestle's handwritten document retyped, and in September 1947 sent it out together with a circular letter to a group of well-known British New Testament scholars, requesting their comments and advice. It is worth quoting extensively from this letter:

> I am planning to bring out a revised edition of the Greek Testament, chiefly for the use of theological students, clergy and missionary translators.

> At present (and since 1904) the Bible Society prints the 4th edition of Eberhard Nestle's text, with an apparatus at the foot of each page which indicates every variation of importance in the resultant text above it, in words, spelling or punctuation, from (1) the Textus Receptus, and (2) the Greek Text which is supposed to underline [*sic*] the English R.V. of 1881.

> The present Bible Society edition is manifestly unsatisfactory now. The Stuttgart edition of Nestle has reached its 17th edition, and I have obtained from Dr. Erwin Nestle, the son of Prof. Eberhard Nestle, (who has been responsible for the recent Stuttgart editions) some proposals for a new Bible Society edition which shall incorporate the new evidence and whose apparatus shall perhaps be more appropriate for the use of students in the English-speaking world.

> I should be glad if you would kindly examine Dr. Nestle's proposals in the light of the requirements of your students and pupils. If you will inform me of your preferences, my Sub-Committee will then have valuable evidence to guide them in their decision. I may add that I have Sir Frederic Kenyon's judgment and experience to guide me in the final recommendations which I hope to place before my Sub-Committee.

Responses to this circular letter came in from several British scholars,[9] and in particular a fairly extensive discussion continued with Sir Frederic Kenyon. On 1 October Coleman reported to the BFBS Sub-Committee 'the receipt of helpful replies from various scholars, giving advice as to the best apparatus to print with the Nestle text, in view of the additional MS evidence available since 1905 [*sic*]'. Even before this meeting of the Sub-Committee, from a shortlist of potential collaborators proposed by Kenyon comprising C.H. Dodd, G.D. Kilpatrick and T.W. Manson the choice had narrowed to Kilpatrick. By the end of September he was working through Nestle's document, sending a response to Coleman early in October.

George Dunbar Fitzpatrick was born in September 1910 in British Columbia of British parents who had moved to Canada immediately following their marriage. Following the death of his father in the First World War, mother and son returned to England to further young George's education. He was educated at the universities of London and Oxford, and ordained to the Anglican priesthood in 1937. He taught in Birmingham, Lichfield, Nottingham and Oxford, where he was appointed in 1949 as Dean Ireland's Professor of the Exegesis of Holy Scripture, a post he held until his retirement in 1977. George Kilpatrick died in January 1989. He was the author of three monographs and a large number of scholarly articles – and also (as we shall see) of two very significant publications for the BFBS.[10]

Kilpatrick's 'Notes on Dr. Erwin Nestle's proposals for a new edition of the Greek N.T.' (undated, but a retyped version has a BFBS office stamp from October 1947) respond to Nestle's document point by point, and add further reflections on a number of issues. On the matter of **text**, for example, Kilpatrick lists the fifteen changes he has noted between Nestle 16 and 17,[11] but also points out that

---

[9] The BFBS archives preserve the replies from, among others, Allen, Bishop, Duncan, Fulton, Hendry, Howard, Hunter, Kenyon, Kilpatrick, Lightfoot, Manson, Moule, Skelton and Sparks.

[10] Kilpatrick's papers are conveniently gathered in the volume edited by J.K. Elliott, *The Principles and Practice of New Testament Textual Criticism: Collected Essays of G.D. Kilpatrick* (BETL 96. Leuven: Peeters, 1990). A biography of Kilpatrick may be found in another volume edited by J.K. Elliott, *Studies in New Testament Language and Text: Essays in Honour of George D. Kilpatrick on the Occasion of his Sixty-fifth Birthday* (Supplements to *NovT* 44. Leiden: Brill, 1976).

[11] Matt. 15:5; Mark 1:4, 7:11; John 1:21, 7:8; Acts 23:20; Rom. 5:1, 14:19; 1 Cor.

No edition of N takes into account critical work after Weiss, i.e. N well represents 19th century views but nothing later (...) This failure to represent 20th century work is the more serious as at any rate in England the work of 20th century scholars who have made the greatest advances in textual criticism (...) has been made public not in new editions of the Gk. N.T. but in articles in periodicals and odd chapters in books.

For the **apparatus**, Kilpatrick proposes that 'the apparatus of N.17 might be taken as a starting point and here and there it might be pruned a little'; that all the variants from the *Textus Receptus* should be kept (since so many collations are made against this base); that the detailed presentation of Westcott and Hort material should be dropped in favour of more recent work by Burkitt / Streeter / Turner,[12] and that 'Conjectures ought to be drastically reduced.'[13] He pleads for the retention of 'variation-signs' in the text, for a smaller reduction in parallel passage references, and for preservation of the text divisions and Eusebian canons.

In a concluding section Kilpatrick offers a number of 'Additional comments'. Firstly he mentions the importance of commercial considerations: a 'peculiar advantage' of Nestle's edition was the fact that large sales enabled frequent revisions which kept the edition up to date 'in a way not attempted by English editions before this summer.[14] (...) If one text were generally accepted in the British Isles, it could, like N, be kept up to date by frequent revision. We would also have an edition which the British Universities could set as a standard text.' Secondly, Kilpatrick reiterates his view that 'practically no text of the Greek N.T. (as distinct from the apparatus) has been published which represents the work of 20th

---

8:7, 15:49; Gal. 6:10; 1 Thess. 3:2; 2 Thess. 2:13; Heb. 6:2; 1 Jn 5:20. As Kilpatrick observes, 'this list is probably not complete'.

[12] Specifically, Burkitt's *The Gospel History and its Transmission*, Streeter's *The Four Gospels*, and Turner's series of articles in *JTS* vols 25–30.

[13] 'Few have more than a transient plausibility; so few need be cited. Thus Hort's conjecture at Col.ii.18, clever as it is, is now known to be unnecessary.' (The details of Hort's conjecture, a possible 'primitive error' θέλων ἐν ταπεινοφροσύνῃ for a conjectured original ἐν ἐθελοταπεινοφροσύνῃ, may be found in B.F. Westcott and F.J.A. Hort, *The New Testament in the Original Greek* (Cambridge & London: Macmillan, 1881), vol. 2 Appendix, pp. 126–7. The conjecture has not generally found favour among scholars commenting on this verse.)

[14] This is a reference to the second edition of Souter's *Novum Testamentum Graece*; see note 4 above.

century scholarship.' Such an edition cannot be produced 'by the mechanical means which gave us the Nestle text', but rather 'the judgment of an editor will have to be followed.'

Even at this early stage, perhaps, there were indications of future disagreements to come. As his 'Questions and propositions' indicate, Nestle was quite flexible concerning both the form and the content of the new edition. BFBS (supported by Kenyon) was in favour of a much simplified edition, aiming at the student market rather than the community of scholars. Kilpatrick on the other hand emphasised already at this early stage the need to provide a vehicle for the insights of British textual scholarship in the twentieth century. As he points out at the end of his 'Notes':

> Myself I have been for long interested in the task of producing a critical text. Over several years, I have been collecting, in an interleaved copy of facts [*sic*], from Burkitt, Streeter, Turner, Wellhausen, Lietzmann's <u>Handbuch</u> and other sources readings which seem to me to have some claim to be correct or at least deserve to appear in an apparatus. There seems on a number of points to be an increasing consensus which goes beyond W.H. or N.

It was to be some years before Kilpatrick's wish to produce his own critical text began to be realised, and the outcome was not a happy one. But this is to jump ahead of our story.

During the latter part of 1947 arrangements and terms were discussed with both Nestle and Kilpatrick. On 10 September Nestle sent to Coleman a detailed 'survey for the possibilities of the new Apparatus' in which he offered four different variants of a critical apparatus for Matthew 1, Mark 1:1–8 and Luke 1:1–25:

1. All variant readings from the apparatus of the BFBS 1904 edition

2. These readings plus their manuscript references, and also all the variants of WH (text, margin and apparatus)

3. Selected readings from 1904 plus all the WH variants

4. A 'free selection' of variant readings based on manuscript witnesses rather than modern editors

As an example we may take the well-known variant υἱοῦ θεοῦ at Mark 1:1. This variation unit is displayed as follows in the four arrangements outlined by Nestle in his 'survey':

1. υιου [του] θεου S Rᵗ

2. Χρ.] add υιου θεου BDμ; h; υι. του θ. λ pm

3. Χρ.] add υιου θεου BDμ; h

4. Χρ.] add υιου θεου BDμ; h; υι. του θ. λ pm; txt S Θ μ Irᵖᵗ Or

In Nestle's suggestion 4, the variants for and against the chosen reading are given and manuscript witnesses are cited; compared with the final form of this variation unit in the BFBS 1958 edition it is more concise and ordered differently (variant – text rather than text – variant).[15] The tension between brevity and comprehensiveness in particular, was to be a feature of the whole process of subsequent work on the edition.

While these matters were being discussed, and in the hope of tackling them face to face, Coleman invited Nestle to attend the first United Bible Societies' (UBS) conference of Bible translators, which was held in the Netherlands in October 1947. This led to a rather awkward exchange of correspondence because Nestle was refused an exit permit by the Military government of the US Sector of Germany in which his home town of Ulm was located. The reason for this refusal was that the issue of Nestle's 'denazification'[16] had not been resolved and so he felt obliged (on 28 September 1947) to write at length to BFBS explaining why he had become a member of the Nazi Party (because membership was more or less

---

[15] Η Καινη Διαθηκη. *Second Edition with revised critical apparatus.* (London: BFBS, 1958). The apparatus entry for Mark 1:1 is as follows: Ιησ. Χρ. ℵ* Θ *28 pc* armᵖᵗ geoᵖᵗ Ir Or Bas Vict Hierᵖᵗ; Rᵐ] *add* Υιου Θεου **BDW** *pc* (Υι. του Θ. **A** f1 f13 *565 700 pm* ς; Rᵗ) latt co

[16] 'In the aftermath of the fighting, or when Allied troops occupied a town or city, denazification began immediately … All Nazis had to be removed from positions of power and responsibility … The term 'denazification' also came to mean the process of removing the stigma of having been a Nazi for those 'lesser Nazis' and led to restitution of full civil rights. This enabled lesser Nazis to vote again in general elections and to have their jobs restored' (Helen Fry, *Denazification: Britain's Enemy Aliens, Nazi War Criminals and the Reconstruction of Post-war Europe.* (Stroud: The History Press, 2010), pp. 12–13). For a detailed account of the whole denazification process see Perry Biddiscombe, *The Denazification of Germany: A History 1945-1950.* (Stroud: Tempus, 2007). Among the family archive materials kept at Freie Theologische Hochschule Giessen there is a file of papers relating to Nestle's own denazification.

obligatory for teachers of religion in public schools) and why his case had
not been resolved (because the higher authorities in Berlin had overruled
the more lenient judgment of the local court in Ulm). He writes about his
own church affiliation under Nazism:

> In my religious position I had nothing to do with the 'German
> Christians', but was always with the 'Confessing Church' (our bishop
> Dr. Wurm). But I was never embarrassed by the Party in my work for
> the Church and therefore I had no reason to retire from the Party; on
> the contrary, as a member of it I could better say somewhat, to dissipate
> misunderstandings and exaggerations in the religious questions, than
> otherwise.

Coleman never referred directly to this issue (remarking on 9 October
only that 'it is regrettable that you are not allowed to go to Holland'). From
the end of October onwards however he began broaching with Nestle the
idea of a possible English collaborator, sending him a copy of Kilpatrick's
Notes (and of Kenyon's letter from the previous month). In a letter to
Coleman on 7 November Nestle comments rather amusingly on the
differences between these two scholars:

> The vote of Sir Frederic Kenyon and Dr. Kilpatrick were very
> interesting for me. That they differ in many points, doesn't matter. Then
> we can do what we think best and we have always an authority with us!
> [As] to the 'Variation Signs' I think to omit them like Kenyon. They are
> as Dr. Kilpatrick says, very useful, but not so necessary, when we have
> not so much variants. In Germany too some scholars would not have
> them. Then these shall use your new edition and the others have
> Stuttgart.

During December terms were agreed with the BFBS for Nestle's
work,[17] and on 1 January 1948 Coleman was able to summarise more or less
formally 'the lines on which we would like you to prepare an edition of your
text':

---

[17] Nestle asked for a small royalty payment on each copy of the edition sold;
BFBS declined this request, citing lack of precedent and offering instead the
payment of an honorarium.

Can you see your way to give us -

1. The text of your 17th edition, but modified sometimes in the direction of your earlier text.

2. Leave the text uninterrupted by any signs but differentiate O.T. quotations and print poetical poetical passages strophically.

3. Supply marginal references.

4. In the apparatus give the chief MSS. evidence for a selection of important readings. (Give only English A.V., R.V., and American Standard Revised agreements, but omit WH and other editors).

5. Omit conjectures. Any that are really important could be collected in a preface or appendix.

6. An English preface to explain how the text has been made and treated.

7. The Eusebian Canons – opinion is divided at present whether to retain them or not.

But if you can agree to point 1–6 above, it will enable you to get on with the work which you have so kindly promised to do for us.

(Nestle's response to this proposal appears not to have survived – however as his continued work demonstrates, he clearly accepted it *de facto*.)

Meanwhile Coleman was also in regular correspondence with Kilpatrick in order to secure his involvement in the project. On 22 December 1947, in response to a request from Coleman for an official confirmation of his willingness to work on the project, Kilpatrick wrote:

In reply to your letter of the 18th, I shall be glad to undertake the task of supplying Dr. Nestle with information about the findings of British scholarship for the New Testament text and will be prepared to assist him in checking and correcting the final proofs when the time comes. I shall be very pleased to send all information either direct to Dr. Nestle or to the British and Foreign Bible Society, as may be most convenient.

On 7 January 1948 Coleman left for a tour of Africa which was to last several months. Tragically, Noel Coleman was killed in an aeroplane crash in the Belgian Congo on the very day (in May 1948) when he was due to return to England. It was to be some time before a new Translations

Secretary was appointed by the BFBS and the momentum of work on the
new edition of the Greek NT picked up once again.

On 20 January 1950 the Revd Wilfred J. Bradnock wrote to Nestle
introducing himself as the new BFBS Translations Secretary and expressing
his support for the Greek New Testament project:

> I am deeply interested in the work which you are doing in conjunction
> with Dr. Kilpatrick and would like to take the matter up with you where
> it was left at Canon Coleman's death.

Nestle however had clearly been far from idle in the intervening two years,
for on 29 January 1951 he wrote to Bradnock that 'I have finished the copy
of the Apparatus, so that it is ready for printing'(!). He goes on to lament
that he has not heard from Kilpatrick for several months – and this
becomes a standard refrain in correspondence over the next months as well.
Clearly Nestle, by now presumably retired from his full-time employment as
a teacher of religion, could devote considerable time and energy to this
work on the BFBS Greek New Testament, while Kilpatrick, who had
recently been appointed to an Oxford professorship, was much involved in
advancing his own career.

Another bone of contention which appears again and again in the
correspondence between Nestle, Bradnock and Kilpatrick in the early 1950s
concerns the extent or size of the critical apparatus. There were already
hints of this disagreement in the position papers prepared by Nestle and
Kilpatrick back in 1947, but now the difference in approach becomes more
clear and open: Nestle has in mind a reduced apparatus to serve an
audience primarily of students and translators (and appealing to the fourth
principle enunciated by Coleman in January 1948: 'In the apparatus give the
chief MSS. evidence for a selection of important readings'), while Kilpatrick
saw the BFBS edition increasingly as a vehicle for pursuing his own plans to
produce a new critical text and apparatus.

In this respect it is notable that relations between BFBS and Kilpatrick
were growing closer. From early in the 1950s Kilpatrick served as member
of the important BFBS Translations and Library Sub-Committee, where all
policy decisions on matters of translation were taken, and a few years later
he became a member of the committee for a 'Translator's Translation'
which was intended to serve as a model for missionary translations in other
parts of the world. This appeared in preliminary form as a series of fascicles

of a *Greek-English Diglot for the Use of Translators*, the Greek part of which was to be Kilpatrick's own new text.[18]

At the same time personal relations between Bradnock and Kilpatrick were also becoming warmer (although it was many years before they went so far as to address each other by their first names!), and this growing warmth tended to make them line up in implicit opposition to Nestle when a difference of opinion arose. Bradnock, for instance, stoutly defended Kilpatrick's view about the size of the critical apparatus – and in general the tone of the correspondence between Bradnock and Kilpatrick is quite different to that of the letters between Bradnock and Nestle.

Kilpatrick was indeed becoming more and more important for the BFBS, especially when in 1952 the news reached London that the American Bible Society in the formidable person of Eugene A. Nida was making plans for an entirely new critical edition of the Greek New Testament to be produced by an international committee. The story of this edition (which became what is now known as the *UBS Greek New Testament*) is an interesting one, but it cannot be told here; suffice it to say that the BFBS in general and Bradnock in particular clearly counted on the prestige and expertise of Kilpatrick to ensure that their edition would not simply be swept aside by this American upstart.

The process of typesetting and proofreading the BFBS Greek New Testament proved a long and tortuous one lasting several years, during which time it becomes clear that Nestle was being gradually edged out of the project in favour of a more prominent role for Kilpatrick. Matters came to a head over the issue of the Introduction to the new edition. In Coleman's original guidelines for the project (see above) the preparation of an introduction to the English edition was understood to be among Nestle's responsibilities; as he did with everything else, Nestle took this assignment very seriously and produced a first draft already at the end of 1951. Little note appears to have been taken of this in either London or Oxford, however, until the process of preparing the whole work for the press was underway, although on 19 March 1952 Bradnock wrote to 'My dear Kilpatrick':

> We should have to give some thought as to the way in which Nestle should be associated with the Introductory Note. In my view it was not

---

[18] Seven brochures for restricted circulation appeared between 1958 and 1964 when the project was discontinued (see below).

our intention that this should of necessity follow the pattern of the Stuttgart editions, thus re-inforcing the impression that the B.N.T. is simply a Junior Stuttgart.[19] I do not think that the propriety of the Bible Society's sponsoring the Introduction with acknowledgement to Nestle could be questioned.

In the end the compromise solution agreed upon was to have the Introduction unsigned, and to have acknowledgement of the work of both Nestle and Kilpatrick in the Preface. In any event the issue continued to rankle, not least because when the book finally appeared in 1958 the surrounding publicity mentioned only Kilpatrick as editor. Nestle protested about this both in his correspondence with Bradnock, and in public at the 1958 SNTS meeting in Strasbourg where Harold Moulton (Bradnock's deputy and later to be his successor as BFBS Secretary for Translations) presented a paper introducing the BFBS edition and the Society's plans for further work. It is ironic and not a little sad to have to record that at the time BFBS was sending a presentation copy of the newly published New Testament with a nicely worded dedication plate to Nestle (Figure 2), Wilfred Bradnock and George Kilpatrick were already considering how to dispense with his further services.

It is not hard to see how this state of affairs came about. Already six years previously, in the same letter from Bradnock to Kilpatrick in March 1952 referred to above, one of the topics was 'whether the Bible Society would be free to treat a revised 1904 text as a basis for future editions independently of Stuttgart'. And, at the same time as Bradnock was placating Nestle in 1958 following the SNTS incident (in a letter of 21 November 1958), he was writing to Kilpatrick (in a letter of 17 November 1958 marked 'Confidential') about a detailed strategy to secure the necessary institutional support for the BFBS Greek New Testament 3rd edition to be produced under the editorship of Kilpatrick alone.

---

[19] Interestingly, in the Minutes of the Board of Management (Verwaltungsrat) of the Württembergische Bibelanstalt, to whom Nestle regularly reported on his activities, the BFBS edition is consistently referred to as the 'Englischer Nestle'. I am grateful to the German Bible Society for allowing access to the relevant sections of these Board Minutes.

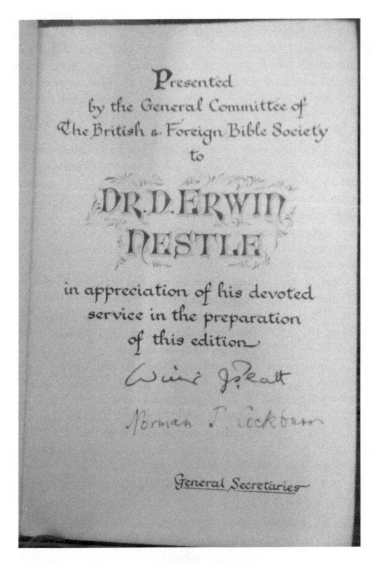

Figure 2. Nestle's presentation copy of the BFBS Greek New Testament (Reproduced by permission of Freie Theologische Hochschule, Giessen)

The strategy mentioned by Bradnock in his letter to Kilpatrick was put into effect at the beginning of 1959, when the BFBS Translations and Library Sub-Committee made a recommendation authorising the preparation of a third edition of the BFBS Greek New Testament under Kilpatrick's sole supervision, and allowing for revision not only of the apparatus, but also 'a moderate revision of the text', including permission 'to follow readings which are supported by modern scholarship or recent discussion, but which are not in any of the editions, versions or translations referred to [*earlier*]'. It is hard to see this recommendation, which was confirmed as official policy by the BFBS General Purposes Sub-Committee in March 1959, as anything other than a determination by the BFBS to continue with its own work on an edition regardless of the project now being undertaken by the American Bible Society (which led to the publication in 1966 of the *UBS Greek New Testament*).[20] Of course it left Nestle out in the cold, an isolation further reinforced by the decision of the Württembergische Bibelanstalt to participate in the American Bible Society project and authorise Kurt Aland to join its editorial committee (a move which led in turn to the decision to adopt an identical base text in the UBS and Nestle–Aland editions).

The planned third edition, however, was not to be. Partly this was for internal UBS reasons (growing international co-operation on the one hand, and the perceived need for a common agreed text of the Greek New Testament on the other), but partly also because of a cooling in relations between the BFBS and Kilpatrick. At the same time as the American Bible Society's 'Critical Greek New Testament' project was gaining significant traction, some unease was being expressed about the Greek text of the BFBS *Diglot for Translators*. In discussion of the 'Translators' Translation' at the meeting of the Translations and Library Sub-Committee on 25 November 1964, it was reported that 'the Greek text of the Diglot had caused surprise and uneasiness among some missionary scholars. These comments had been passed on to Prof. Kilpatrick.' Relations with Kilpatrick however seemed to be deteriorating. In his report to the Sub-Committee:

> Mr. Bradnock stated that as early as 1962 he had spoken to Prof. Kilpatrick about this kind of comment, and had reminded him that it had been agreed that the Greek would be a moderate revision. Prof. Kilpatrick had promised a brochure setting out clearly the principles on

---

[20] The 1966 edition appeared in the name of the Bible Societies of the USA, Scotland, the Netherlands, Germany and the BFBS. Subsequent editions bore the imprint of the United Bible Societies.

which the revision had been made. Such an explanation had been repeatedly asked for by translators. It is still awaited.

The upshot of all this was a decision to formally rescind the resolution of 1959, and to take steps gradually to disengage from Kilpatrick. Evidently, neither the Translations Department of BFBS, nor the missionary translators with whom they were working in the field, were ready for a Greek New Testament text constructed according to the principles of thoroughgoing eclecticism.[21]

Kilpatrick had been given advance notice of this decision, and he sent a strongly worded letter to be read to the Sub-Committee, in which among other things he stated that he regarded the 1959 resolution to be a contractual matter and that he would continue his work. But by this time the writing was on the wall. The BFBS discontinued the Diglot project, dropped Kilpatrick's Greek text from the *Translators' Translation*,[22] and finally came on board the American Bible Society's Critical Greek New Testament project ten years after this had been initiated by Eugene Nida. The 1958 'Nestle-Kilpatrick Greek New Testament' had been overtaken by events, and finally turned into something of a dead end.

What lessons can be learned from the story of the BFBS Greek New Testament, and in particular from the relations between the Bible Society and Erwin Nestle? Apart from the truism about those who do not learn from history being condemned to repeat it, we may suggest that there are at least three specific conclusions which can be drawn from the saga outlined in this paper.

First, the making of any Greek New Testament edition is a complex and occasionally fraught process, especially – as is almost bound to be the case – when strong personalities and personal interests are involved. The BFBS edition of 1958 discussed in this paper (and indeed the UBS edition of 1966 as well) underwent numerous twists and turns over the course of more than a decade in both cases.

---

[21] On thoroughgoing eclecticism in general, and the role of Kilpatrick in developing this approach, see J. Keith Elliott, 'Thoroughgoing Eclecticism in New Testament Textual Criticism', in Bart D. Ehrman and Michael W. Holmes, *The Text of the New Testament in Contemporary Research: Essays on the Status Quaestionis*, 2nd edn (NTTSD 42. Leiden: Brill, 2013), pp. 745–770 (especially pp. 749–750).

[22] This was finally published in 1973 as *The Translator's New Testament*, in English only.

Secondly however, many of the questions discussed in the late 1940s and early 1950s between the BFBS, Nestle and Kilpatrick (positive versus negative apparatus, extent of versional and patristic citations, matters of spelling, punctuation and orthography) are among those which have to be faced by any editor of the Greek New Testament, and so it is of practical as well as theoretical interest to see how they were resolved for this particular edition; one need only think, for example, of the arguments about citation of editions versus citation of manuscript witnesses in the debate following publication of the SBL Greek New Testament.[23]

And thirdly, the commercial aspects of Greek New Testament editions which may hope to be widely circulated give them a special importance for their publishers, whilst offering visibility and possible prestige to their editors. In view of this it is not surprising that tempers may occasionally fray, and that the players involved may not be above scheming against one another. In this respect the story of Erwin Nestle and the BFBS is something of a cautionary tale.

---

[23] See Michael Holmes, David Parker, Harold Attridge and Klaus Wachtel, 'The SBL Greek New Testament: Papers from the 2011 SBL Panel Review Session', *TC: A Journal of Biblical Textual Criticism* 17 (2012), http://rosetta.reltech.org/TC/v17/TC-2012-PR-Holmes.pdf (accessed 27 September 2013).

INDEX OF MANUSCRIPTS

Greek New Testament manuscripts are listed according to their Gregory–Aland number.

Other manuscripts are given by library:

INDEX OF BIBLICAL PASSAGES

INDEX OF SUBJECTS

INDEX OF GREEK WORDS